A DYNASTY IN BLUE

25 YEARS OF
MICHIGAN FOOTBALL GLORY
(1969-1994)

EDITED
BY
FRANCIS J. FITZGERALD

Nashville, Tennessee

Portions of this book have been previously published. Listed below is their original source of publication:

Chapters 1, 2, 4, 5, 7, 8, 10, 11, 12, 14, 15, 18, 20, 21, 22, 24, 27, 28, 29, 33, 37, 38, 39, 41, 42, 44, 45, 47, 48, 51, 53, 54, 57, 58, 61, 63, 67, 68, 70, 71 and 75 have been previously published in *The New York Times*. Reprinted by permission of The New York Times Company.

Chapters 3, 6, 13, 17, 19, 25, 26, 31, 35, 46, 59, 64, 66 and 74 have been previously published in *Sports Illustrated*. Reprinted by permission of Time Inc.

Chapters 9, 23, 34, 40, 43, 50, 52, 64 and 73 have been previously published by *The Associated Press*. Reprinted by permission of The Associated Press.

Chapters 16, 32, 36, 60 and 72 have been previously published in *The Washington Post*. Reprinted by permission of The Washington Post Company.

Chapter 30 has been previously published by *The Los Angeles Times*. Reprinted by permission of The Los Angeles Times Syndicate.

Published by
Athlon Sports Communications Inc.
220 25th Avenue North
Nashville, Tennessee 37203

The Team, The Team, The Team . . .

CONTENTS

INTRODUCTION

It all began 25 years ago when a fiery, determined — and largely unknown — coach, who had been shaking up things and building a modest powerhouse at Miami U., a football coaching outpost, was chosen to take the reins of the long esteemed, but then struggling Michigan gridiron program.

The Wolverines were indeed at a crossroads: Wanting big-time football success but only having played in the Rose Bowl once in the previous 18 years and needing to overcome the growing popularity of their Big Ten Fraternity brothers, Ohio State and Michigan State. Little did anyone in the Maize and Blue faithful realize what a dramatic impact that a man by the name of Glenn E. (Bo) Schembechler would soon have on their lives.

In one short season, Schembechler, who was a disciple of both Woody Hayes and Ara Parseghian, quickly installed a strong dose of courage and commitment into the wandering Wolverines. Initially, though, the going would be tough, with Michigan posting 3 wins and 2 losses in the first five games of 1969. Yet by late November Schembechler's crusaders had put together a 5-game winning streak and along the way had overthrown both the Buckeyes and the Spartans for supremacy of the Big Ten and earned a Rose Bowl invitation to meet U.S.C. on New Year's Day.

Life would never again be the same in Ann Arbor.

In all, 15 more Big Ten championships and 10 more Rose Bowl dates would follow for the Wolverines. The contests against longtime rival Ohio State and the Buckeyes' football mentor, Woody Hayes, would also be elevated to a new status: An annual War Between the Yardsticks which was viewed on television in late November by millions. For Michigan fans, there would be plenty of winning and glory and laughter and memories.

Remarkably, following the 1979 season, when the beloved Schembechler decided to retire after 21 years at the helm of the Michigan Blue Machine, and his longtime, trusted assistant Gary Moeller was tapped to lead the

Den, this dynasty would continue without interruption.

A Dynasty in Blue: 25 Years of Michigan Football Glory is the story of Bo, Mo & Company and a celebration of their special period in college football history. It was penned by several of America's finest sportswriters.

A Dynasty in Blue will bring to life many of those wonderful college football Saturdays of our past. Yet for a few of us, it will also be a journey back to the salad days of our youth, when a college football team that wore those Maize and Blue uniforms with the unmistakable Roman warrior-like winged helmets, ran and passed and blocked and tackled its way into a special place in our hearts, remaining ever since as trusted and cherished memories.

It is a trip that I believe that you will find worth taking.

Francis J. Fitzgerald
Washington, D.C.
September 29, 1994

A DYNASTY IN BLUE

25 YEARS OF
MICHIGAN FOOTBALL GLORY
(1969-1994)

1

MICHIGAN GAINS ROSE BOWL AS OHIO STATE STRING ENDS AT 22

By NEIL AMDUR
Special to The New York Times

ANN ARBOR, Mich., Nov. 22, 1969 — In a year of impossible dreams, from the Jets to the Mets to the moon, Michigan upset Ohio State, college football's No. 1 team, 24-12, today and ended the Buckeyes' 22-game winning streak and their chance for a second consecutive national title.

Before a roaring record crowd of 103,588 in Michigan Stadium, the inspired, twice-beaten Wolverines won a share of the Big Ten Conference championship, a postseason trip to the Rose Bowl and respect they have not enjoyed in almost two decades.

The architect of college football's upset of the year was Glenn (Bo) Schembechler, a 39-year-old coach who spent five years as a graduate assistant and line coach under Woody Hayes, the Ohio State mentor, and is in his first season at Michigan.

"We knew we were going to win from the very beginning," Schembechler said, after excited Michigan players carried him across the synthetic Tartan playing surface. "We said after our last game that we were going to win."

'All Good Things End'

The defeat was a bitter ending for a team that some coaches had termed "super" and "the greatest ever." Ohio State was ineligible for the Rose Bowl this year and Hayes had used a national championship as an incentive during the season.

"All good things must come to an end and that's what happened today," said the 56-year-old coach, who wore a short-sleeved shirt throughout the game. "We just got outplayed and outpunched. Our offense in the second half was miserable. We made every mistake you could possibly make."

Ohio State's setback throws the national championship picture into turmoil with three major teams ranked among the top 10 still unbeaten — Penn State (9-0), Texas (8-0) and Arkansas (8-0). Texas and Arkansas meet

Dec. 6, but a definitive national champion may not be determined now until after the postseason bowl games are played.

All the scoring came today in the first half, and Michigan, beaten only by Missouri and Michigan State in 10 games, wiped out deficits of 0-6 and 7-12.

So tenacious and effective was the Michigan defense and secondary in the second half that Ohio State's deepest penetration until the closing minutes was to the Wolverine 44-yard line.

Kern Passes Backfire

The alert Michigan secondary intercepted four passes thrown by Rex Kern, the Buckeyes' junior quarterback and Heisman Trophy candidate. With 6 minutes 55 seconds left in the final quarter, Hayes replaced his frustrated starter with another junior, Ron Maciejowski.

Maciejowski fared little better, throwing two more interceptions, including the third of the game by Barry Pierson, a defensive back, whose performance Schembechler called "one of the greatest I have ever seen."

Michigan was defiant from the time Ohio State stepped onto the stadium Tartan for pre-game warmups. Wolverine students pelted Buckeye players with snowballs and taunted Hayes with chants of "Good-bye Woody" in the last 10 minutes.

Michigan's offense produced what Purdue lacked last week in a 42-14 loss to Ohio State — a strong, controlled running game. With Wolverine offensive linemen firing out quickly on the slick synthetic surface, Michigan backs broke through for 266 yards rushing.

Don Moorhead, an unheralded but highly capable 6-foot-3 junior quarterback, carried for 68 yards in 17 keepers, including a 1-yard run for the third Michigan score, after Pierson ran 60 yards with a punt.

A 15-point favorite, Ohio State had averaged 46 points a game en route to eight easy victories this year. Last season, the Buckeyes thrashed Michigan, 50-14.

But this time Michigan was not impressed. After Jim Otis put Ohio State ahead, 6-0, with a 1-yard plunge in the first quarter, Michigan took the kickoff and marched 55 yards in 10 plays. Garvie Craw scored the first of his two touchdowns on a 3-yard plunge.

When Frank Titas converted the extra point (Ohio State missed its fourth extra point in two games after the first touchdown), it marked the first time any team had scored on the Buckeyes in the first period and the first time they had trailed all season.

Kern was at his best after the next kickoff, methodically moving his team 73 yards, the last 22 on a scoring pass to Jan White, the tight end, 8 seconds into the second quarter.

But 3 minutes and nine plays later, Michigan had pushed the Ohio State defense into the end zone again with a 67-yard drive. Pierson's punt return and Tim Killian's 25-yard field goal signaled the beginning of the end.

Kern's Bid Fails

Michigan defensive determination peaked with 13 minutes left on a Buckeye fourth-down gamble at their 42. Needing only a yard, Ohio State turned its back on Otis, who gained 144 yards rushing in a dynamic effort, and called on Kern.

The 190-pounder faked to his fullback, kept the ball on a run to the left but was smothered for a 2-yard loss by Pete Newell, a defensive tackle.

"The strategy was to contain Kern," Schembechler said, "because we knew Otis would get his yardage. Kern couldn't, and that was the difference."

Score By Periods

Michigan	7	17	0	0 —	24
Ohio State	6	6	0	0 —	12

13

2

VICTORY ASSURES WOLVERINES UNDISPUTED BERTH

By NEIL AMDUR
Special to The New York Times

ANN ARBOR, Mich., Nov. 22, 1969 — Michigan would have turned down a chance to play in the Rose Bowl if the Wolverines had lost to Ohio State, coach Glenn (Bo) Schembechler said today.

"We wouldn't have wanted to go if we lost and they wouldn't have wanted us," the 39-year-old Schembechler said, after Michigan ended Ohio State's 22-game winning streak, the longest in college football, with a stunning 24-12 victory. "Now, we're going as co-champions of the Big Ten Conference."

Ohio State, by virtue of its appearance in the last Rose Bowl, was ineligible to return this time under Big Ten rules. The conference runner-up usually gets the honor in a case when one team wins successive championships.

Had the Buckeyes won today and taken sole possession of the crown, Purdue, which also won today, and Michigan would have shared runner-up honors, forcing the Big Ten to choose between them for the trip to Pasadena.

Michigan's triumph and New Year's Day berth in Pasadena caps a remarkable success story for the blond, stocky Schembechler, who was such a surprise selection as the new Michigan coach this year that the word among alumni was "Bo Who?"

Cradle for Great Coaches

Schembechler's background belies a tag of obscurity. Besides spending five years as an assistant under Woody Hayes at Ohio State, Schembechler compiled a 40-17 won-lost record in six seasons at Miami University in Oxford, Ohio. He also played offensive tackle under Hayes at Miami. Miami of Ohio, as everyone knows, has become the cradle for great coaches.

"It was a very emotional game," Schembechler said. "We felt other teams made mistakes early against Ohio State and had no momentum. We were going to run the ball and we wanted to keep it close at halftime, because if it were close, we felt we could take it."

Schembechler said "great plays on defense" saved Michigan in the second half. Barry Pierson, a defensive back who intercepted three passes and returned a punt 60 yards, agreed.

Curtis Sets Mark

"We knew we were going to win," said Pierson, a 6-foot, 175-pound senior. "We've been ready since last Monday. We saw in the films we could stop them by playing our type of game. Our pressure on (Rex) Kern made the difference. They had to go to things they hadn't gone to before."

Tom Curtis, another defensive back, intercepted two Kern passes and set a National Collegiate career record for pass-return yardage with a three-year total of 431 yards.

"As soon as we stopped their running game we knew we had them," Curtis said. "And the crowd never stopped shouting. They were really behind us. I couldn't believe it."

3

BYE-BYE, NO. 1

By KAYE KESSLER and WILLIAM F. REED
Sports Illustrated

NEW YORK, Dec. 1, 1969 — Even in the dying seconds the idea persisted throughout Michigan's cavernous old stadium that Ohio State, the awesome Buckeyes, would pull it out. After all, weren't they No. 1 in the nation, winner of 22 straight games and (people were beginning to joke) a worthy opponent for the Los Angeles Rams? Surely the real Rex Kern would expose that hapless impostor wearing No. 10 and wriggle through the whole Michigan defense for a couple of life-giving touchdowns. Or, failing that, surely the real Jack Tatum would rise up from wherever he had spent most of the afternoon and knock loose a couple of fumbles. Or, finally, surely some magic play, or piece of wisdom, would spring from a cranny in old Woody Hayes' fertile mind, where it had been stored away for just this kind of emergency. So everyone waited, and waited, and then suddenly delirious Michigan fans were rolling on the new Tartan Turf rug and tearing the north goal post right out of its concrete base.

The numbers on the scoreboard were MICHIGAN 24, OHIO STATE 12, but the big winner in sunny Ann Arbor was the Rose Bowl. Now, instead of having the second or even third best team from the Big Ten, the Rose Bowl will get a Michigan team that not only is the league co-champion but earned its way in style, whipping the Buckeyes head to head. As Michigan's bright young coach, Bo Schembechler, told the press after the game, "Nobody here wanted to go as the No. 2 team. That would have been tough. It was an emotional thing for us. Now we're going as co-champions of the Big Ten — and don't forget that."

And the Buckeyes? They will sit at home New Year's Day, as they would have been forced to anyway, but now they will not even have the consolation of being No. 1. Who knows what went wrong — why they had looked so flat all afternoon, even when leading. Perhaps it was a letdown after getting so high for Purdue the week before. Perhaps it was overconfidence or that lack of a Rose Bowl incentive. But a lot of it was Michigan.

The door to Ohio State's locker room remained shut long after the game, except for the 18 seconds it took Hayes to conduct what had to pass for a press conference. Opening the door a crack and thrusting out his gray, jowly head, Woody said: "All good things must come to an end and that's what happened today. We just got outplayed, outpunched and outcoached. Our offense in the second half was miserable and we made every mistake you could possibly make." With that, Woody shut the door again, and for the time being that was as close as the waiting world would come to finding out how Ohio State felt.

There were 103,588 witnesses to the upset, the largest crowd ever to see a college game, and what they saw was Michigan playing Ohio State's game better than Ohio State, a turn of events that was by no means accidental. Schembechler, 39, was Ohio State's line coach under Hayes for five years. Even as a young man learning at the master's knee, he displayed such a passion for Hayes' tactics, both psychological and physical, that his peers dubbed him "Little Woody," a nickname that has stuck even though Schembechler himself is not particularly fond of it.

The Schembechler game plan had gone into effect a week earlier, right after Michigan had drubbed Iowa, 51-6, its seventh win in nine starts. "We knew right then that we were going to beat Ohio State," he said later. Schembechler personally kept the fires burning, even to the point of making the players on his "scout" team wear a tiny No. 50 on their practice jerseys, a gentle reminder of Ohio State's 50-14 rout of the Wolverines last year.

Around his home Schembechler, like Hayes before big games, was a monster. He not only ignored his wife Millie, but he made her sleep in the baby's room so that neither woman nor child would disturb his concentration. Even on Thursday night, when Millie fixed his favorite dish, Southern-style chicken and dumplings, Bo showed only a glimmer of appreciation. "He was completely preoccupied," Millie said, laughing as wives do on these occasions. "He couldn't remember what he had told me from one day to the next."

The way to beat Ohio State, Schembechler had decided, was to concede fullback Jim Otis his yardage and concentrate on stopping Kern, the Buckeyes' superb quarterback. "We didn't want Kern running the football," Schembechler said, "so we set our defenses for him. We felt that our secondary could stop his passing, and we felt that we could score against their defense by running at 'em, which is something nobody has done." Sound familiar? You can look it up in the Woody Hayes textbook

17

on winning: always attack an opponent at his strongest point.

As Schembechler was quick to point out, too, Michigan had a few Jack Tatums and Rex Kerns of its own. There was the pass defense, built around Tom Curtis and Barry Pierson, and there was the passing attack, with quarterback Don Moorehead and tight end Jim Mandich. But the surprise find of the season was tailback Billy Taylor, a boy from Schembechler's home town of Barberton, Ohio, who in Michigan's first five games had played only enough to work up a good sweat. But after fumbling on his first two plays against Minnesota, Taylor gained 151 yards in little more than a half and the Wolverines had themselves a runner.

On Saturday, during the pre-game warmups, a few of the Michigan fans pelted Ohio State players with snowballs and everyone was amused until the Buckeyes' first play from scrimmage, when Kern rolled out around left end for 25 yards to the Michigan 31. "We didn't want Kern running the football," said Schembechler later, "so what does he do on the first play? Break a pass pocket and run for 25 yards, that's all." Before Bo had time to seriously doubt his game plan, however, Michigan's defense rose up and stopped Ohio State at the 10, and that was the first inkling of what was to happen throughout the afternoon.

"We knew we had 'em right there, when we stopped their regular stuff," said Pierson, who was to play a big role later.

Even after Ohio State's second series of downs, when Otis plunged in from the 1 for a 6-0 Buckeye lead, the Wolverines remained confident. Working to the short side of the field, quarterback Moorhead passed the Wolverines 55 yards in 10 plays to take a 7-6 lead, putting the Buckeyes behind for the first time this season. Twice Moorhead hit Mandich with key passes and once he found wide receiver Mike Oldham. An 11-yard reverse by wingback John Gabler helped, and senior fullback Garvie Craw got the final 3 yards on a dive. What was especially noteworthy was that Michigan had made no special effort to work away from Tatum, the Buckeyes' peripatetic cornerback. "Sure, we wanted to go into their short side, then hit Mandich when they single-covered," said Schembechler in his postmortem. "Tatum just happens to play the wide side, but you can't really run away from him — he'll hunt you down."

The Buckeyes weren't dead yet. They came right back to take a 12-7 lead on the first play of the second quarter, Kern passing to tight end Jan White. Ohio State's Stan White kicked the extra point, but Michigan was offside. Taking the penalty, the Bucks went for 2 points but Kern was smothered by Michigan's defensive end, Mike Keller, a sight that was to become routine before the end.

18

During the rest of the quarter Michigan pushed the Buckeyes around as no one has done all year. The Wolverines moved to the Ohio State 27, and Taylor, breaking three tackles, ran to the 5, setting up Craw's scoring smash two plays later. That made it 14-12. When Ohio State could not move and had to punt, Pierson ran back up the middle to the Ohio State 3 in what was perhaps the single most important play of the game. Two plays later Moorhead went over, and now even Woody Hayes would have admitted that Ohio State was in deep trouble.

And the Wolverines pressed on. After scoring what was apparently another touchdown on Moorhead's 3-yard pass to Mandich with 1:15 left in the half only to have it nullified on a holding penalty, junior Tim Killian kicked a 25-yard field goal, making it 24-12.

So that was it. The Ohio State defense braced in the last half, reducing Michigan's offense to four missed field goals by Killian. But Ohio State's offense, that once awesome machine, was moribund. The Wolverine ends, Keller and Cecil Pryor, kept Kern so well contained that he gained only 28 yards in 11 runs after his initial 25-yard gainer. And when the Bucks ditched the little passes to White — the first three had been successful — and began going for the long ones, the Wolverine defenders were there to intercept six times, three by Pierson. Only Otis was up to his usual form, gaining 144 yards in 28 carries, but then Schembechler had decided to leave him alone hadn't he?

While Ohio State was behind Woody's closed door, trying to figure out what had gone wrong, the Michigan team was laughing it up, singing a lusty if somewhat off-key version of "Hail to the Victors" and waving a bunch of plastic red roses. There were so many reporters waiting to see Schembechler that when the coach finally showed up at the interview room he could squeeze in no farther than the doorway. His Michigan sweater and slacks were wringing wet from the traditional shower his players had given him, and his old football knee was aching because the players had dropped him off their shoulders during the post-game victory ride. But Little Woody didn't care. He was the only thing his players had dropped all day.

4

U.S.C. BREAKS DEADLOCK
TO DEFEAT MICHIGAN, 10-3

By BILL BECKER
Special to The New York Times

PASADENA, Calif., Jan. 1, 1970 — The Southern California Trojans, scoring on a 33-yard touchdown pass from Jimmy Jones to Bob Chandler, upset the favored Michigan Wolverines, 10-3, today before a record crowd of 103,878 spectators in the 56th Rose Bowl game.

It was the first defeat in the Rose Bowl for Michigan, the Big Ten co-champions and winners of four straight here previously.

Noted throughout the season for their fine defense, the Trojans today throttled Michigan's vaunted running attack in clutch situations.

Moreover, U.S.C. uncorked some fine running by its tailbacks, Clarence Davis and Mike Berry, to take control of the game away from Don Moorhead, the Wolverines' all-round quarterback.

However, it took a third-quarter break to dissolve a 3-3 tie. Sandy Durko, the alert Trojan cornerback, supplied it with a diving interception of a Moorhead pass at the Trojan 49-yard line.

From there, Jones, a sophomore quarterback from Harrisburg, Pa., passed 14 yards to Chandler. After two running plays, Jones hit Chandler with a 23-yard pitch on the Michigan 10. Chandler, a junior flanker, broke a tackle by Brian Healy, a safetyman, and dodged two other Wolverines to score.

Ron Ayala, who had kicked a 25-yard field goal in the first quarter, added the conversion.

Michigan's only points came on a 20-yard field goal by Tim Killian in the second period.

Moorhead thrice marched Michigan deep into Trojan territory in the fourth period, but each time the Trojans, led by its hard-charging forwards, the Wild Bunch, prevailed.

A 54-yard drive was halted on the U.S.C. 13 early in the quarter. Later a 48-yard march was stopped on the 9, with the Trojans taking over.

In the final 2 minutes 25 seconds Moorhead resourcefully ran and passed his squad 50 yards to the Trojan 34 but under heavy pressure, his final three passes sailed incomplete as the clock ran out.

Playing without their coach, Bo Schembechler, who was hospitalized with a stomach ailment, the Wolverines had a 20-16 edge in first downs.

Michigan Holds on Its 14

But Southern Cal, making a fourth straight Rose Bowl appearance, came up with the big play and wound up with its 12th victory against five defeats in the original New Year's Day bowl.

For John McKay's Trojans, it was a happy climax to an unbeaten season. They finished with 10 victories and one tie (14-14 with Notre Dame) and figured to move up a notch or two in the final Associated Press ratings which had them fifth nationally at the end of the regular season.

It was McKay's third Rose Bowl success against two defeats. Jim Young, the Michigan defense coordinator, was the acting coach in place of the stricken Schembechler. The Wolves finished their year with eight triumphs and three losses.

The Trojans, showing they were more than a defensive club, carried a brisk ground attack to the Wolverines in the first quarter. With Davis carrying the first six times, U.S.C. marched 30 yards before Michigan held for downs on its own 14-yard line.

Late in the opening period, Jones, the flashy quarterback, used the option play well, moving the Trojans 57 yards in 15 plays before settling for Ron Ayala's 25-yard field goal.

Moorhead marched the Wolves 76 yards in 18 plays in the second period, and Tim Killian, a reserve junior center, booted a 20-yard field goal to tie the score at 3-all.

Big plays of the drive were Moorhead's own 10-yard dash on fourth down and a holding penalty against U.S.C. that took the ball to the Trojan 9.

Just before the first half ended, Ayala tried a 34-yard field goal which sailed wide and to the left, leaving the score tied at intermission. Covering most of a 55-yard drive, Jones passed 12 to Evans, 9 to De Kraai and 8 to Davis in the series.

Chandler, who wound up with three catches for 78 yards, was selected player of the game. It was a heartening finish to an injury-riddled season for the Trojan receiver.

Jones completed 10 of 17 passes for 128 yards, Moorhead 14 of 32 for 127. Moorhead also ran for 60 yards to lead the Wolverine attack. Davis led all rushers with 76 yards in 15 carries for a 5-yard average.

Davis gave the huge crowd its biggest thrill by breaking away on what appeared to be a 96-yard touchdown run in the final period. But an official ruled he was brushed out of bounds by Ed Moore, a linebacker, at the U.S.C. 21, cutting the gain to 17 yards.

On defense, Jimmy Gunn and Charlie Weaver, ends; Al Cowlings and Tody Smith, tackles, and Tony Terry and Bubba Scott, guards, did a superb job of containing Billy Taylor, the hard-running sophomore tailback who riddled Ohio State. Taylor netted 56 yards in 18 tries.

McKay also gave a large share of credit to his linebackers and defensive backs, particularly Durko and Tyrone Hudson, whose ball-hawking foiled Moorhead's long-range barrage in the waning moments.

This was the lowest-scoring Rose Bowl game in 17 years. Southern Cal was involved in that one, too, beating Wisconsin, 7-0, in 1953.

"This is our best-ever defensive team," said McKay in the dressing room. "We played very crippled against Ohio State last year (U.S.C. lost, 27-16) in the Rose Bowl. This year we had more people ready. I didn't see us do too many things wrong."

Young, the stand-in loser, said, "We missed Bo's leadership and the decision he might have made."

The pro-tem coach added: "All of us were playing under difficult circumstances. There was a definite effect from the standpoint of leadership."

However, Young praised U.S.C. as "stronger physically on defense than Ohio State."

SCORE BY PERIODS

U.S.C.	3	0	7	0 —	10
Michigan	0	3	0	0 —	3

5

STRONG GROUND ATTACK PROPELS BUCKEYES OVER MICHIGAN

By NEIL AMDUR
Special to The New York Times

COLUMBUS, Ohio, Nov. 21, 1970 — The long agony of defeat became instant ecstasy for Ohio State today as the unbeaten Buckeyes powered past Michigan, 20-9, en route to a berth in the Rose Bowl on New Year's Day.

Spurred by a howling record crowd of 87,331 in Ohio Stadium, the Buckeyes reversed the lone blemish on their football record in the last 31 games. They did it convincingly in the awesome, aggressive style that has become the trademark of Ohio State football teams for two decades.

At times Ohio State appeared almost "superpsyched." Four times in the first 12 minutes the Buckeyes lined up with only 10 men on the field. On one series Coach Woody Hayes, ebullient and anxious, in a white, short-sleeve shirt and his familiar black baseball cap, lost track of the action and sent in his punting team on second down.

But the Buckeyes did what had to be done to redeem the torment of last year's stunning 24-12 setback by Michigan at Ann Arbor, a defeat that ended their 22-game winning streak and chances for a second successive national championship.

Only 12 Passes Thrown

On offense today they slammed at the strength of a Wolverine interior ranked fifth nationally in rushing defense. Hayes called 12 pass plays to 65 rushing attempts, but one was a 26-yard touchdown toss from Rex Kern to Bruce Jankowski. It was Jankowski's first scoring reception of the season.

Attacking the Michigan defense with two tight ends instead of one, Ohio State amassed 242 yards rushing. By contrast the superb Buckeye defense continued its consistently magnificent play and limited the Michigan running attack to 37. In nine earlier victories the Wolverine ground game had averaged 274.

In Front to Stay

Ohio State scored first with Fred Schram's 28-yard field goal after having recovered a Michigan fumble on the opening kickoff. The Wolverines matched that 3-pointer with a 31-yard placement by Dana Coin on the first play of the second quarter.

But after Kern hit Jankowski behind Bruce Elliott in the end zone late in the first half, the Buckeyes were in front to stay. Michigan moved to within a point, 10-9, midway through the third quarter on a 13-yard scoring pass from Don Moorhead to Paul Staroba.

But Tim Anderson took a running start and crashed through to block Coin's extra-point kick — it was only his second miss in 17 attempts — and the Buckeyes tacked on another Schram field goal, from 27 yards, and a 4-yard scoring run by Leo Hayden in the final quarter.

The ultimate display of State's superiority and muscle came in the final 4 minutes 58 seconds, after the Buckeye defense had stopped a Michigan drive at the Ohio State 24. Hayes called 11 straight rushing plays, and the offensive line produced the punishing format that has characterized recent State teams. Hayes calls it "grinding meat."

The Buckeyes ground out the remaining time with two first downs. As students and fans poured onto the field after the game, Hayes symbolically found his way to the game ball, grabbed it, clutched it tightly in his right arm like a fullback and ran off the field with a police escort providing interference.

Michigan appeared loose in workouts yesterday in contrast to the intensity within the Ohio State walls. But the Wolverines fumbled three times today and completed only 12 of 26 passes for 118 yards. An interception by Stan White led to Ohio State's final touchdown with 8:14 left.

The Wolverines also were penalized six times, including a 15-yarder for grabbing a face mask that nullified a wind-aided 73-yard punt by Staroba in the second quarter that would have pushed the Buckeyes back to their 18.

Instead Michigan had to punt again. Ohio State gained 36 yards on the exchange and took control on the Michigan 46. Kern's crucial 4-yard run on a fourth-and-3 situation from the Michigan 29 maintained the momentum; the pitch to Janowski was the only pass in the drive.

Michigan's last chance typified the Wolverines' frustration during the 40-degree afternoon. After recovering a fumbled punt, which Hayes insisted his player did not touch, Michigan moved to the State 26.

Three plays gained 2 yards. On fourth down Moorhead threw perfectly to Glenn Doughty at the State 12. In another stadium on another day, perhaps at Ann Arbor, Doughty might have caught the ball, for it plopped squarely in his stomach. But he dropped it, and so went Michigan's slim hopes for a national title and conference crown.

Ohio State's Rose Bowl opponent will be Stanford, and another national championship again appears within the Buckeye grasp. Ohio State won the mythical title in 1968 with many of the same fine players (Kern, Jack Tatum, Jim Stillwagon, Jan White, Mike Sensibaugh) who were in their final regular-season game today.

Kern's leadership on offense was evident throughout. His slick faking and ball handling continually kept the Michigan defense from keying too heavily on one back. His perfect option pitch to Hayden produced the last Buckeye score.

SCORE BY PERIODS

Ohio State 3	7	0	10	—	20
Michigan 0	3	6	0	—	9

6

NOBODY STANDS UP TO MICHIGAN

By ROY BLOUNT Jr.
Sports Illustrated

NEW YORK, Oct. 25, 1971 — Ann Arbor sounds like a nice place to bring a girl named Ann but is a terrible place to bring a football team. A hitting and running group there known as Bo and the Wolverines (featuring the Mellow Men, the Wolfman, Big Ed and others) just destroys football teams.

No one has beaten a Bo Schembechler outfit in Michigan Stadium since early October 1969, and during the past two years the Michigan student cheering section has been able to relax in the first quarter and devote the rest of the afternoon to passing around captured cheerleaders and bottles of apple wine. In the last six games held in Ann Arbor the composite Michigan-opponents score is 272-6.

Last Saturday the unbeaten Wolverines were hospitable enough to offer the winless University of Illinois two touchdowns (one of which the Illini accepted) within the first 2 minutes, but still won handily. As Schembechler said afterward, "It is nice to have a game where you don't play as well as you can and still win, 35-6."

It was an unusual Michigan game in two respects: Michigan passed and Michigan made mistakes. Schembechler's position on passing is the same as a rooster's on flying: He will do it only if forced. Schembechler's position on mistakes is that only the other team is allowed to make them. In the five games preceding Illinois the Wolverine defense had caused 23 turnovers while the Wolverine offense had suffered only five. Imagine the general consternation, then, when on the first play from scrimmage, sophomore quarterback Tom Slade threw a pass and Illinois caught it, giving the Illini the ball on the Michigan 12. They scored in three plays. Quarterback Mike Wells — a placekicker who last year made eight of 10 field goals, some from far out, yet curiously only nine of 16 extra points — missed the extra point, but then Michigan came roaring back with a fumble, surrendering the ball on its 14. This time the defense held, and from then on Illinois netted 67 yards to Michigan's 355. Slade threw only six passes after his opening gaffe, but he completed five of them, and the second Michigan touchdown came on three straight pass plays, all completions, the third one a Slade-to-Glenn Doughty 19-yarder. As usual the big ground during the day was gained by senior tailback Billy Taylor, whose 103 yards brought him within 85 of the Michigan career rushing record held by Ron Johnson, who presented Taylor with the blue suede shoes he runs in. Taylor was ably abetted by sophomore fullback Big Ed Shuttlesworth, a 6-foot-2, 237-pounder who reliably produces 4 yards and a cloud of linemen, and Doughty, a wingback who had been confined to blocking assignments all year. This time he ran and caught passes for three touchdowns.

As one-sided as it was, it was by far Michigan's sloppiest game, and the feat of advancing one's record to 6-0 by depressing another team's to 0-6 is not calculated to improve one's national standing. Illinois, trying to build, and Michigan, shooting for a No. 1 ranking, ought to have each other's schedules this year. The Illini, having played five teams that are or have been ranked in the top 20, are better than their records indicate. The Wolverines, having played only one opponent of real repute so far — Northwestern, a 21-6 victim in the first week of the season — and with only two more coming up — Purdue and Ohio State — are probably better than they will have a chance to prove.

That would disappoint the Mellow Men: Taylor, guard Reggie McKenzie, Doughty, linebacker Mike Taylor (the best in the country, claims Schembechler), safety Tom Darden, defensive end Butch Carpenter and split end Mike Oldham. They all live together off campus in a white house known as the den of the Mellow Men.

"We started hanging tight our freshman year," says McKenzie. "We all lived in the west quad, and everybody there was running around in a big controversy over pledging fraternities. So we decided to form our own group. To be a member, you had to have three jazz albums."

"We also set ourselves some goals," says Billy Taylor. "We were going to win a Big Ten championship, win the Rose Bowl, have an undefeated season and rank No. 1 in the nation."

As sophomores the Mellow Men and their teammates won the Big Ten title, but Schembechler suffered a heart attack the day before the Rose Bowl, and Michigan lost to Southern Cal, 10-3.

As juniors they lost the title, the undefeated season and a shot at the national title to Ohio State at Columbus in the last game of the season. This year the Mellow Men don't plan to fall short in any particulars.

If they do, it won't be for lack of hitting. Schembechler likes to emphasize hitting. On defense this theme is perhaps best articulated by senior defensive back Frank Gusich, known as the Wolfman because that is the name of his position (some teams would call him the Ripper or the monster). He is also called Superman, because when he changes into his head-busting clothes he is transformed from a mild-mannered, Mass-attending, nice person (he was elected last year to Churchmen's All-American) to a fellow who lives for the moment when he catches a fullback in the flat just looking up to catch a pass. At such a moment Gusich goes, as he puts it himself, "berserk." The fullback goes end-over-end.

For the offense, let McKenzie speak. "You can't shuck and jive, you can't lollygag," he says. "You got to hit." Searching for an analogy to the satisfaction he gets from really stunning someone, he says, "It's like . . . when you bite into a good piece of apple pie and say, 'Ohhhhhh, that's good.' Lots of times I'll be sitting talking, and I'll just get to shivering, from thinking about loving to hit."

During the week before the Michigan State game, the Spartan defensive tackle who was to play opposite McKenzie declared that if Michigan State didn't win he would eat a towel. Michigan State did prove more formidable than its reputation, but McKenzie's performance against the tackle was later graded at 92%, and Michigan won, 24-13.

"I want to see him eat a towel," McKenzie was yelling after game. "Hey Bo, can I go across the hall? I want to see him eat a towel." "Be humble in victory, Reggie," said Schembechler. "Michigan State did all the woofing," said Billy Taylor, "and we did all the whupping."

The Mellow Men do a good deal of woofing, too, though. After the Illinois game — as they have after every game since they moved into the white house as juniors — the seven of them and their parents and brothers and sisters and nephews and friends and coaches and their parents' old P.T.A. associates convened for "dinner at the den." Name tags reading "guest of the den" were distributed; fried chicken, barbecued ribs, green beans, turnip greens, cornbread, macaroni and cheese, chicken and rice, black-eyed peas, baked beans, sweet-potato pie, lemon pie and chocolate cake cooked by the parents and brought in from Detroit, Flint and Highland Park, Mich., as well as Cincinnati, Sandusky and Barberton, Ohio, were hit almost as hard as the Illini had been. Mike Taylor's father danced to James Brown's "Hot Pants." Carpenter's girl friend, Pat Batson, a professional singer, was prevailed upon to sing her Mellow Men song, with Billy Taylor, McKenzie, Darden and Doughty moving and going "woom badoom awoom" in the background. Some of the words went like this:

"There's an endless giving of love and affection,
"And if you're lost, they'll give you directions —
"Take a boat or a plane, a jet or a train,
"Turn the highway to dust, cut a class if you must,
"But go to the den, the den of the Mellow Men."
Just try telling that one to some of the football teams that have visited Ann Arbor recently.

7

WOLVERINES UPEND BUCKEYES BEFORE 104,016

By NEIL AMDUR
Special to The New York Times

ANN ARBOR, Mich., Nov. 20, 1971 — Stunned by an 85-yard punt return and stymied by an aroused Ohio State defense, unbeaten Michigan scored a touchdown with 2 minutes 7 seconds to play on a 21-yard run by Billy Taylor today for a thrilling 10-7 victory over the Buckeyes.

Before an overflow crowd of 104,016, one of the largest ever to attend a college football game, the Rose Bowl-bound Wolverines went 72 yards for their decisive score, which reversed last year's loss to Ohio State and preserved their chances for a national championship.

Strange, Almost Bizarre

It was a strange, almost bizarre game that began in gusty rains and snow and finished with the sun shining and Woody Hayes, the Ohio State coach, almost as hot inside his bright red windbreaker.

In an unusually fiery display of temperament that typified his coaching intensity, the 57-year-old Hayes rushed on the field in the last 90 seconds to protest a Michigan pass interception that thwarted Ohio State's final offensive series at the Wolverine 49-yard line.

Tom Darden, a Michigan defensive back, had leaped in front of Dick Wakefield, the Ohio State pass receiver, for the crucial interception at the Wolverine 32 with 1:25 left.

Apparently contending that Darden had interfered with Wakefield, Hayes confronted the referee, Jerry Markbreit, and had to be restrained by assistants and players.

The Buckeyes were penalized 15 yards for Hayes' misconduct. They lost another 15 yards when Hayes, still shouting at officials on the sidelines, tore up the first-down and sideline markers, to the bewilderment of Lou Lehman, the field judge.

'A Great Interception'

Afterward, as more snow fell and a brilliant rainbow capped the afternoon, Hayes refused to comment on the play. But Darden and Bo Schembechler, the Michigan coach and a former pupil under Hayes, defended the coverage.

"I just jumped over him," said Darden, who picked off two State passes. "He was going down for the ball, and I was trying to just go around him, but I finally jumped over him.

"I knew I would either knock the ball down or catch it. We were in zone coverage and they ran cross-cuts. I didn't see Wakefield until he was wide open so I just picked him up. I still have the ball and I'm going to keep it."

Schembechler, who termed his defense "superb," said Darden's interception "was one of the greatest I've ever seen. I don't need to look at films to know that."

The last-minute demonstration typified the tenseness that prevailed in the second half, after Dana Coin, the Michigan kicking specialist, had put up the only points of the first half with a second-quarter, 32-yard field goal.

Ohio State, besieged by injuries all season, had no offense to loosen the tenacious Michigan defense, ranked third nationally and first against scoring.

The Buckeyes gained more yards on Tom Campana's five punt returns, 166, than they could with 51 running and passing plays.

Campana, an offensive back converted to defense this year, stunned the crowd and the Wolverines on his weaving 85-yard return, only the second touchdown scored against Michigan in the third period.

Campana's effectiveness in shaking away from onrushing tacklers was more an instinctive reaction to the Wolverines' aggressive coverage, which came down quickly, protecting the outside lanes, but left daylight up the middle.

Ohio State's inability to control the ball, or "grind meat," as Hayes calls it, gave Michigan its chance with 7:06 left in the last quarter.

Neither team had shown any imagination or effectiveness on crucial third-down plays. Ohio State fluffed 12 of 14. When Michigan came out with third and 7 at its 31 and 6:08 left, it had muffed 12 of 15 earlier tries to hold the ball.

Billy Taylor Scores

On this series, however, Billy Taylor, the Wolverines' fine halfback, bulled determinedly for the first down.

Another possession down, third and 4 at the 45, gave Larry Cipa, a reserve quarterback who replaced the injured Tom Slade, the opportunity to complete his only pass in seven attempts. It was a 22-yarder to Bo Rather, a wide receiver, off a fake draw play.

Now Michigan was at the Buckeye 33, and the crowd, conspicuously quiet since Campana's electrifying run, roared encouragement.

Three plays gained 9 yards. On fourth down, stopped once before in a similar situation, Fritz Seyferth dived over right guard for a first down.

With the ball at the State 21, Cipa pitched out to Taylor, who turned the right side. When Seyferth put a perfect block on Campana, Taylor sped down the sidelines for the score. The clock read 2:07.

Mobbed by teammates and fans, Taylor ran off the field, his index finger waving the familiar No. 1.

It was not until Darden's interception, however, that Michigan fans could settle back. And even then, Hayes' outburst produced a mob scene at midfield.

Despite a series of injuries that had sidelined 11 starters since the start of the season, Ohio State limited Michigan to its lowest first-half scoring total in 11 games.

The Buckeyes also produced a 50-yard punt return by Campana after Michigan's first offensive series that must have unnerved Schembechler, who several days ago had praised his team's kicking game as one of the country's finest.

The Wolverines had allowed only 88 total yards in 22 punt returns, but Campana shook off two blockers and bolted through a small opening to the Michigan 28 before many in the large crowd found their way to seats. Mike Taylor caught him to save a touchdown.

The Buckeyes, however, fumbled away the scoring threat at the Wolverine 17. The first of two fumbles by Billy Taylor in the opening half gave Ohio State its other opportunity at the Michigan 28.

Fred Schram's 38-yard field-goal attempt with 10 minutes left in the half had sufficient distance but drifted to the left of the crossbar.

Michigan's offense sputtered after Slade, the regular quarterback, left the field in the first quarter with a hip injury. Slade returned in the second period and marched Michigan's version of the wishbone offense 65 yards in 13 plays to the Buckeye 22. The Buckeye defense stiffened and the Wolverines had to settle for Coin's seventh field goal of the season.

Ohio State's ability to contain the Wolverines was remarkable in view of the various adjustments the Buckeyes had to make in recent weeks. Only this morning, Tom Marendt, a sophomore defensive end and starter, was rushed to a local hospital with an appendicitis attack.

SCORE BY PERIODS

Michigan 0	3	0	7	—	10
Ohio State 0	0	7	0	—	7

8

STANFORD UPSETS MICHIGAN IN LATE RALLY

By BILL BECKER
Special to The New York Times

PASADENA, Calif., Jan. 1, 1972 — In a Rose Bowl game they'll be talking about for another 70 years, Stanford finally caught up with Michigan today for the 49-0 pasting it took in the 1902 contest, the first of this postseason football series.

The Stanfords used a 31-yard field goal in the final 12 seconds by little Rod Garcia to upset the undefeated Big Ten champions, 13-12, and they accomplished this after virtually handing the game to the Wolverines on a safety a few minutes earlier.

It was the second straight upset victory for the Indians from Palo Alto, Calif., and their coach, John Ralston. Ralston likes to play it cool and loose — but not quite this loose.

103,154 See Game

However, he had Don Bunce, a rifle-armed quarterback, who completed 24 passes for 294 yards to more than match the vaunted Wolverine running attack led by all-American Billy Taylor. Bunce may be a shade behind Jim Plunkett but he did the job almost as well as Plunkett did last New Year's Day against Ohio State.

The loss was the second for Michigan and its coach, Bo Schembechler, in their last two trips. The Wolverines had four consecutive victories here starting with that 1909 inaugural. But they hadn't met Stanford since then.

A crowd of 103,154 was treated to one of the hardest-hitting of the 58 games in the Rose Bowl series. Tough defenses nullified the best thrusts of both teams for three quarters. Dana Coin kicked a 30-yard field goal to give the Wolverines a 3-0 halftime lead before Garcia tied it with a 42-yarder in the third period.

Long Drive at Start

The final period started with Michigan's 71-yard drive producing a 1-yard touchdown plunge by Fritz Seyferth, fullback. Coin's conversion made it 10-3.

But Ralston, a gambler at heart, let his boys run from punt formation on fourth and 10 at their 33-yard line midway in the period. Jackie Brown swept right end for 31 yards and a minute later broke off right tackle for 24 yards and a touchdown. Garcia's conversion tied it, 10-all.

Michigan recovered a Bunce fumble on the Stanford 35 to set up a 46-yard field-goal try by Coin, which fell short.

However, Jim Ferguson, a sophomore safety, tried to run the ball back and was knocked back into the end zone by Ed Shuttlesworth's tackle for a safety. Michigan took the lead, 12-10, with 3 minutes 18 seconds left.

After one exchange of kicks, the Indians got the ball at their 22 with 1 minute 48 seconds to go. Bunce, the riverboat shifty, passed 13 to Bill Scott, a tight end, 16 and 12 to John Winesberry, the shifty flanker; 11 to Miles Moore, a split end; 14 to Reggie Sanderson, the fullback, and there was Stanford on the Michigan 14 with 14 seconds left.

On third down and 7 to go and with Steve Murray holding, Garcia, who led the nation's field-goal kickers with 14 in 1971, kicked his biggest. It was a 31-yard bull's-eye requiring only 2 seconds. A kickoff later, Stanford was returned the 13-12 victor.

Bunce Hits 24 of 44

Bunce completed 24 of 44, with several near interceptions, but kept the Indians rolling with 22 first downs, compared to 16 for Michigan. Stanford rushed for only four first downs, but the Wolverines got no first downs passing, with Tom Slade, a sophomore, showing more skill as a runner.

Ralston hailed the victory "as just as satisfying" as last year's. This made it three straight for the Pacific 8 over the Big Ten for the first time in this series. Michigan lost, 10-3, to Southern California, in 1970.

Schembechler conceded, "Stanford deserved to win because we didn't get first downs when we needed them."

The Indians made a goal-line stand inside their 5-yard line at the start of the third period, then marched downfield to set up Garcia's first field goal.

They consistently gang-tackled Taylor, the workhorse who carried 32 times for 82 yards, and refused to break under the pounding rush attack of the Wolverines.

The Michigan coach singled out the fake punt as a key play that swung the momentum to Stanford. Ralston said the play was one he had picked up from a fellow coach. The ball was snapped to the fullback, Reg Sanderson, instead of the punter, Murray. Sanderson then handed it to Brown, who took off.

Ralston also praised Bunce and "all those fine receivers." Especially outstanding was Winesberry, the sophomore from Tulsa who caught eight for 112 yards. Bunce said all the plays on the final drive were audibles. "We were really pulling some plays out of the air," the quarterback told reporters. "I was so excited I didn't even know what I was calling."

Stanford, it should be added, played without Hillary Shockley, the fullback hobbled by ankle injury. Sanderson and others took up the slack.

Stanford now has won five games, lost five and tied once in 11 Rose Bowl appearances.

SCORE BY PERIODS

Stanford 0	0	3	10	—	13
Michigan 0	3	0	9	—	12

9

LANTRY KICKS WOLVES TO VICTORY OVER PURDUE

By THE ASSOCIATED PRESS
The New York Times

ANN ARBOR, Mich., Nov. 18, 1972 — Mike Lantry, who earlier had missed a key extra point, kicked a 30-yard field goal with 1 minute 4 seconds remaining today to give undefeated Michigan a 9-6 football victory over Purdue.

It was the Boilermakers' last chance to stay in contention for the Big Ten title.

Randy Logan intercepted a pass by Purdue's Gary Danielson at the Michigan 42-yard line with 3:03 to go and the Wolverines drove to the Purdue 12 in five plays to set up the winning kick.

It was Michigan's 10th victory, and seventh in the Big Ten. Purdue is now 5-2 in the conference and 5-5 over all.

The Boilermakers went out into a 3-0 lead on a 25-yard field goal by a sophomore, Frank Conner, at 6:22 of the first quarter.

That advantage held up until Dennis Franklin hit Paul Seal with an 11-yard Michigan touchdown pass that capped an 80-yard, nine-play drive following the second-half kickoff.

But Lantry's conversion attempt went under the crossbar and on the last play of the third quarter, Conner tied the game with a 20-yard field goal.

Michigan had a rough time moving on the ground.

However, on the first two plays after Logan's interception, Franklin ran up the middle for 17 yards and Chuck Heater crashed over left guard for 22 more to the Boilermaker 19.

Michigan will now face Ohio State at Columbus, Ohio, next Saturday for the Big Ten championship and a trip to the Rose Bowl. The Buckeyes, who defeated Northwestern, 27-14, today, have a conference record of 6-1.

Michigan's touchdown was set up by a 52-yard pass play from Franklin to Clint Haslerig that put the ball on the Purdue 11. The scoring pass to Seal came after two incompletions.

The usually overpowering Michigan ground game was cut short at 100 yards net, with another 52 yards in rushing losses. The tenacious Purdue defense was led by a linebacker, Mark Gefert, the middle guard, Greg Bingham, and an end, Steve Baumgartner.

SCORE BY PERIODS

Michigan	0	0	6	3 —	9
Purdue	3	0	3	0 —	6

10

BUCKEYES FRUSTRATE MICHIGAN AT GOAL LINE

By NEIL AMDUR
Special to The New York Times

COLUMBUS, Ohio, Nov. 25, 1972 — Two incredible goal-line stands led aroused Ohio State to a 14–11 victory over previously unbeaten Michigan today for a share of the Big Ten Conference championship and a berth in the Rose Bowl.

In an upset that must have warmed the heart of Woody Hayes, the Ohio State coach who thrives on tenacity and whose hero is Gen. George Patton, the Buckeyes stopped Michigan's powerful rushing attack on six different downs at the 1-yard line, including four successive downs near the end of the first half.

It was the ninth triumph in 10 games for Ohio State, and it may have been one of the most satisfying moments for Hayes, who was severely criticized for tearing up first-down markers and temperamental outbursts in a controversial 10-7 defeat by the Wolverines last year in Ann Arbor.

Michigan, which had visions of a national championship game against unbeaten, top-ranked Southern California on New Year's Day, scored on a 35-yard field goal and controlled possession for most of the game before a raucous capacity crowd of 87,040.

But the Wolverines could not break the unrelenting spirit of the Buckeye defense, and the futility of the Michigan offense was symbolized in the last 6 seconds when George Hasenohrl, a 262-pound Buckeye defensive tackle, collared Dennis Franklin, the Michigan quarterback, attempting to pass on fourth down from the State 41-yard line.

The Wolverines started offensive series at the State 29 and 37 in the final period and could not score. Their last series, with 1 minute 20 seconds left, followed a futile 47-yard Buckeye field-goal attempt.

Three first downs reached the Ohio State 41-yard line with 40 seconds remaining. But the Buckeyes stiffened and Michigan turned over the ball while elated Ohio State rooters tore down both goal posts.

The tempo of the game was hot, despite cold, sleet, rain and snow, from the moment Ohio State players ran on the field for the opening kickoff and began jumping up and down and leaping in a furious circle in front of the Buckeye bench.

Not to be outdone by Hayes, his former boss, Glenn (Bo) Schembechler, the Michigan coach, let his players match State with a similar psyching ceremony at midfield.

But Hayes won this war, too. Buckeye players went the Wolverines one better with still another circle of dancing, yelling and backslapping and maintained the psychological momentum throughout, particularly during the critical goal-line stands.

Michigan gained only 208 yards rushing against the State defense and was forced to pass 23 times, double the per-game average the Wolverines had settled for en route to nine consecutive earlier victories.

"Our defense grows to magnificent heights," Hayes said afterward.

Asked to comment on the goal-line stand in the first half, with the Buckeyes leading, 7-3, the Ohio State coach said, "Yes, it was the greatest I'd seen — until the one in the second half."

Hayes also said that the first goal-line stand probably was the game's "turning point," since the Buckeyes retained their lead at halftime and extended it with a third-quarter score.

'We Should Have Scored'

Michigan ran 83 plays to Ohio State's 44 and had possession over 39 minutes. Besides the goal-line stands, the Wolverines also were stopped on a fourth-and-1 situation at the Buckeye 20 two plays into the fourth quarter when Richard Middleton, a linebacker, submarined an attempted plunge at the heart of the State defense.

"Their defense bent, but it wouldn't break," Schembechler said, in tribute to Michigan's fiercest Big Ten rival in a series that has seen the home team win the last four games, all by close scores.

Asked why he shunned the almost certain field goal that could have tied the game in the fourth quarter, Schembechler said tersely, "Because I thought we could score. We should have scored."

The teams traded third-quarter touchdowns after Ohio State drove 78 yards for a score that made it 14-3 less than 3 minutes into the second half.

A 35-yard run by Greg Hare, the junior quarterback from Cumberland, Md., preceded a 30-yard, quick-opening burst over right tackle by the freshman Archie Griffin, for the touchdown.

Michigan matched the State score with a 10-play touchdown drive that consumed almost 9 minutes and ended with the second goal-line confrontation of the game, this time from the State 5.

Three plays netted 4½ yards. On fourth down, Ed Shuttlesworth hammered through right guard for the score. Shuttlesworth, nursing a tender ankle in the past few games, had been inserted in the lineup on the preceding play only after Neal Colzie, a Buckeye defensive back, had sent Bob Thornbladh to the sidelines with a head-on tackle after a pass play.

Logan Intercepts

Sensing that a tie could still send them to the Rose Bowl, the Wolverines went for a 2-point conversion over the extra-point placement. Franklin sprinted out and completed the pass to Clint Haslerig that reduced the Buckeye margin to 3 points. A pass interception by Randy Logan of an underthrown toss by Hare put Michigan in possession at the State 29 for the tying field goal or winning touchdown early in the final quarter.

The Wolverines again reached the Buckeye 5-yard line on first down, the 4 on second down and the 1-yard line on third.

But Harry Banks, a 177-pound running back, was stopped without a gain as he attempted to wrestle free from four State tacklers.

Shunning an almost certain field-goal conversion that might have assured their trip to Pasadena and perhaps a national championship, the Wolverines went for the touchdown on fourth down.

Franklin took the snap and tried to push in for the touchdown. But he was hit in his tracks and stood up by four State tacklers — Randy Gradishar, Doug Plank, George Hasenohrl and Shad Williams — and the Buckeyes again had held, this time with 9 minutes left.

Michigan had two more opportunities in the closing minutes, one after a Buckeye punt had given them possession at the State 32-yard line.

But again the aggressive Buckeye defense swarmed Franklin, and a fourth-down pass went incomplete.

Michigan controlled the ball for 11 minutes 23 seconds in the first quarter and ran 22 plays to only six for the once-beaten Buckeyes.

But the Wolverines could not score until the third play of the second period when Mike Lantry, their placekicking specialist, converted a 35-yard field-goal attempt. Lantry had missed a 44-yarder on the preceding series.

Ohio State finally rushed for its initial first down of the game on a 19-yard run by Hare that ended up with Hayes being knocked down on the sidelines as players from both teams rolled out of bounds. Michigan held at its 44, but Gary Lago's punt put the Wolverines deep in their territory and helped

41

give the Buckeyes excellent field position for a 46-yard scoring drive. The big gainer was an 18-yard burst over right tackle to the Michigan 4-yard line by Griffin. A Michigan offside penalty on third and 1 — the Wolverines' third such infraction of the half and most costly — gave the Buckeyes a first down at the Michigan 22.

Champ Henson's 20th touchdown of the season came on a third-down burst behind John Hicks, a 254-pound junior right tackle, who blocked with the power and efficiency of such other great Buckeye offensive linemen as Dave Foley, Rufus Mays, Jim Parker and Bob Vogel.

The touchdown came with 4:30 left in the half and touched off wild cheering by the capacity crowd. For the next 12 plays of the half, however, State rooters watched anxiously as Michigan drove to the Buckeye 1-yard line only to be repelled on one of the great goal-line stands of the season.

A 35-yard pass play from Franklin to Paul Seal, his favorite receiver, contributed most of the yardage, after Franklin, a 6-foot-1 sophomore from Massillon, Ohio, froze two Buckeye defensive backs with a marvelous fake.

Another pass play, 14 yards to Haslerig, put the ball at the Ohio State 11 with 43 seconds left, and a 10-yard slant off right tackle by Chuck Heater moved the ball to the 1, with a go-ahead touchdown seemingly imminent and 33 seconds on the clock.

But Heater lost 1 yard on a pitchout and slipped on the slippery synthetic surface on an attempted sweep to the right side. On third down, with Shuttlesworth, the team's leading ground-gainer standing next to Schembechler on the sidelines, Thornbladh, the Wolverines' No. 2 fullback, was stopped on a plunge into the middle of the red-shirted Buckeye defense.

Michigan called time out with 11 seconds left, but the pressure apparently was too great for Franklin. He fumbled the fourth-down snap, fell on it, and State's defensive unit left the field to a tumultuous standing ovation.

SCORE BY PERIODS

Ohio State 0	7	7	0	—	14
Michigan 0	3	8	0	—	11

11

MICHIGAN RALLY TIES OHIO STATE, 10-10

By BILL BECKER
Special to The New York Times

ANN ARBOR, Mich., Nov. 24, 1973 — Michigan rallied for 10 points in the fourth quarter, but missed two long field-goal attempts in a frantic final minute that would have broken a 10-10 tie with top-ranked Ohio State today.

The dramatic deadlock between the two undefeated Big Ten Conference powers delayed a decision on the league's Rose Bowl representative until tomorrow afternoon, when votes of the various athletic directors will be tabulated.

But Ohio State's failure to win almost assures college football of a true national championship game between Alabama and Notre Dame in the Sugar Bowl, if both teams survive their final regular-season encounters.

Alabama, unbeaten and ranked No. 2 this week, must play Auburn next Saturday. Notre Dame, No. 5 in the polls, faces Miami of Florida on Saturday.

The largest crowd to attend a regular-season college game in modern times, 105,223, watched an ironic wind-up to this much-awaited meeting.

It saw Ohio State, which had tried 49 consecutive running plays and rejected the forward pass even in obvious passing situations, desperately trying to break the tie in the closing minute with passes by a reserve quarterback, Greg Hare, who had not played earlier in the game.

Hare's first attempt, thrown off-balance and while backing up, almost cost the Buckeyes the game. It was intercepted by Tom Drake at the State 40-yard line and returned to the 33 with 52 seconds left.

Out of time-outs and missing their No. 1 quarterback, Dennis Franklin, who had been hurt on the preceding series, the Wolverines tried one running play for a 6-yard gain and threw an incomplete pass, which stopped the clock with 28 seconds left.

"We didn't want to hurry our kicker, we wanted to take our time," Bo Schembechler, the Michigan coach, said of his decision to shun another play and attempt a field goal on third down.

Mike Lantry, the Wolverines' place-kicking specialist, had kicked a 30-yarder on the second play of the final quarter and missed a 58-yarder on fourth-and-two from the Buckeye 41 with 1:06 left.

The snap was good, Lantry got good distance into his kick with the aid of 20-mile an hour wind, but the ball sailed wide to the right.

Realizing that its national championship hopes would end with a tie, Ohio State went for broke with three more desperation passes from its 20-yard line. But all three were incomplete, a symbolic gesture of futility for a team that won its first nine games by throwing only 75 passes during its 695 plays.

Ohio State built a 10-0 half-time lead on a 31-yard field goal by Blair Conway and a 5-yard scoring burst from Pete Johnson, a 6-foot-1-inch, 227-pound freshman from Long Beach, L.I.

The Buckeyes amassed 143 yards rushing in the first half, with Archie Griffin, their fine sophomore, piling up 99. The closest thing to an Ohio State pass play was a routine pitchout from Cornelius Green to Griffin for an outside sweep.

Michigan made its first serious penetration into Buckeye territory on its opening series of the second half, but was turned back on an end-zone interception by Neal Colzie.

The tempo changed late in the third period when Michigan stopped the Buckeyes on successive running plays — third-and-seven from the Wolverine 39 and fourth and inches from the 33.

A 50-yard drive produced Lantry's fourth-quarter field goal. When Ohio State again shunned a pass on third-and-seven from its 26, the Wolverines drove 51 yards in six plays for the tying score.

Franklin ran the final 10 yards on a fourth-and-three keeper after luring State defenders inside with a fake to Ed Shuttlesworth, a workhorse all day at fullback.

Ohio State took the next kickoff and reached third-and-six at the Michigan 47. But again the Buckeyes lacked enough confidence to attempt their first pass and Griffin was stopped short of the first down.

Michigan might have scored on its next series if Franklin had not suffered a broken collarbone while being thrown to the ground after completing a seven-yard pass to Shuttlesworth.

The play carried to the State 49. Without Franklin's versatility, the Wolverines tried three running plays that gained eight yards before Lantry's 58-yarder failed.

"I'm disappointed that we didn't win, but I'm really proud of this team," said Schembechler, whose club had won its first 10 games enroute to a No. 4 national ranking. "They came out at the half and were great."

SCORE BY PERIODS

Ohio State 0	10	0	0	—	10
Michigan 0	0	0	10	—	10

12

MICHIGAN STEAMS AS OHIO STATE WINS BOWL VOTE

By GORDON S. WHITE Jr.
Special to The New York Times

NEW YORK, Nov. 26, 1973 — Ohio State was voted into the Rose Bowl by the Big Ten athletic directors yesterday and Bo Schembechler, Michigan's football coach, reacted quickly and bitterly, accusing these conference administrators of being guided by "petty jealousies."

Undefeated Ohio State and undefeated Michigan, ranked first and fourth, respectively, in the nation last week, struggled to a 10-10 tie at Ann Arbor, Mich., Saturday in a game that was to decide the Big Ten championship and the league's entry in the Rose Bowl. Big Ten rules stipulate that in case of a tie for the title, the athletic directors shall vote to select their Rose Bowl team.

Wayne Duke, the Big Ten commissioner, conducted a telephone vote from his Chicago office yesterday morning. Duke refused to divulge the count in favor of Ohio State, but indicated the majority was persuaded by the fact that Dennis Franklin, Michigan's quarterback, suffered a broken collarbone late in the game and would probably be unavailable for the New Year's Day game at Pasadena, Calif.

Thus the majority of Big Ten officials did not take into account the fact that underdog Michigan rallied in the fourth quarter to tie Ohio State and finish the game with an edge in statistics. Ohio State scored 10 points in the second quarter, Michigan scored its 10 in the final period with Franklin making the tying touchdown on a 10-yard run just before he was hurt.

The Wolverines gained 312 yards to 247 for Woody Hayes' Buckeyes and Michigan had 16 first downs to nine for Ohio State.

But Ohio State, not Michigan, will meet Southern California on Jan. 1 in a rematch of last winter's Rose Bowl, which the Trojans won, 42-17. Southern California became the Pacific Eight Rose Bowl team when it upset U.C.L.A., 23-13, on Saturday.

Schembechler lashed out at the athletic directors and said, "I'm very bitter and resentful. Petty jealousies were involved and they just used the injury to Dennis Franklin as a scapegoat.

"I'm very disappointed in the administration of the Big Ten. It hasn't been very tough and it hasn't been very good."

Don Canham, the Michigan athletic director, backed up his coach, saying, "We're shocked. That's a sad situation that they used the injury. If we're deep at any position it's at quarterback. And who is to say Franklin won't be healthy by the time of the Rose Bowl?

"We feel the underdog that ties the favorite team should get the credit. We have Larry Cipa, who has played a lot this year behind Franklin. He's the one, you remember, who led us to the win over Ohio State two years ago."

Although most athletic directors would not disclose their vote, Michigan got at least two — Canham's and that of Paul Giel, the Minnesota director of athletics.

Giel said, "I voted for Michigan because Ohio State was the team that most recently went to the Rose Bowl. I called Don Canham before casting my vote and he told me Michigan really wanted to go even though Franklin was hurt so I cast my vote for Michigan."

Bill Orwig, Indiana's athletic director, said, "I won't tell. But I didn't let the injury influence me at all. I just voted for the team I felt was the best representative."

Bump Elliott, Iowa's athletic director and a Michigan alumnus, said, "I don't think it's right to divulge anything about the vote."

Schembechler said, "I would really like to know how those schools voted and particularly how our sister school Michigan State voted." Burt Smith, Michigan State's athletic director, was unavailable for comment.

Edward Weaver, Ohio State's athletic director, obviously voted for his team. The other directors, who did not disclose their vote, are: Cecil Coleman of Illinois, Elroy Hirsch of Wisconsin, Dick Ordyna of Purdue and Tippy Dye of Northwestern.

Hayes, Ohio State's coach, said immediately after the game Saturday: "We had to win this one to go and we didn't. If they vote Michigan, Michigan deserves to go."

But after the vote was announced yesterday, Hayes said: "I'm delighted. I couldn't be happier.

"You have to remember that we played an even ball game on an uneven field." He was alluding to the fact that the game was played at Michigan Stadium before a record crowd of 105,223 persons.

Hayes said, "What probably influenced the athletic directors more than Franklin's injury was the fact that most of the coaches who faced our team and Michigan had said Ohio State was the tougher opponent of the two."

When John McKay, Southern California's coach learned of the Big Ten decision, he said: "I don't know whether it's a surprise or not. They must have decided to pick the most representative team and Ohio State was No. 1 in the nation by a wide margin going into Saturday's game."

But McKay knows what happens to a No. 1 team that plays a tie. His Trojans were first at the end of the 1972 season and, after the Rose Bowl victory over Ohio State, started this season favored to repeat as No. 1. But Oklahoma and Southern California battled to a 7-7 tie, last Sept. 29, and the Trojans were replaced at the top by Ohio State.

13

OHIO STATE MAY BE NO. 1, BUT DON'T TELL MICHIGAN

By TEX MAULE
Sports Illustrated

NEW YORK, Oct. 21, 1974 — Second best? What's with this second best, Michigan would like to know. Up in Ann Arbor, some 175 miles north of Columbus, the Wolverines were staking their own claim to the national championship, disposing easily of traditional rival Michigan State. Sure, the score was not nearly as eye-popping as the Buckeyes', but 21-7 might easily have been, say, doubled. Second best? Michigan begs to differ.

It was apparent almost immediately that Michigan State was no real match for Michigan in speed, size or skill. The Spartans are a young, lively team, but Michigan had more of everything, including incentive. Burt Smith, the Michigan State athletic director, provided the latter at the end of the 1973 season when he voted to send Ohio State to the Rose Bowl instead of Michigan; this was particularly galling to Michigan since the final vote for Ohio State, which had tied Michigan for the conference championship in the final game of the season, was six to four. Had it been five and five, Michigan would have gone, because Ohio State had been to Pasadena the previous year.

Coach Bo Schembechler was understandably upset. Dennis Franklin, the Michigan quarterback, had suffered a broken collarbone in the Ohio State game, and Smith, like the other athletic directors who sided with him, wanted a victory after four consecutive Big Ten defeats in the Rose Bowl.

"I thought the Bowl trip was a reward for the team, win or lose," Schembechler said then. "Why penalize the whole team for one injury?"

"We remember," one Wolverine player said. "We don't talk about it, but we remember." Bumper stickers on the Michigan campus suggested BURT SMITH FOR QUARTERBACK with a nail through the name.

But the Wolverines really did not require that incentive. The first time they got their hands on the ball, Franklin took them 48 yards on a neatly put together drive that ended with a pitchout to one of the few small men on the team, tailback Gordon Bell. Bell, 5-foot-9 and 175, skipped down the sideline for 13 yards and a touchdown as the formidable Michigan blockers worked over would-be Spartan tacklers.

By halftime Michigan led, 21-0. Franklin, whom Schembechler has called the best quarterback in collegiate football, had gone a long way toward proving it. He is quiet and self-contained, with enough confidence to argue with Schembechler about football philosophy and enough discipline to yield to his coach's wisdom. On the option play, which is the backbone of the Wolverine attack, Franklin's preference is to pass, something Schembechler looks on with about as much enthusiasm as does Woody Hayes. But, although he is given considerable freedom in play selection, Franklin uses the pass with admirable prudence. In this game he threw only nine times and completed five.

One of the completions was on a rare long throw, a gamble Schembechler felt justified in taking with only 6 seconds left in the half and Michigan on the State 44-yard line. Franklin, who has an exceptionally strong arm, dropped back and hit split end Jim Smith, who had been overlooked by the Spartan defense, on the 5-yard line. Easy touchdown.

After the game, breathing painfully from bruised ribs which forced him out in the fourth period, Franklin seemed almost apologetic for having scored on so atypical a play.

"Usually there's no use in a play like that," he said. "You just put it out there, and hope someone runs under it. I did, and he caught it."

Schembechler, an intense driver with an extraordinary talent for organization, was not really pleased with the victory, although it must have been a particularly satisfying one.

"I was quite disappointed with the second half," he said. "We didn't move the ball well. It was bad coaching, and I don't blame the kids, I blame myself. I didn't let our offense run at them and I tried to get too fancy with a 21-0 lead. When you get a little older, like I am, I guess you get a little frivolous."

Michigan's second touchdown might be termed a bit frivolous, but it was not a Schembechler operation. Tom Birney, the Spartan punter, missed a one-hop snap from center on his 21, was crunched by defensive end Dan Jilek and fumbled the ball all the way into the end zone, where Jilek pounced on it.

Jilek was one of the few Michigan players who admitted special satisfaction in the victory. "It was good to get the touchdown," he said later. "And it was especially good to beat Michigan State. Coach Schembechler never said anything about the vote during the week, but he didn't have to. It was in the back of all our minds. You never forget a thing like that."

And so it seems certain that an undefeated Michigan again will be playing an undefeated Ohio State for the Rose Bowl and, possibly, for No. 1. Although it is no longer true that the Big Ten is the Big Two and eight also-rans, the rest of the conference has not yet caught up to these schools.

A great deal of the credit for the Wolverines' success over the past few seasons belongs to Schembechler, who has lost only six of 60 games since coming to Michigan five years ago from Miami of Ohio. His attention to detail is so meticulous that it extends to charting the position of players and coaches for the annual team picture, and he has a Lombardi-like quality for inspiring players.

Schembechler was brought to Ann Arbor by Michigan athletic director Don Canham, who used to be the school's head track coach. Like Schembechler, Canham is an efficient organizer who owns a successful manufacturing company and runs the Michigan athletic department like a business. He hired Schembechler on recommendations by of all people, Sonny Werblin, then owner of the New York Jets, and George Allen, the coach of the Washington Redskins, neither of whom knew Bo personally.

"George had looked at movies of Miami games, looking for talent," Canham says. "He told me that the club was exceptionally well drilled and well organized, and the coach was doing a hell of a job.

"Then I went East to try to get Joe Paterno for the job, but he did not want to leave Penn State. I ran into Sonny Werblin in Toots Shor's, and he said he had been looking at film and *his* coaches liked the way Miami looked. 'I don't know what the coach's name is, but I'd look him up,' he said."

So, if Michigan can manage a victory over Ohio State and Franklin can stay healthy, the Wolverines may make it to the Rose Bowl and the national title by way of a New York saloon.

51

14

BUCKEYES DEFEAT MICHIGAN, 12-10

By **GORDON S. WHITE Jr.**

Special to The New York Times

COLUMBUS, Ohio, Nov. 23, 1974 — Ohio State acted just like a member of the National Football League today as it failed to score a touchdown but won the biggest game of the season when Tom Klaban kicked four field goals to beat Michigan, 12-10.

This left Ohio State and Michigan, which suffered its first loss of the season, in a tie for the Big Ten title. But the result of this regular-season finale before 88,243 persons filling Ohio Stadium left unanswered for 24 hours the question of who will represent the Big Ten in the Rose Bowl game, Jan. 1.

Because coach Woody Hayes' Buckeyes won, the 10 conference athletic directors will meet tomorrow near Chicago's O'Hare Airport to vote on whether Ohio State or Michigan will go to the Rose Bowl. The fact that the victory was by only two points and the fact that the Buckeyes never crossed the Michigan goal line may play an important part in Michigan's favor in the vote.

When Michigan's placekicking specialist, Mike Lantry, missed a 33-yard field-goal attempt with 18 seconds remaining in the game, the Ohio State players and fans jumped with glee and surely felt they deserved the trip to Pasadena, Calif. But strange things have happened in previous voting, such as last year when these powers finished in a 10-10 tie and co-champions of the conference. The Buckeyes were voted to the Rose Bowl then, even though they had gone just the year before.

This year's big game resembled one of those professional struggles the N.F.L. has so often. After Michigan scored a touchdown on its opening drive, the two college powers slugged it out and let their placekickers settle the issue. What it amounted to was that Klaban, a junior born in Czechoslovakia and raised in Cincinnati, proved to be a better field-goal kicker today than Lantry, a senior from Oxford, Mich.

Lantry booted a 37-yarder with five minutes to go in the first quarter, giving the Wolverines a 10-0 lead. But the left-footed, orthodox kicker missed three other field-goal attempts — of 51 and 58 yards as well as the final 33-yarder.

Klaban, meantime, kicked field goals in the second quarter of 47, 25 and 43 yards, tying a Buckeye record of three field goals in a half. Then the right-footed soccer-style kicker hit the winner — a 45-yarder at 4:51 of the third quarter.

Michigan, one of four remaining major college teams to be undefeated and untied before today, finished the regular season with a 10-1 won-lost mark and the all-important loss in the Big Ten Conference. Ohio State, which was upset by Michigan State in conference play two weeks ago, finished with a similar mark of 10-1.

Defenses Take Over

Today's game, which was nationally televised, never produced the spectacular ground thrusts characteristic of both teams. This may have been largely because the two defenses took control, particularly in the second half.

Archie Griffin, Ohio State's star tailback, picked up 111 yards in 25 carries, increasing his National Collegiate record to 22 straight games in which he has picked up over 100 yards. But Michigan's little tailback, Gordon Bell, just about matched Griffin in effort by carrying 25 times and picking up 108 yards.

These two junior runners epitomized the equal strengths of the two offenses. The teams finished in a dead heat for team rushing yardage at 195 each and were on a par in passing, with Ohio State gaining 58 yards in the air and Michigan 96. But the most notable similarity of their passing games was that neither was effective when it counted most.

Griffin's biggest single gain was an 18-yard burst early in the first period. The fact that he and other good Ohio State runners never scored attested to the fine defense up front for the Wolverines.

Two of the real standouts of the contest were Ohio State's Pete Cusick, a huge but quick defensive tackle, and Michigan's Jeff Perlinger, an equally huge and mobile defensive tackle. Perlinger was obviously assigned to Griffin all game long. He stuck to coach Bo Schembechler's orders and rode down the running star many a time at the line of scrimmage, sometimes even catching Griffin from behind.

Cusick destroyed some of the best-laid plans of the Wolverines at key moments, such as third-down plays when Dennis Franklin, the Michigan quarterback, had to pass. Perlinger hit Ohio State's quarterback, Cornelius

Greene, so hard that Greene lost the ball on a running play and Michigan's Tim Davis recovered at the Wolverines' 26.

Franklin Directs Drive

From that point, Franklin directed the best sustained drive of the day for Michigan. He sent Bell on sweeps right and left in which he pitched way out to the scampering tailback for good gains. This got the visitors to the Ohio State 21 in just 10 plays. After Franklin failed on two consecutive passes into the end zone, Lantry booted his only successful field goal.

Shortly before Lantry's field goal, Franklin had his big moment of the day. On a first down at Ohio State's 42, he hit Gil Chapman, the wingback, at the Buckeyes' 22. Chapman kept right on running and turned the pass play into a 42-yard touchdown for the only successful move into either end zone all day.

Lantry kicked the extra point and Michigan had its 7-0 lead.

After that sudden move and the long drive for the field goal, Michigan could not get within an easy strike of a touchdown the rest of the way. But Ohio State never really threatened either. The closest the Buckeyes got was to the Michigan 7-yard line for a third-down-and-6 play.

This came about when a Franklin pass early in the second period was intercepted by Bruce Elia, a sparkling linebacker today. Elia ran the ball 11 yards to the Wolverines' 44.

Griffin then ran on seven of Ohio State's next nine plays to get the ball inside the 10-yard line. But on the third down from the 7, there was big Jeff Perlinger again to help Rick Kolschalk, the middle guard, throw Greene for a short loss. This forced Ohio State to go to Klaban's second field goal.

Klaban kicked his first field goal (47 yards) on the first play of the second period to conclude a drive that Ohio State began on its own 20 following Michigan's field goal. Michigan turned this moving offense into a field-goal settlement when Dan Jilek, a Wolverine defensive end, sacked Greene for a 7-yard loss to the Michigan 35.

After a gain of 5 yards by Greene on the next play was not good enough for a first down, Ohio State went to a fourth-down field goal and trailed, 10-3.

Then came Elia's interception and the ensuing field goal. This was followed by a 26-yard pass from Greene to Dave Hazel that got Ohio State to the Michigan 26. But Perlinger was there again to nail Griffin on the next play for no gain and with just six seconds remaining in the first half, Hayes ordered Klaban to kick his third field goal.

54

Thus Michigan took a 10-9 lead into the locker room at halftime. What turned out to be the winning field goal came in the third period after a 20-yard drive by Ohio State from the Michigan 48 to the 28. Forced to a fourth-and-5, Ohio State once again asked for Klaban to produce, and he did with a 45-yard kick that may get the Buckeyes into the Rose Bowl.

Michigan's final chance came with 57 seconds to go as the Wolverines took an Ohio State punt at the Michigan 46. Franklin immediately hit Jim Smith for a 23-yard pass and a first down at the Buckeyes' 31. Now there were 52 seconds to go, and Franklin tossed high and out of bounds to stop the clock.

Then Bell's replacement, Rob Lytle, ran a draw for 10 yards and a first down with 25 seconds remaining. Another run by Lytle and the ball was at the Ohio State 16 with 18 seconds to go.

This set up Lantry's final field-goal attempt which failed to make the difference.

SCORE BY PERIODS

Ohio State	0	9	3	0 —	12
Michigan	10	0	0	0 —	10

15

BUCKEYES TRIUMPH, 21-14, ON LATE TOUCHDOWNS

By **MURRAY CHASS**
Special to The New York Times

ANN ARBOR, Mich., Nov. 22, 1975 — Just as everyone figured, a lad named Griffin was the difference in today's annual Big Ten championship war between Ohio State and Michigan, both unbeaten and both bowl-bound.

But, surprise — it wasn't Archie, the prolific ball-carrying machine, who sparked Ohio State to a 21-14 victory and a record, fourth consecutive Rose Bowl appearance. Not at all. An alert, swarming Michigan defense saw to that, limiting Archie to 46 yards in 19 carries and snapping his collegiate record string of 31 straight games in which he had rushed for more than 100 yards.

The difference in this battle waged before a record 105,543 fans at Michigan Stadium was Archie's younger brother, Ray, a sophomore safety whose pass interception late in the fourth quarter set up the touchdown that capped the Buckeyes' comeback victory. Ray also made a game-high 10 unassisted tackles, helped on four others and broke up two other passes.

Pete Johnson's touchdown burst from 3 yards out with 2 minutes 19 seconds left, stunned the scrappy Wolverines who only a minute before had led, 14-7, and were certain they finally had broken Ohio State's domination of the Big Ten spot in the Rose Bowl.

However, after holding top-ranked Ohio State to no first downs and a net of only 28 yards in a span of 36 minutes 50 seconds — from State's first play in the second quarter until 7 minutes remained in the game — the Wolverines crumpled and wound up with the consolation prize — a $700,000 trip to the Orange Bowl.

Ohio State will go to Pasadena, Calif., where it will earn $1.4 million, to be allocated among all Big Ten teams, as the icing to a season of 11 victories and no defeats. Michigan concluded its regular-season efforts with eight victories, one loss and two ties, but its 41-game unbeaten streak at home, dating to 1969, also was ended.

This was an unusual game involving these two teams because they generally play the type of football that cavemen played in another era. Together, the teams had averaged 17 passes a game this season. In this contest, though, they passed a total of 37 times.

In the end, it was three passes by Cornelius Greene and one by Rick Leach, Michigan's freshman quarterback, that decided the game.

Stifled by the Michigan defense, the Buckeyes finally awoke midway through the fourth quarter and ripped off first downs in five straight plays. Greene, their quarterback, hit on three consecutive passes to Brian Baschnagel (17 yards) and Lenny Willis (14 and 18). Then Archie Griffin ran for 11 yards and Greene kept the ball for another 12.

That placed the ball at Michigan's 8-yard line and Ohio State, ignoring Griffin, the elder, as if he had the plague, scored the tying touchdown on the last of Johnson's four straight runs, a 1-yard smash.

Only 3:18 remained and the Wolverines, ranked fourth and fifth in the various polls, tried desperately to pull out the game because a tie still would have sent Ohio State and its better over-all record to the Rose Bowl.

"When the score is 14-14, you've got two choices to make," Bo Schembechler, the Michigan coach, said. "You either play conservatively or you play to win. We decided before the game not to play for a tie so we had to gamble late in the game and you all know what happened when we had to go to the air."

On third and 19 from the Michigan 11, Leach fired a pass over Jim Smith's head and Ray Griffin caught it at the 33.

Leach bumped the 19-year-old converted safety (he was a running back like Archie) out of bounds at the 3-yard line, but Johnson scored on the first play, sending all those Michigan fans into shock.

Archie Griffin suffered a huge shock himself from such aggressive Michigan tacklers as Dave Devich, Don Dufek, Dwight Hicks and Calvin O'Neal.

Hayes credited Michigan with having played the best defense ever against Griffin, who wound up his four-year regular-season career with a record total of 5,177 yards. He hadn't gained so few yards in one game since the ninth contest of his freshman year. His 31-game, 100-yard streak started in the first game of his sophomore season.

Overlooked in the outcome was a fine performance by Gordon Bell, Michigan's 5-foot-9 tailback. Bell ran for 101 yards in the first half, ended with 124 and tossed an 11-yard touchdown pass to Smith in the second quarter that tied the game, 7-7. The pass was a play put in especially for this game and it was the first pass Bell had thrown in his four-year col-

57

legiate career.

Michigan went ahead, 14-7, in the fourth quarter when Leach bulled across from the 1. An offside penalty against Aaron Brown, the Ohio State linebacker, on an errant third-down pass, kept the Michigan 43-yard drive alive.

Earlier, in the second quarter, the Wolverines squandered four scoring chances. They lost the ball twice on fumbles and once on an interception, all in Ohio State's half of the field. Then, after Archie Griffin fumbled the kickoff at his 21 following the tying touchdown, Michigan could not get a first down and Bob Wood's 37-yard field-goal attempt was slightly wide to the left.

Another missed opportunity hurt Michigan on Ohio State's 11-play, 80-yard tying drive in the fourth quarter. On second and 10 from his 20, Greene escaped a frenzied chase by Tim Davis, the middle guard, in the end zone and let fly with a desperation pass. Four Wolverines touched the ball, but none could hold it. And from then on, Michigan couldn't hold the lead.

SCORE BY PERIODS

Ohio State	7	0	0	14	— 21
Michigan	0	7	0	7	— 14

16

SOONERS VICTORS IN ORANGE, 14-6

By MARK ASHER
Special to The Washington Post

MIAMI, Jan. 1, 1976 — Oklahoma overpowered Michigan, 14-6, tonight in the Orange Bowl football game and became the strong favorite to be voted No. 1 in the final Associated Press ranking to be announced Saturday.

All-America linemen Leroy Selmon and Jimbo Elrod led a defensive charge that stopped the nation's No. 2 rushing game.

Wishbone quarterback Steve Davis ended his career by engineering two touchdown drives. He passed 40 yards to Tinker Owens to set up Billy Brooks' 39-yard end-around reverse for a second-quarter touchdown. Davis scored the other touchdown on a 10-yard run on the first play of the final quarter.

Oklahoma, 10-0 this season and 31-1-1 over the past three seasons when it was on N.C.A.A. probation, was ranked third going into the game. No. 1 Ohio State lost to U.C.L.A., 23-10, earlier today; No. 2 Texas A & M lost to Arkansas and Southern Cal following the previous poll.

Michigan got its touchdown with 7:06 to play when tailback Gordon Bell ran 2 yards following the Wolverine recovery of reserve fullback Jim Culbreath's fumble on the prior play. Quarterback Rick Leach, who sat out the third quarter with a slight concussion, was stopped on an attempt to run for 2 points by Dewey Selmon.

The opening kickoff was delayed, for television, until the end of the Ohio State-U.C.L.A. game. So Oklahoma started the game knowing a victory probably would assure it the national championship.

Michigan had more scoring chances in the first half, but Oklahoma struck suddenly in the second quarter for the half's only touchdown and a 7-0 lead at intermission.

The Sooners went 79 yards in two plays, with Billy Brooks running 39 yards on an end-around reverse for the touchdown one play after quarterback Steve Davis completed a 40-yard pass to Tinker Owens, who Brooks replaced for the next play.

Defensive end Dan Jilek overran the 202-pound senior in the Sooner backfield. Then Brooks took advantage of some good downfield blocking around the 30 to break loose. Tony DiRienzo kicked the extra point, and Oklahoma led, 7-0, with 5:07 left in the half.

Oklahoma has been successful with the same play in other big contests. Owens ran the end-around reverse for 10 yards and a first down in the winning drive against Texas this year. Last season Brooks ran the same play for 40 yards for the tying touchdown against Texas and DiRienzo won the game, 16-13, with a field goal.

The Davis-to-Owens connection did not compromise coach Barry Switzer's philosophy of running whenever possible. It was second down and 22 following a holding penalty on the Sooners two plays earlier. Davis threw only two other passes in the half, completing one.

Rick Leach, Michigan's freshman quarterback, did not complete a pass in seven attempts before he was knocked ajar by Oklahoma cornerback Jerry Anderson late in the half. He walked groggily to the locker room as Mark Elzinga completed the half with two incompletions.

Then Bob Wood's 43-yard field-goal attempt was partially blocked by Terry Peters. Michigan had taken over at the Oklahoma 31 following Owens' 16-yard punt with 16 seconds left in the half.

Early in the half, left-hander Leach had split end Keith Johnson open on a long pass down the sideline with plenty of open space ahead of him. But Johnson dropped the pass. The Wolverines had driven from their 5 to the Oklahoma 42.

Faced with fourth and inches at the Oklahoma 33 after Leach's 11-yard run, the Wolverines lined up to go for the first down. But movement in the left side of their line cost Michigan an illegal motion penalty and the Wolverines punted.

The Oklahoma offensive line started controlling Michigan's defense on the next two possessions. An Elvis Peacock fumble cost the Sooners at the Michigan 34 on the first.

But the Sooners drove 67 yards in 11 plays, with Davis scoring on a 10-yard run on the first play of the fourth quarter. DiRienzo's conversion kick gave Oklahoma a 14-0 lead.

Two plays earlier, Culbreath ran 21 yards to make a first down at the Michigan 9 by a yard.

Culbreath is Oklahoma's third-string fullback. No reason was announced for starter Jim Littrell's second-half absence. Horace Ivory was disciplined and did not make the trip.

Leach's injury was diagnosed as a slight concussion and Elzinga started

60

the second half for Michigan.

After Michigan failed to get a first down on its first possession, reserve fullback Jim Culbreath fumbled on Oklahoma's second play and Jilek recovered at the Sooner 26.

It was Oklahoma's first turnover of the game.

But the Sooners escaped damage. Sidney Brown intercepted Gordon Bell's tailback-option pass in the end zone on third and 3 from the Oklahoma 9. Brown appeared to try to run the ball out of the end zone and was apparently tackled on the playing side of the goal line.

SCORE BY PERIODS

Oklahoma	0	7	0	7	—	14
Michigan	0	0	0	6	—	6

17

'IDIOTS' CAN KILL YOU QUICK . . . AND SO CAN NO. 1-RANKED MICHIGAN

By BUD SHRAKE
Sports Illustrated

NEW YORK, Oct. 25, 1976 — From his office at a corner table in a joint on State Street in Chicago last Friday night, Big Tom the bookie said, "I make this out to be the worst mismatch since Pearl Harbor. Michigan has got the fastest backfield in the history of the Big Ten. Northwestern has got scholars. The line says Michigan by 33. But you can't hardly get none of my colleagues to book it. You know why? The numbers are too high. What kind of a idiot would give 33 to any team in the world? But what kind of a idiot would take Northwestern and 33 against Michigan? In my business you want to do heavy trade with suckers. You can get killed fooling around with idiots."

Judging from the screaming and imploring and general button-busting racket at Northwestern's Dyche Stadium the next afternoon, there must have been an army of bettors on both sides of the line. Considering that only 31,045 people showed up for the Michigan-Northwestern game in the first place, the last couple of minutes reached a level of loudmouth usually found only in those games that match fire against water.

The question was: Would Northwestern score? Would the poets, artists and drama majors, who had lost 11 games in a row, actually make a touchdown or even kick a field goal against the No. 1 team in the nation?

That the question involved more than pride or curiosity could be detected by shouts of "Kill 'em! Kill 'em!" and "Fumble! Fumble!" and "Please, God, give me just one break in this life!" Such shouts accompany the finish of a game with a wager on it. Ordinarily you would not observe such behavior in a home crowd whose team is behind 38-0 with about a minute to play. Ordinarily the crowd would have been out in the parking lot honking at each other by then.

With a fourth and 3 at the Michigan 13, Northwestern quarterback Randy Dean threw a pass to Wally Kasprzycki for 5 yards. Bedlam. It was Dean's 10th pass completion. For a quarterback with a broken arm, that is about halfway remarkable, no matter what class the opposition.

Actually, it wasn't Dean's whole arm that was broken. It was his wrist. And it was his left wrist, whereas he throws with his right. But it is against N.C.A.A. rules to play wearing a cast, so Dean's left arm from elbow to fingertip was wrapped in tape, bandages and sponge rubber. Every time Dean fell on his left arm you wanted to cry out in sympathetic pain. Or else you wanted to cry out that one of the top engineering students at Northwestern ought to have more sense.

Northwestern's best runner, the school's all-time rushing leader, tailback Greg Boykin, tore up his knee in the first quarter two weeks ago while the Wildcats were being shut out by Indiana. Boykin will not play again this year. Dean isn't sure when he broke his wrist. Maybe it was against Indiana, maybe before. "My adrenaline gets to rushing so fast that I forget my wrist hurts," Dean says.

Anyhow, there were three running plays and then a timeout was called with 34 seconds left, fourth and goal from the 4. The crowd going crazy. What to do?

Whatever small success opponents have had against the Michigan defense this year has come from passing. Scott Yelvington of Northwestern, on that fourth down, needed one more catch to tie Pat Richter of Wisconsin as the Big Ten's 10th all-time receiver.

Dean threw a pass to Yelvington for a touchdown.

Dyche Stadium broke up with noise. Far to the south you could see the skyline of Chicago wobble as the reverberations busted into the smog. Over to the east the whitecaps on Lake Michigan shuddered.

"They ought to call *this place* the Windy City," said Big Tom the bookie. His nose was blue from the cold but his heart was warm from the day's work. Big Tom had booked the game. Most of the action that came into his office on State Street was giving the points. The score was 38-7, Michigan. Giving the points was a loser.

But those who took the points, or even those who were interested in the metaphysical implications of scoring a touchdown against Michigan after all these years, were winners. Long into the night they whooped and chatted. "Never have I seen so many people claim a team that got beat 38-7 done so good," said Big Tom. "On the other hand, never have I heard so many people who give the 33 points bitch that their side wasn't trying to throw the bomb on the last two plays of the game."

Bo Schembechler, the Michigan coach, was not trying to hold down the score, if that is consolation to those on the wrong end of a wager. Because Bo used to be a roommate at Miami of Ohio of Northwestern coach John Pont doesn't mean Bo froze on the trigger. Michigan had beaten Stanford, 51-0, and Navy, 70-14, and had outscored the opposition 234-51 heading into the Northwestern game. Near the end of the first half, leading Northwestern by 31-0, Michigan called a timeout with 8 seconds left on the clock and tried a 55-yard field goal. That does not sound like cooling it with the scoreboard.

Neither does keeping most of the Michigan first team on offense in the game deep into the fourth quarter. Bo did yank the defensive first team with a mere 38-0 cushion. But he thinks that may have been a mistake.

"I probably should have taken out the offensive first unit and left the defense in there to hold Northwestern back," Schembechler said.

To preserve the shutout? "I don't care that much about shutouts," he said. To protect the point spread? "What point spread? I don't pay any attention to point spreads," he said.

Schembechler was grinning and nodding and drinking a soft drink out of a can. His yellow shirt was smudged. He had his meet-the-public face on. But you could see he was tired and bothered by the way he would duck his head and his eyeballs would sink for a moment. After all, this is Bo's first time to be No. 1 in the nation, right from the opening forecast straight on through more than half the season. And Bo is a certified heart case. Bo had his heart attack the day his Michigan team went to the Rose Bowl and lost, in 1970. The old blood pump is still tricky enough that Schembechler had to lay out of spring training this year. If he sat by himself for a while on a locker room bench after the Northwestern game and allowed his head to dangle and his eyes to shut who should be surprised?

His quarterback, Rick Leach, had spent much of the spring playing baseball and there was no question his attention was divided. As a high school senior in Flint, Leach was said to have been offered a $100,000 bonus to sign with the Phillies. To get him to Ann Arbor, Bo had to promise Leach that he could play baseball, too. Last year as a freshman it was said of Leach that his passing style belonged in the other sport. In the spring Leach cut loose with a hard, low, one-bounce throw from center field to third base to catch a runner. "That's the way you throw a football," somebody yelled from the stands. "One bounce!"

Last year Michigan went ahead of Ohio State, 14-7, in the fourth quarter, but Leach threw a couple of interceptions and Michigan lost. Then Leach did not complete another pass until the fourth quarter of an Orange Bowl loss to Oklahoma. In the Orange Bowl, Bo had Leach throw nothing but long passes for fear of interceptions. Now Schembechler says Leach has become something of a passer, at last. Against Northwestern, Leach threw seven passes, completed three and had two intercepted. At one point Leach threw passes two plays in a row. "We were afraid he might get a sore arm," Bo said. But Leach's three completions covered 101 yards, scored one touchdown and set up another. Besides, it is Leach's shorter passes, his pitchouts, that are vital to the Michigan offense.

Against Northwestern, the Michigan fullback, Rob Lytle, moved to tailback for much of the game. Lytle is a compact 6-foot-1, 195 pounds, a sprinter on the track team who is often used as a blocker for fellow sprinter Harlan Huckleby, the regular tailback. Against Northwestern Lytle rushed for 172 yards in 18 carries. With a hurt right knee.

"People hear I'm a Big Ten fullback and they look past me, wondering who is being talked about," Lytle said. (By comparison, the Ohio State fullback, Pete Johnson, is 247 pounds.) "But my style of running probably fits more as a fullback than it does as a tailback. Playing tailback, the thing that scares me most is the pitchout. I'm concentrating on that defensive guy. That's one of the places where Rick is terrific. His pitchouts are soft and they come right into your hands."

Seven of the Michigan starters — including offensive guards Mark Donahue and Gerry Szara and tackle Mike Kenn and wingback Jim Smith (perhaps the team's best athlete, according to Schembechler) — are from the neighborhood of Dyche Stadium. Lytle, however, is from Fremont, Ohio, in Woody Hayes territory. For five generations Lytle's family has owned a clothing store on Front Street in Fremont. When Rob chose Michigan over Ohio State, people came into the store and said from now on they would rather go naked than buy a Lytle garment. "But they were mostly kidding, and my family is not that rah-rah about football anyway," says Lytle.

Woody also once courted Huckleby, inviting him down to watch the Ohio State-Michigan game when Huckleby was a high school senior in Detroit. Ohio State won the game, 12-10, when Michigan missed a field goal. "I tried to be neutral, but I'm from Michigan and I couldn't help it. That game made up my mind," Huckleby said.

Schembechler said the thing that is bothering him now is that this season has been too easy. "We need a slugfest," he said. "We need to have it hanging in the balance. We need to need continuity snap after snap, to know we've got to drive it out, with the heat on. We need to give up the idea that we can score from anywhere on the field at any moment. We are going to run into some of those slugfests in the last part of the season. Nobody will know how good we are until we find out ourselves."

"I can tell him one thing," said Big Tom the bookie. "It didn't hurt him none to call it off in the second half against Northwestern. Lytle didn't run but three times for 30 yards in the second half. Leach didn't throw but one pass, and it was intercepted. The scholars looked real good in the second half. Now we will wait for the numbers to come down while Ohio State approaches on the Michigan schedule, and then we will see where the business comes from. Suckers and patriots, it's all the same. With idiots, I'm happy to have got out a winner."

18

WOLVERINES TROUNCE OHIO STATE FOR ROSE BERTH

By NEIL AMDUR
Special to The New York Times

COLUMBUS, Ohio, Nov. 20, 1976 — The frustration finally ended for Michigan today with a convincing 22-0 victory over Ohio State.

Five years after their last triumph over the Buckeyes had sent them to the Rose Bowl, the once-beaten Wolverines again qualified for the New Year's Day game with a second-half scoring surge that silenced a record Ohio Stadium crowd of 88,250.

This was the first shutout against a Buckeye team in 123 games, dating back to another Michigan victory, 10-0 in 1964.

It also provided a satisfying moment for coach Glenn (Bo) Schembechler, who had undergone open-heart surgery earlier this year. Michigan had been considered the nation's No. 1 team until losing to Purdue, 16-14, two weeks ago.

"It was a great victory," Schembechler said after having been carried off the field on the shoulders of his players in what may have been his finest victory since he began to rebuild a sagging Michigan in 1969. "We have always played well against them, but they have held us back. We felt there was no way they could do that for this game."

Michigan's dominance after a dull, scoreless first half, was a result of a strategic adjustment. Instead of trying to ram the ball down the Buckeyes' throats, as the Wolverines had done unsuccessfully in the opening two quarters, they utilized the option offense that had won nine of 10 previous games and produced college football's most prolific ground attack.

With Rick Leach, the sophomore quarterback, keeping the ball, pitching it back to Rob Lytle or handing off inside to Russell Davis, Michigan rushed for 259 yards in the second half, including third-quarter scoring drives of 80 and 52 yards that consumed 11 minutes 6 seconds of the period.

Michigan attempted no passes in either of the two drives, and completed no passes all day. But the threat of the option kept the Buckeye defense from aggressively penetrating the line of scrimmage and allowed the Wolverines greater flexibility, particularly for their outside game.

Two Big Plays

A 20-yard scramble by the 6-foot-1, 180-pound Leach on third and 3 at the Buckeye 47-yard line, after he had appeared to miss a handoff, sustained the first, 11-play drive.

On the second drive, a reverse to Jim Smith, a wingback, caught Ohio State flat-footed on second and 12 at the Buckeye 25 and resulted in a 16-yard gain.

Davis scored the first two touchdowns, on 3-yard runs. Lytle, the game's leading rusher, with 167 yards in 29 carries, ran 3 yards for the clincher with 8:13 left after Jerry Zuver had intercepted a James Pacenta pass and returned it 11 yards to the Ohio State 15.

The defeat left Ohio State with a won-lost-tied record of 8-2-1 for the regular season. It also again dramatized the Buckeyes' futility as a catch-up club.

State's only scoring threat, late in the second quarter at the Michigan 10, ended with a pass that should not have been thrown. Pacenta, under pressure all afternoon, threw into a crowd, and Jim Pickens, a defensive back, made a leaping interception in the end zone.

In the second half, Michigan, its offensive line firing out quickly on the synthetic turf, ran 43 plays, to 22 for Ohio State. The Buckeyes, who have always scorned the pass, were limited to 173 total yards, only 63 in the last two quarters. When they had to pass, trailing by 15-0, the Buckeyes could not execute. Often Michigan's line, led by two aggressive tackles, Greg Morton and Jo Hennessy, hurried Pacenta into misfiring.

"Michigan will get my vote as the No. 1 team in the country," said Woody Hayes, Ohio State's coach, who had run onto the field and protested what he considered illegal motion after the Wolverines' first touchdown.

That was the closest thing to controversy today in a rivalry that had produced its share of intense moments. Michigan lost a perfect season by bowing to Ohio State in 1972, then lost the Rose Bowl bid despite tying the Buckeyes in 1973, a decision that still rankles Schembechler. Ohio State won the last two years, but by close scores.

Hayes, in a rare admission, blamed himself for the interception that probably cost the Buckeyes 3 points in the first half.

"It was my call all the way," Hayes said, "and it was just a bad call. We put that pass in earlier this week but when they shot a linebacker in, our quarterback had to rush his throw. If we had scored then, it might have affected the second-half outcome. But I don't want to take anything away from them. They were a fine team today."

Schembechler conceded that Michigan "didn't play good offense in the first half." Hayes said Michigan's second-half outside game had been the difference.

"They hurt us badly with Lytle's speed," the Ohio State coach added. "Then, when we adjusted to the outside game, they hurt us inside.

"Last year when they tried to go outside," Hayes went on, "they made some mistakes. But they didn't make any this year. Any team that beats us as soundly as they did deserves to be No. 1."

With today's result, each team finished the regular season with a Big Ten record of 7-1, the best in the conference. Since Michigan won today's contest, it receives the invitation to the Rose Bowl, where the Wolverines will play the Pacific 8 Conference champion.

SCORE BY PERIODS

Michigan 0	0	15	7	—	22
Ohio State 0	0	0	0	—	0

69

19

FOR ALL THE MARBLES–AND ROSES

By LARRY KEITH
Sports Illustrated

NEW YORK, Nov. 29, 1976 — Last Friday evening in Columbus, Ohio, while Woody Hayes and his Ohio State Buckeyes were watching yet another inspirational John Wayne movie — this time "The Shootist" — Bo Schembechler was tucking his Michigan Wolverines in for a long night's sleep. It is Bo's custom on these occasions to rap lightly at each player's door around 9 p.m. to make sure no one is doing anything outrageous, like ordering a garlic pizza or sneaking out the window for a night on the town. But when the night watchman came to one room he took the liberty of inviting himself in, sitting himself down and having a bedside chat with Greg Morton, a defensive tackle, and Calvin O'Neal, a middle linebacker. Schembechler wanted to give them something to dream about — namely, a victory over Ohio State.

Morton and O'Neal are both players of distinction, but even as fifth-year seniors, they had never seen their team defeat Ohio State. Michigan had been unbeaten before each of the previous four games with a chance to represent the Big Ten in the Rose Bowl. But after losses in 1972, '74 and '75 and a tie in '73, it was the Buckeyes who went West for New Year's.

"Gentlemen," Bo began, "here we are again. You know how close we've come in the past, but something has always happened to stop us. Some people are even saying we've choked. Now we know that's not true. We've just made some mistakes we shouldn't have made. But tomorrow we're not going to make those mistakes because tomorrow we're going to win."

The following afternoon, before a record and hostile Ohio Stadium crowd of 88,250, that dream became a reality as Michigan did win, 22-0. It took the Wolverines two full quarters to get their offense in gear, but once under way they were relentless, driving to three touchdowns in the second half and being thwarted on their other two possessions by an interception after reaching the 16 and by the clock after getting to the 12. During the same 30 minutes the Buckeyes were minus 7 yards net on the ground, throwing an interception, losing the ball on a fumble and never penetrating past the Michigan 38.

"Any team that can beat us that badly," said gracious Woody Hayes afterward, "has got to be No. 1." And Hayes threw a special bouquet to Schembechler. Recalling that his old protege had undergone open-heart surgery before the season began, Hayes boosted him for Coach of the Year. "It is almost unbelievable what he has done," said Woody. "It was the most courageous job in football this year."

Only three weeks ago courageous Bo and mighty Michigan were everybody's No. 1. But that was before a 16-14 loss to Purdue. Because Ohio State was unbeaten in the Big Ten (although losing to Missouri, 22-21, and being tied by U.C.L.A., 10-10, outside the conference), the Wolverines needed a victory Saturday just to be co-champion. The Buckeyes had been in that position twice before in recent years and won. Now that Michigan has finally done the same, the Wolverines can take their half loaf to Pasadena to play U.S.C., while the Buckeyes head to the Big Ten's unofficial runner-up berth in the Orange Bowl.

This is the eighth time in the last nine years that the Michigan-Ohio State game has divvied up the the conference spoils, leaving nothing at all for the Little Eight. Until Saturday the Wolverines had won only two of the games, upsetting the Buckeyes in 1969, Bo's first year, and winning in 1971, when Ohio State was out of the running and the result did not matter as much. Michigan's repeated, almost predictable failures had some people thinking it might never beat Ohio State again. Even back home in Ann Arbor a clothing salesman admitted that his store's $14 short-sleeved sweater with the school insignia "might be half price after the game on Saturday."

Schembechler was thinking more positively. The close scores of the last four games (14-11, 10-10, 12-10 and 21-14) indicated that "We've never played badly and they've never dominated us. In fact, the score is the only thing that's really gone against us. I'm not going to sit back and say they've beaten the heck out of us, because they haven't. We've been playing well enough to win, so now we have to play well and win as well."

Publicly at least, Schembechler went around radiating the good disposition of a man who knew his number would be drawn in the next lottery. But then, Bo is smiling more these days. His heart attack seven years ago and the surgery last May have given him a better perspective on life. "I'm not as uptight as I used to be," he says. "I know that losing a football game is not the end of the world." Losing the Ohio State game can be something else, of course — the end of the universe, at the very least — so he fudged

71

a little on his doctor's standing orders to watch his diet, get plenty of exercise and take a nap every noon. He is still gung ho, as one of his players put it, but as another said with relief, "He's also more relaxed, and this week — that made it better for all of us."

Hayes was putting in extra hours too, even passing up "Patton" on television the Sunday night before the game for a staff meeting. "We started thinking about this one after the Rose Bowl last January," he said. "This is the best team we'll face this year and we always point to beat the best team." The Buckeyes had already clinched at least a share of their fifth straight conference title, but they figured to be a touchdown underdog against the Wolverines. A Columbus sportswriter who dared to predict a Michigan victory was hung in effigy at a meeting of a local booster organization. Woody answered such defeatist talk by saying, "When you're an underdog you play from your heart. It involves your ability, determination and just damn meanness to go on every play." Well, if meanness is all it takes, defensive tackle Eddie Beamon promised, "We'll crush 'em."

Those were hollow threats, though. Wolverine quarterback Rich Leach and wingback Jim Smith are a deadly (if infrequent) passing combination, and speedy running backs Rob Lytle, Russell Davis and Harlan Huckleby came into the game averaging roughly 6 yards a carry. Ohio State, on the other hand, had a fullback (Pete Johnson) with two bad ankles, a senior quarterback (Jim Pacenta) with only three career starts and a tailback (Jeff Logan) who was pretty good but was no Archie Griffin. "I had the feeling we could blow those guys out," said O'Neal when the game was over. "They just didn't seem to have the offensive threat they've had in the past."

In the first half, neither team did. It was conga football at its most absurd — one, two, three, kick! — everything the Ohio State-Michigan game usually is, only worse. The Buckeyes' Tom Skladany punted four times, and the Wolverines' John Anderson three before Michigan made the game's initial first down. When it finally was accomplished, on a 9-yard run by Lytle with 12 minutes gone, it seemed totally out of place. How *quaint!* The Buckeyes did not muster a 10-yard drive of their own until their sixth possession. Later in the half, though, they put together a serious march to the Michigan 10. Then, on a second down and 8, Pacenta faked a handoff and, under extreme pressure from an unexpected blitz, looped a pass in the approximate direction of tight end Greg Storer. Unfortunately, Storer was neither alone nor very close to the football, and one of two Wolverines accompanying him, Jim Pickens, picked the ball off. It was a horrible decision by Pacenta — most high school quarterbacks in Ohio would have taken the 8-yard loss — and an odd call by a coach who had said just two days before, with much pride, that "only rushing teams win the Big Ten title." Later, even Woody admitted, "I don't have an alibi. I just called a bad play. But I will always wonder what might have happened if we have been able to score." A fair guess is 22-3.

The scoreless first half did not dishearten Schembechler. "Coming into the game," he said later, "I felt there was no way they were going to stop us. Then at halftime I honestly didn't believe they'd score. I knew that our defense could hold them if we didn't give up the ball deep in our own territory. As for ourselves, I felt we could score if we just straightened out and started executing what we'd done all year."

Entering the game, Michigan ranked first nationally in rushing, scoring and yards gained per offensive play. It had a strong option attack featuring Leach, a sophomore on the path to greatness, and Lytle, a senior whom Schembechler considers "the best back I've ever coached." Whether operating as a tailback (as he did against Ohio State) or at fullback (as he did last year and much of this season), the 195-pound Lytle had been outstanding. He entered the game as the school's record ground-gainer (3,085 yards) and with the best yards-per-carry average (7.1) in the country. He is durable, too, never missing a single practice or game with an injury and admitting to two cracked ribs suffered before the season began only after they had knit.

However, despite the best efforts of Leach and Lytle, Ohio State contained the Michigan outside game in the first half. "We were getting some yardage on them inside," said Lytle, "but it was sporadic. In the second half they tried to shut off the middle more and it left the option and pitch open. But a lot of it was my fault, too. I kept looking for the big play even though it wasn't there. I just told myself in the second half that I'd better get my butt in gear."

On the first play of the third quarter Leach went right for 9 yards. Three plays later Lytle went left for 15. Then it was Leach right for 20 and Lytle right for 11. Their speed was spreading Ohio State's defenders like a rubber band. Fullback Davis finally capped the 80-yard drive by slipping through right tackle from the 3.

After the kickoff the Buckeyes waited three plays before unleashing their most potent weapon, Skladany, the punter, who finished the day with a 52-yard average on eight kicks. But another of several fine returns by Smith gave the Wolverines the ball at their 48, and it took them only 5 minutes to score again. Lytle started the drive with a 16-yard burst around the right side, and wingback Smith kept it alive when he picked up 16 more to the

Buckeye 9 on a tricky reverse pitch to the left. Davis scored his second touchdown on another 3-yard bolt off tackle. Schembechler had promised "another dull game just like the others," but after the touchdown he tried an unorthodox and risky twist. Realizing that a 14-14 tie would deny his team the Rose Bowl again, Schembechler ordered a 2-point attempt. But not just any 2-point play. No, on this one, added especially for the game, Michigan lined up in kicking formation and let the holder, Jerry Zuver, race the ball around right end for a 15-0 lead.

Zuver also played a decisive role when he intercepted a Pacenta pass and returned it 13 yards to the Buckeyes' 15. Three plays later Lytle scored from the 3, his 15th touchdown this season.

Lytle finished with 165 yards in 29 carries as the Michigan offense bettered its 362-yard rushing average by 4. The defense, led by Morton's 14 tackles, held Ohio State to 104 yards total offense, 225 yards below its average.

Although it was Michigan's fifth shutout of the year, it was the first time Ohio State had been blanked since a 10-0 loss to the Wolverines in 1964. In fact, as Bo himself was quick to point out, the Buckeyes did not score a touchdown against them at home two years ago either, kicking four field goals in their 12-10 victory. "You know, I got more and more confident about this game as the week went on," Schembechler said. "I would have been sick if we hadn't won. Now I can envision the Rose Bowl being for the national championship."

Now there's something to *really* dream about.

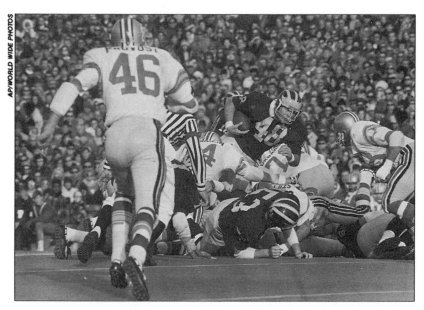

Wolverine fullback Garvie Craw (48) scored two touchdowns in Michigan's 24–12 upset of Ohio State in 1969.

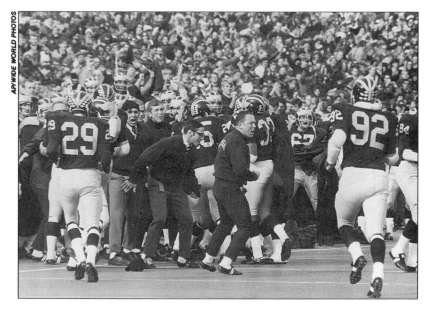

As Michigan began to take the upper hand against the Buckeyes in the 1969 thriller, the excitement on the Wolverine sideline grew to a fevered pitch.

Following the Wolverines trouncing of Ohio State, a weary, but happy Bo Schembechler addresses reporters in the Michigan locker room.

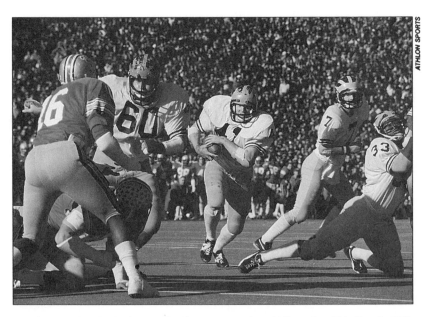

Running back Rob Lytle (41) runs for big yardage up the middle against Ohio State in 1976.

Harlan Huckleby (25) teamed up with Russell Davis and Rob Lytle in the Michigan backfield to pound out a 22–0 victory over Ohio State in 1976.

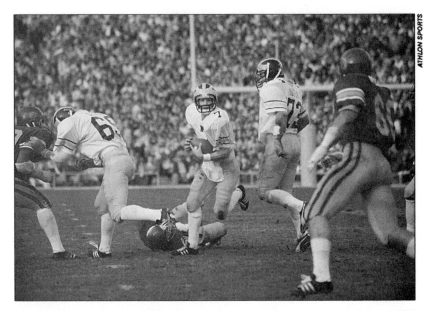

Wolverine quarterback Rick Leach (7) scampers up the middle against U.S.C. in the 1977 Rose Bowl.

Dom Tedesco (99) applies pressure to Trojan quarterback Vince Evans in the 1977 Rose Bowl, which Michigan lost, 14–6.

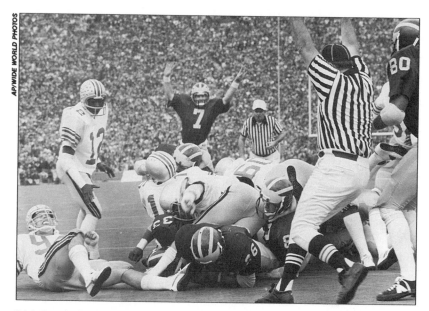

Rick Leach (7) signals a touchdown as Roosevelt Smith (26) submarines through the Ohio State line to score in 1977.

Anthony Carter (1) makes another miraculous reception for the Wolverines in the 1980 contest against Notre Dame.

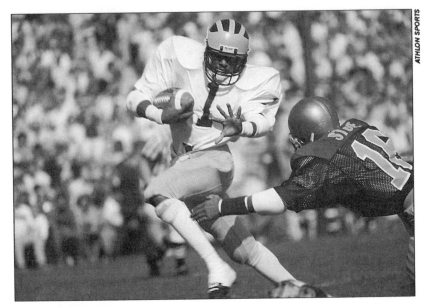

Anthony Carter (1) shows off his Heisman potential as he evades Notre Dame defensive back Jim Stone (16).

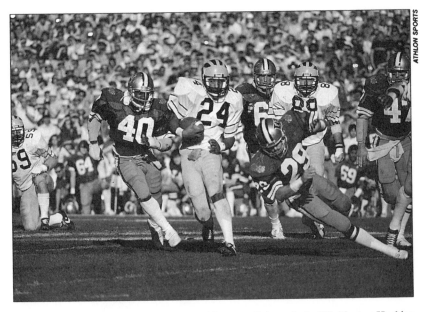

In the 1981 Rose Bowl, Butch Woolfolk (24) romped through the Washington Huskies defense.

After receiving a handoff from quarterback Steve Smith (16), Michigan fullback Stanley Edwards (32) barrels through the grasp of a Buckeye tackler in 1981.

Steve Smith (16) connected on a 71-yard bomb to Anthony Carter which sparked the Wolverines to a 25-7 victory over Notre Dame in 1981.

20

MICHIGAN FALLS TO TROJANS, 14-6

By WILLIAM N. WALLACE
Special to The New York Times

PASADENA, Calif., Jan. 1, 1977 — The University of Southern California had the quarterback, Vince Evans, who could do everything today, and Michigan did not. That was the difference in the 63d Rose Bowl game, won by the Trojans, 14-6, before the largest football crowd of the season, 106,182.

The two teams, champions of the Pacific-8 and Big Ten conferences, were playing for glory, perhaps for fun, but not for No. 1.

Because undefeated Pittsburgh, ranked as the No. 1 college team in the nation, had decisively defeated Georgia, 27-3, earlier today in the Sugar Bowl, the victor here has no chance to move to the top in the polls conducted by The Associated Press and United Press International. These polls decide who is No. 1, No. 2 and so on.

Southern California was ranked No. 3, behind Pitt and Michigan, going into its final game, and the Trojans will undoubtedly move up to No. 2 in the last balloting next week. But the team's opening-game defeat, by 46-25 to Missouri on Sept. 11, cost it the unofficial national championship. The Trojans won all the others, 11 in a row. Michigan wound up with 10 victories and two defeats.

Both coaches, John Robinson of U.S.C. and Bo Schembechler of Michigan, claimed the national title for the Trojans when the action had concluded, but that kind of pitch is not going to change many votes of the other coaches and the sportswriters who do the balloting, especially in western Pennsylvania.

Both coaches also agreed that the game had been a good one, hard fought and well played by two wonderful teams, and the the quarterbacking of Evans had made the difference. More to the point was that the Pac-8 team had beaten the Big Ten representative for the seventh time in the last eight Rose Bowl contests and for the eighth time in the last 10.

Unless Ohio State and Michigan, whose teams have lost seven of these games since 1970, run into stronger competition within their conference, which will force their coaches to build all-round offenses, Big Ten fortunes are not going to improve at Pasadena on New Year's Day. Rick Leach, the Wolverine quarterback, was the example today.

Wolverines Lack Passing Attack

Schembechler had spent hundreds of hours drilling Leach in the delicate timing of the pitchout play in the veer offense, an attack that worked well up to a point today. That point concluded as the fourth quarter began and Southern California took command. Schembechler had spent far fewer hours teaching Leach, his left-handed sophomore who is a good baseball player, how to throw a spiral pass.

When Michigan falls behind, which is not very often against the likes of Iowa and Northwestern, its ball-control ground offense is in trouble because it lacks a passing attack and consumes time. That is what happened against the Trojans.

Gary Jeters' block of a conversion kick in the second period kept the Wolverines' short-lived lead to 6-0, and it put them behind, 7-6, after the Trojans had scored their first touchdown, also in the second period. They stayed behind.

Leach, otherwise an admirable player, completed only four of 12 passes, and only one put fear into U.S.C.'s, defense, a 32-yard spiral to Jim Smith, the wingback, in the 13th minute of the fourth quarter.

Meanwhile, Evans, voted the player of the game by the press-box occupants, ran and passed. He scored the Trojans' first touchdown on a daring rollout to his left on fourth down from the 1-yard line, and he completed 14 of 20 passes for 181 yards. Said Schembechler:

"Evans was tremendous. He could roll one way and throw another, and he stepped around our pass rush. He made the big plays, and we didn't."

Evans had a lot of help, but very little from Ricky Bell, U.S.C.'s great halfback, who had run for 1,459 yards in 11 prior games. Bell made only 16 in four carries before leaving this game in the fourth minute of the opening quarter after having received a blow to the head.

Charles White, a 19-year-old freshman, replaced Bell and worked hard, carrying the ball 32 times and gaining 122 yards. He scored the second U.S.C. touchdown on a 7-yard run with 3 minutes to go in the final quarter.

White too had help, and his scoring run was symbolic of today's play, because he ran between the strong blocks of Marvin Powell and Dennis Hickman, a tackle and guard who carried 520 pounds of thrust at Michigan's John Anderson and John Hennessy.

When the Trojans needed yards, they sent White on the heels of Powell and Hickman, with other blocking help from Mosi Tatupu, the Samoan fullback.

Michigan's reply was its fine runner, Rob Lytle, who gained 67 yards in 18 rushes; scored the Wolverines' only touchdown, on a 1-yard run, and was hit hard all afternoon. All kinds of people in the maroon and gold jersey's hit him, most notably Rod Martin and David Lewis, the linebackers, and Walt Underwood and Jeter, the tackles.

Defensive players on both sides had the pro scouts' attention. U.S.C. would have scored more points had it not been for the play of Calvin O'Neal and Jerry Meter, the Wolverine linebackers, and Dwight Hicks, a safety.

SCORE BY PERIODS

Southern California . . . 0	7	0	7	—	14
Michigan 0	6	0	0	—	6

21

RECORD CROWD SEES BUCKEYES STYMIED BY LATE FUMBLE

By GERALD ESKENAZI
Special to The New York Times

ANN ARBOR, Mich., Nov. 19, 1977 — Amid a constant roar produced by the largest crowd in the history of regular-season college football, Michigan won the Rose Bowl trip today with a 14-6 victory over Ohio State.

The 106,024 fans who filled Michigan Stadium, which has 101,701 seats and is 90 rows high, were part of a spectacle that saw the game end with thousands of Wolverine fanatics dashing onto the field, some climbing the goal posts and tearing them down.

Silently, the 6,000 Ohio State rooters watched from one end of the field, almost all of them wearing red Buckeye jackets.

Just a few minutes before, they had had a chance for a tie, which would have sent them to Pasadena, Calif., home of the Rose Bowl. With four minutes remaining Ohio State had moved from its 10-yard line to Michigan's 8, only to lose the ball on a fumble.

Most of the game was also seen by 30 million television viewers, but not the opening seven minutes. Instead, the American Broadcasting Companies showed the historic arrival in Israel of Egypt's President, Anwar el-Sadat. And an ABC official said by telephone from New York, "We received thousands of telephone complaints for missing the kickoff."

The Drama Begins Early

What the TV viewers missed was the opening of a Midwestern drama that is played out every year on the last day of the two clubs' season. These teams always meet in their finale, and for eight of the last nine years the trip West for New Year's has been at stake.

This time each wound up with a 7-1 won-lost record in the Big Ten. So the Wolverines go, to meet the champion from the Pacific-8 Conference, on the basis of winning the showdown today. Ohio State accepted a bid tonight from the Sugar Bowl to play Alabama, the Southeastern Conference champion.

The crowd, the players and the bands were at an emotional peak rarely approached in other sports in other places. The TV viewers also failed to see the Michigan players massing in the tunnel on the 50-yard line, leaping faster and faster and higher and higher until they exploded like popcorn from the runway onto the field.

There they jumped under the "Go Blue" banner that, a minute earlier, coach Woody Hayes and his Ohio State players had sacrilegiously touched.

The unpredictable Hayes, wearing shirtsleeves in the 42-degree chill, had led his players out. Then he suddenly went under the Michigan banner. Quickly, he and the players were surrounded by fist-waving Michigan students, who shoved some of the players.

Hayes laughed as he took off for the sideline. He wasn't finished, though.

He led Ohio State's backers in a pre-game cheer, and then, after his players had left, following the warm-ups, he gathered his staff of coaches around him for an emotional huddle.

All this appeared to have worked. For the Buckeyes launched a drive that consumed half the first quarter, and they led, finally, on a 29-yard field goal by Vlade Janakievski, a Macedonian whom Hayes spirited away from Ohio State's soccer team.

The feared option attack was working perfectly, with Rob Gerald, the junior quarterback, befuddling the usually quick Michigan linemen.

Meanwhile, the Wolverines showed no attack in the opening quarter. They ran only five plays from scrimmage in the period, as the Ohio State defense appeared to get to the ball quicker than the Michigan backs did.

Slowly, though, the game turned. The Michigan defense stiffened against the country's leading rushing team, which had entered the game with an average of 332 yards on the ground. Then Roosevelt Smith of the Wolverines, playing for the injured Harlan Huckleby at tailback, scored on a 1-yard burst in the second quarter to cap a 46-yard drive, and Gregg Willner kicked the extra point.

Rick Leach, the Michigan quarterback, was now able to move his backs and hit with his passes.

In the third quarter Ron Springs of State fumbled, giving the ball to Michigan only 20 yards from a score. Leach soon went over, and the extra point extended Michigan's edge to 14-3.

Later in the quarter Janakievski's 44-yard field goal cut the edge to 14-6.

Then came the drama in the last minutes, when a touchdown and a 2-point conversion would have created a tie, left Ohio State unbeaten in conference play and sent the Buckeyes to the Rose Bowl, to be played Jan. 2.

Instead, John Anderson hit Gerald just as he attempted to pitch out to

Spring, the ball squirted loose, and it was snared by Derek Howard. Michigan used up most of the remaining time and then punted, and the Buckeyes could get off only three plays.

"This is by far the best game we ever played and lost," Hayes said later, and the statistics tended to support him. The Buckeyes had the edge in first downs (23 to 10), number of plays from scrimmage (74 to 51), rushing yardage (208 to 141) and passing yardage (144 to 55).

Hayes Punches TV Man

That fumble by Gerald sent Hayes into a characteristic tantrum. A TV cameraman put the camera into the coach's face at that critical moment, and Hayes punched him.

"How would you like it if they did this to you all the time?" Hayes said later, putting his fists in a newsman's face.

Hayes then signaled that the post-game news conference was over by exiting, not laughing.

He had switched his team to new shoes for Michigan's Tartan surface, which is different from his field's artificial surface. The players had difficulty with the shoes.

"They're not ordinary shoes," said Anderson. "You have to file the edges off them. They were slipping in them."

Bo Schembechler's Michigan team, wearing the same old shoes, wound up with a 10-1 record over all, while State was 9-2. But Hayes should not be unduly distressed. Since Schembechler took over here in 1969, Michigan has dropped only two games in its stadium.

The regular-season college record broken by today's crowd was set here two years ago at the Ohio State-Michigan game, attended by 105,543. The overall college football record is 106,182, set at last season's Rose Bowl, between Michigan and the University of Southern California.

And there is more. Michigan's home average of 104,203 fans a game this season also set a National Collegiate mark. The previous record was 103,159, set here last year. And today's crowd was the 16th straight of more than 100,000 here.

The intense Schembechler-Hayes rivalry, which began in 1969, is now tied at four games apiece, with one tie.

Michigan was not always this good, and the crowds were not always this large.

"I can remember," said a visitor from Detroit, "when they used to draw only sixty or seventy thousand."

Score By Periods

Michigan 0	7	7	0	—	14
Ohio State 3	0	3	0	—	6

22

LATE WOLVERINE COMEBACK FAILS IN ROSE BOWL, 27-20

By **WILLIAM N. WALLACE**
Special to The New York Times

PASADENA, Calif., Jan. 2, 1978 — The Pacific Eight, this year represented by the University of Washington, again deflated the Big Ten Conference in the Rose Bowl game today as the Huskies upset Michigan, a two-touchdown favorite, 27-20, before a crowd of 105,312.

This one was supposed to be easy for the Wolverines, ranked as the fourth best team in the nation. But the Huskies played the Wolverines off their feet in a tremendous first half to lead, 17-0, and increased their advantage to 24-0 in the third quarter.

The Wolverines then produced three touchdowns in a magnificent rally that ended at the Washington 2-yard line with 81 seconds to play.

It was the ninth time in the last 14 years that a Pacific Eight team had defeated the Big Ten entry in the Rose Bowl and the fifth time Michigan had lost in the last eight years. This Michigan team had won 10 of its first 11 games this season while Washington had lost four of 11, although it had won six of its last seven as the Huskies took the conference championship for the first time in 14 years.

Play That Backfired

Bo Schembechler, the Michigan coach, whose teams now have an 0-5 bowl game record, said later, "I was certain we were going to win this game at the end." But Schembechler, not known for risk-taking, took a chance on a play call near the end and it backfired.

Michigan's offense, dormant for the first 40 minutes of play, was rolling in the final quarter and the Wolverines had a first down at the Washington 8 with their three timeouts intact and 1 minute 28 seconds left.

Schembechler sent in a pass play for Rick Leach, his quarterback, and Leach passed to a freshman running back, Stanley Edwards.

Edwards did not quite catch the ball and Mike Jackson, the Washington linebacker, stole it out of his hands for what was ruled an intercepted pass.

Jackson said Edwards was two steps behind him and 2 yards from scoring the likely winning touchdown when "Leach put it (the football) in his hands. The ball popped up, hit his helmet, rolled down his back and I saw I could snatch it. So I did."

"It was my fault" said Schembechler. "Blame me. It was a good call but it didn't work."

Interception Ends Threat

Aaron Wilson, the Washington punter, then got a good kickoff from his end zone and Michigan had a final chance.

But Leach's last pass from midfield, a long one intended for Ralph Clayton, was intercepted by Nesby Glasgow at their 7 with 32 seconds left and that play preserved the Huskies' well-deserved victory.

The stars of the game were the Washington quarterback, Warren Moon, and his spectacular receiver, Spider Gaines, a world-class hurdler.

The spirited Huskies were full of vim and Moon rocked Michigan, an excellent defensive team, at the beginning. He completed seven of 14 pass attempts in the first half, three to Gaines for 94 yards, and Moon also scored two touchdowns on 2- and 1-yard runs.

Schembechler said he was shocked at the ease with which the Huskies moved the ball on the Wolverine defense. "We just go down too far," he said with reference to the 24-0 deficit his team faced before it got going in the third quarter. "I was impressed with the way the Michigan team came back. Ricky Leach can play catch-up football. People don't think he can. But he can."

Schembechler disdains the pass but Leach had to throw in the second half to catch up and he did well, completing 10 of 18 attempts for 195 yards and two touchdowns. Those figures had to be milestones for the recent Big Ten Rose Bowl teams, Michigan and Ohio State, which have lost here year after year to superior passing teams and have suffered criticism for their stodgy offenses.

Washington, an emerging national football power under coach Don James, came into the game with a high-risk offense. "I knew if we were going to win we would have to gamble," said James. "A lot of good things happened to us in the beginning. We executed. But I didn't think the 17-0 lead would hold up. I thought we'd need three and a half touchdowns to win and I wasn't far off. Yes, I thought before the game Michigan had a better team than we did."

Apart from Moon, the senior quarterback, and one of a number of players James recruited from the Los Angeles area, the coach cited two defensive performers.

They were the outside linebackers, John Kerley and Antowaine Richardson, who in the first half of this two-part game harassed Leach and stopped the Michigan offense.

So Michigan lost again in the Rose Bowl and this time before its distinguished alumnus, former President Gerald R. Ford, the grand marshal of the Tournament of Roses parade. Was Schembechler bitter?

"Every defeat is bitter," he said.

SCORE BY PERIODS

Washington 7	10	10	0	—	27
Michigan 0	0	7	13	—	20

23

WOLVERINES RALLY TO BEAT IRISH

By **THE ASSOCIATED PRESS**
The Washington Post

SOUTH BEND, Ind., Sept. 23, 1978 — Rick Leach hurled three second-half touchdown passes, two to Doug Marsh and a 40-yard clincher to Ralph Clayton, to lead fifth-ranked Michigan to a 28-14 victory over Notre Dame yesterday.

It was the second loss in a row for the Irish and the first time they have lost two consecutive regular-season games in 15 years. In 1972, the Irish lost their last game of the regular season and lost in the Orange Bowl. The victory was the second straight for the Wolverines, who opened last week with a 31-0 triumph over Illinois. Notre Dame, the defending national champion, was unable to come back from its 3-0 loss to Missouri two weeks ago.

Trailing at the half, 14-7, the Wolverines turned a recovered fumble and two pass interceptions into second-half touchdowns.

The Irish struck for a quick lead when Russell Davis of Woodbridge, Va., fumbled on the first play from scrimmage and, three plays later, Joe Montana hit Dennis Grindinger with a 3-yard touchdown pass.

Leach bolted 4 yards for a touchdown in the second quarter to pull Michigan into a tie but Notre Dame came right back with a run.

The Irish took the second-half kickoff and marched to the Wolverine 26 before Vagas Ferguson fumbled and Curtis Greer recovered.

Leach directed a 71-yard drive in 15 plays, culminating it by hitting Marsh with a 5-yard touchdown pass.

Jerry Meter then picked off a Montana pass and returned 14 yards to the Irish 33. Five plays later, on the opening play of the fourth quarter, Leach connected with Marsh for 17 yards and a touchdown. Gregg Willner missed the conversion attempt and Michigan led, 20-14.

Mike Harden then intercepted a Montana pass and two plays later Leach unloaded with his bomb to Clayton to put the game out of reach.

Michigan failed to make the conversion, but with only 1:08 remaining

Greer tripped up Montana in the Irish end zone for a safety.

Scott Zetick recovered Davis' first-period fumble on Michigan's 17-yard line. Jerome Heavens carried twice for 11 yards before Montana connected with Grindinger for the score. It was the first career reception by Grindinger, a senior.

Early in the second quarter, the Wolverines marched 49 yards for a touchdown capped by Leach's 4-yard slant into the end zone. Harlan Huckleby headed the drive with runs of 11 and 13 yards. Willner's conversion tied the game at 7-7.

The Irish took the kickoff and went 75 yards for a 14-7 halftime lead in a drive paced by Ferguson, who went the final 4 yards for the score. Montana hit Nick Vehr with a 23-yard pass to get the drive rolling and Ferguson carried six times for 34 yards and accounted for three first downs.

SCORE BY PERIODS

Michigan	0	7	7	14 —	28
Notre Dame	7	7	0	0 —	14

24

MICHIGAN WINS 3d STRAIGHT OVER BUCKEYES TO EARN ROSE BOWL BID

By WILLIAM N. WALLACE
Special to The New York Times

COLUMBUS, Ohio, Nov. 25, 1978 — The largest crowd in the 56-year history of Ohio Stadium, 88, 358, most of them Ohio State rooters, waited and waited for something to happen today in the football game against Michigan. Not much happened, except that Michigan beat the Buckeyes, 14-3, in routine fashion.

Rick Leach, the Wolverines' all-America quarterback, completed touchdown passes in the first and third quarters. And in the second half the Buckeyes made only one first down. They couldn't muster a rally even by switching quarterbacks, as the Wolverines beat them for the third year in a row. That had never happened before to Wayne Woodrow Hayes, Ohio State's coach. Michigan thus tied for the Big Ten championship with Michigan State and received the nomination to go to the Rose Bowl as Southern California's opponent on New Year's Day.

The Wolverines ended the regular season with a 9-1 won-lost record and 7-1 in the conference. Michigan State was the only team to beat Michigan, but the Spartans are on probation for recruiting violations and thus are forbidden to accept bowl invitations.

Losers in Gator Bowl

Ohio State, in defeat, made good its provisional acceptance of a bid to play Clemson in the Gator Bowl at Jacksonville, Fla., on Dec. 29. Hayes and his lads would have preferred Pasadena to Jacksonville, but had to beat Michigan to get there.

The Buckeyes wound up fourth in the conference behind Michigan, Michigan State and Purdue, the lowest placing for a Hayes team since 1966. Their record was 7-3-1.

By playing so well defensively in the second half, Michigan took all the excitement out of the game, especially after having made its second touchdown. That took place 11 minutes into the third period and all the

Buckeye fans then suspected their cause had become hopeless because the Michigan defense had figured out the Ohio State offense and buried it. Leach was conspicuous. The left-handed passer from Flint, Mich., starting his fourth game against Ohio State, executed coach Bo Schembechler's conservative game plan flawlessly. Conservative?

Yes, by conventional standards, but for the Michigan coach it was almost radical because Schembechler, an avowed foe of the pass, let Leach throw a few.

He is a good passer and he finished with 11 completions of 21 attempts for 166 yards, no interceptions, and touchdowns on tosses of 30 yards to Rodney Feaster and 11 to Roosevelt Smith. It was obvious from the pregame statistics that Ohio State had encountered much trouble defending against the pass this season. Leach confirmed that on a swift four-play, three-pass scoring drive of 70 yards in the first period.

But Schembechler did not overdo it against his old coach, Hayes, and Michigan played safe, sane football after having established its 11-point lead. The Wolverines missed another touchdown just before halftime when Gene Johnson, after catching a pass, fumbled one stride from the end zone. And Greg Willner missed a 43-yard field-goal attempt in the last quarter.

Ohio State's points came on a 29-yard field goal by Bob Atha in the first period when it looked like the game might develop some memorable qualities.

Freshman Is Broken In

This Ohio State season will principally be remembered as the one in which Hayes broke in a freshman quarterback, Art Schlichter (pronounced SCHLEE-ster). He was an outstanding high school passer whom Hayes expects to make into an outstanding running quarterback.

Schlichter's fancy footwork sparked three first-half drives that ended with an unsuccessful field-goal attempt, a successful one and a lost fumble. When it became essential that the Buckeyes pass, Schlichter failed his mentor, who then called on Rod Gerald. He is a senior and last year's quarterback who played wide receiver this year. Gerald ran two series from the Buckeye 1 and 26 and nothing happened.

"We just didn't do a thing," said George Chaump, the offensive coach.

That was largely because of the efforts of Ron Simpkins, Curtis Greer, Mike Jolly and the others on the Wolverine defensive unit. All the Wolverines were proud of themselves because they had had difficulty preparing for the game due to injuries. Harlan Huckleby, the leading running back the last two years, didn't play. But the Wolverines had enough other backs to make it look easy.

The Rose Bowl might be something else. Michigan teams have lost there four times in four games since 1970, once to Washington and Stanford and twice to Southern Cal.

SCORE BY PERIODS

Michigan	7	0	7	0	—	14
Ohio State	3	0	0	0	—	3

25

THE WOLVERINES HAD
A NAME TO REMEMBER

By **RON FIMRITE**
Sports Illustrated

NEW YORK, Dec. 4, 1978 — The subject of Woody Hayes' rambling discourse before the Buckeye Boosters of Columbus on the eve of last Saturday's Ohio State-Michigan game was, as best anyone could determine, "The Lost Art of Communication." "Students come up to me and tell me they're majoring in something called 'Communications,' and all I hear from them is 'like' and 'you know,' " the Ohio State football coach lamented. According to Woody, the country has not had a really first-class communicator since Emerson. Thoreau, the coach cavalierly dismisses as "strictly a mama's boy," but old Ralph Waldo could jaw with everyone from "highfalutin Harvard types" to hinterland rustics.

Midway through these reflections, Woody espied an apparent Emersonian in the audience. "Now there is a man out there who can communicate," he announced happily. Then, disastrously, he drew one of those blanks familiar to us all. "I may not remember your name, sir," he went on lamely, "but I admire you. Would you stand up, Mr. Chief Justice?"

The Chief Justice of the Ohio Supreme Court rose and waved to the crowd. Then he addressed the speaker. "The name is Leach, Woody. Bob Leach."

Ah yes, Leach. Woody knew the name as well as his own, which, unless memory fails, is Wayne Woodrow. Leach. It was a name he would hear time and again the next afternoon, a name he had cause enough to suppress from conscious thought. This second Leach was Rick, the Michigan quarterback, who would communicate to him the sorry message that the Wolverines, not the Buckeyes, would be traveling to the Rose Bowl New Year's Day to confront Southern California. On Saturday, quarterback Leach, no relation to Justice Bob, led Michigan to a tidy 14-3 win, the third year in a row he had beaten Woody. In these three games Ohio State had scored nary a touchdown against Michigan. When that intelligence was communicated to Hayes during a post-game press conference, this staunch advocate of clear speech launched into a snarling diatribe against his informant, a Chicago newspaperman.

Hayes need not have been so sensitive. His Buckeyes were in no way equal to the team coached by his onetime protege and current nemesis, Bo Schembechler. Ohio State already had been beaten by Penn State and Purdue and tied by Southern Methodist and, entering Saturday's contest, had given up 18.5 points per game, the highest average by a Hayes-coached O.S.U. team and the highest for any O.S.U. team since 1946. For that matter, the loss Saturday dropped the Bucks to fourth place in the Big Ten behind co-champions Michigan and Michigan State (currently on N.C.A.A. probation and ineligible for bowl games) and Purdue. Still, by prior arrangement, O.S.U. will play Clemson in the Gator Bowl on Dec. 29. Had the Bucks beaten Michigan, *they* would have been the co-champs and Rose Bowl representatives and the Wolverines would have gone to the Gator. Because of a little Schembechler deception, this was not to be.

It is common knowledge that Hayes teams can neither pass nor defend against the pass. This has also been true of Schembechler teams, as the Pac-10 has happily discovered. As a result, recent games between Michigan and Ohio State have been no more progressive than the one they played in 1900, which ended zip-zip. Indeed, the devious Schembechler acknowledged afterward that "what I wanted to do was give them the illusion that this would be the same old Ohio State-Michigan game" — which is to say the ball would be airborne about as often as an ostrich. In its first two possessions Michigan dutifully stayed on the ground, advancing minimally. The second time Ohio State had the ball it scored its only points of the day, a field goal by Bob Atha from the Michigan 19 with 1:13 remaining in the first quarter.

Now the illusionist chose to reveal a little of his guile, and 1 minute 4 seconds later Michigan was on the scoreboard — a lightning stroke by any standards.

Starting from the Wolverine 30 after the kickoff, Leach called a thrust into the line — for no gain — by tailback Harold (Butch) Woolfolk, a freshman playing for the injured Harlan Huckleby (Michigan players all seem to have been named by Dickens). Then, on second down, Leach faked a handoff and hit tight end Doug Marsh on a sideline pattern for a gain of 26 yards. On yet another play-action pass he found Woolfolk in the middle for 14 yards. Schembechler sent in an option play on the next down, but Leach, observing that the Buckeyes were virtually in an eight-man line — five linemen down, three linebackers stacked — called an audible at the line of scrimmage. He connected perfectly with Rod

Feaster in the middle of the field, and Feaster, shaking off Mike Guess, loped in for the score. Gregg Willner converted, and, for all purposes, the game was over.

The Buckeyes took their best remaining shot late in the second quarter, advancing on eight plays to the Michigan 21, where they promptly came a cropper. Tackle Keith Ferguson was called for illegal motion. After a run up the middle, freshman quarterback Art Schlichter, harassed all afternoon, was sacked by blitzing linebacker Jerry Meter. He fumbled as he was hit, and another linebacker, Andy Cannavino, recovered on the 32. From there Leach, alternating passes and runs, took the Wolverines to the Ohio State 14, where on third and 1 he hit tight end Gene Johnson on the 2 with a perfect pass down the middle for what appeared to be a second touchdown. But Johnson was stripped of the ball a yard later by safety Vince Skillings, who then recovered it in the end zone for a saving touchback.

Skillings' heroic defense seemed to offer Buckeye fans new hope, and at that precise juncture the sun burst through a dirty gray sky. But it shone not on Ohio State. The Buckeyes would not cross the 50 until the final 3½ minutes of the game, and then only by a yard. The Wolverines would score once more on a Leach pass, this a dinky 11-yard, safety-valve toss to tailback Roosevelt Smith with 4:12 left in the third quarter.

In the fourth quarter Michigan quit fooling around and returned to the "same old Ohio State-Michigan" trench warfare. "We were more interested in controlling the ball than scoring more points," said Leach, who was himself replaced by B. J. Dickey with 5:51 left in the game. This seemed dubious strategy at the time until it was learned that Leach had pulled the hamstring muscle in his left leg way back in the second quarter. Schlichter was also replaced for two series by Rod Gerald, Ohio State's starting signal caller last year, a wide receiver this year. Gerald, Woody believed, could better elude the fierce Michigan pass rush, though not necessarily to pass. It is significant that when warming up for his quarterback chores, Gerald practiced more pitchouts than passes. He threw only once, for 5 yards, and ran three times for a net gain of 7 yards. So much for Gerald. As for Schlichter, one practiced Buckeye-watcher observed of the freshman, "He has a pro arm with playground pass patterns."

The left-handed Leach might have impressed more pro scouts as a college passer if he had been called upon to pass more. "I can pass as well as anyone," he stoutly maintains. His second-quarter injury, incurred during a rare sack, took away Schembechler's preferred option attack, which "is predicated on the movement of the quarterback." Deprived of movement, the dauntless Leach utilized play-action passes and simple handoffs to backs running at him from myriad sets — pro, wishbone, power I. He completed 11 of 21 passes for 166 yards. The two TD passes gave him 16 for the season and brought the total of touchdowns he has accounted for, passing and running, to an N.C.A.A.-record 81. He has quarterbacked more wins — 38 — than anyone in college football history. If he does not win the Heisman Trophy, says Schembechler, then it does not deserve to be given. Leach, affable, good-looking, is more circumspect. "I won't be disappointed if I don't win the Heisman," he says. "There are a lot of guys worthy of it. Whatever happens, happens."

Leach has the athletic options open to one adept at two sports. A center-fielder, he led the Big Ten in hitting this year, and may well have more potential in baseball than in football. To his coach's everlasting gratitude, he opted for four years of college rather than sign a pro baseball contract. In his conference he is the quarterback ideal, but in four years as a starter he has averaged only slightly more than 130 pass attempts a season, about what a Pac-10 quarterback will throw in a month. In the N.F.L., Leach might find himself spending more time on the bench than his namesake in the judiciary. But, as he established last Saturday, he can do whatever is asked of him. Just ask Coach What's-his-name.

26

WHOOPING IT UP FOR THE WOLVERINES

By **JOHN PAPANEK**
Sports Illustrated

NEW YORK, Dec. 4, 1978 — It seems a small enough claim to fame, but University of Michigan grads like to boast that their school has more living alumni, some 250,000, than any other university in the country. If this is true, the chief beneficiary is Bob Ufer, the self-styled Voice of the Wolverines on Detroit radio station WJR. As Ufer bellows into his microphone every football Saturday, "We support you, *Meech*igan. And so does everybody from coast to coast — from the coast of Lake Michigan to the coast of Lake Erie."

Bob Ufer is now 58. He has been broadcasting Michigan football games for 34 years, and, apparently, his on-the-air frenzy continues to rise. As spiritual leader of those hundreds of thousands of alumni, he comes with a guaranteed audience. Last week's Michigan-Ohio State game in Columbus was Ufer's 337th straight play-by-play broadcast. It was beamed to a hookup of 30 stations, and heard in such hamlets as Alpena and Bad Axe and Climax, on what Ufer hails as "the very maize and blue *Meech*igan football network."

A former Wolverine track star — he was an all-American in 1943 and 1944, and set an indoor world record of 48.1 in the 440 in 1942 — Ufer calls the Michigan games the way he sees them. He sees them with impassioned idolatry, outrage or grief, depending on how the game is going. He lives in Ann Arbor in a house once owned by Fritz Crisler and shares a birthday (April Fool's Day) with Michigan's current coach, whom Ufer calls Bo George Patton Schembechler.

"If you spend your whole adult life around Fritz Crisler, Bennie Oosterbaan, Bump Elliott and Bo Schembechler," Ufer says, "you learn that football is a religion and Saturday is the holy day of obligation." Ufer once did his holy-day routine at a pre-Rose Bowl banquet at which Don Meredith was to have been the featured speaker. Meredith got up, shaking his head, and said, "Now, how am I supposed to follow *that* guy?"

Some fans say that Ufer's finest hour came in 1969, when Michigan upset heavily favored Ohio State, 24-12. In his euphoric post-game summary, Ufer crooned:

Ohio came to bury Michigan, all wrapped in maize and blue;
The words were said, the prayers were read, and everybody cried.
But when they closed the coffin, there was someone else inside. . . .
Twenty-two Michigan Wolverines put on the gloves of gray,
And as Revelli played The Victors, they laid Woody Hayes away.

Ufer moaned and cried on the air when Ohio State beat Michigan, 20-9, the following year, but listen to his call of Billy Taylor's touchdown that beat Ohio State, 10-7, in the final minutes of the 1971 game: "Taylor's to the 20, down to the 15, down to the 10, the 5. Four, three, two, one. Touchdown Billy Taylor. *(Ufer's voice cracks.)* Touchdown Billy Taylor! *(Ufer now sounds like Laurel blubbering to Hardy.)* Billy Taylor scored a touchdown from 21 yards out . . . ! Old man Ufer's been broadcasting for 27 years, and I have never seen anything like this . . . ! Oh. Oh, my eyes! I'm an old man. I've got maize and blue spots in front of me right now."

The 1972 game had a much darker ending. Ohio State won at Columbus, 14-11, but Ufer and his legions will always remember the third-down plunge by Harry Banks that was ruled no touchdown by the officials. "Franklin hands off to Banks and it's a touchdown Michigan! Hey, wait a. . . . Aren't they gonna raise their hands? He was into the end zone! It's just like 1954: I can see Dave Hill taking the handoff from Lou Baldacci at the same end of the field and he went in. . . . and they claimed he didn't then — and he didn't now, 18 years later! God darn it! What do you gotta do down here to score a touchdown . . . ? Ohhh, I can't believe it! Oh, that's the rottenest deal I've ever seen in football!"

Then came 1974 at Columbus. Ohio State was ahead, 12-10, with 23 seconds to go, and Michigan's Mike Lantry could win the game with a 33-yard field goal. "Here we have it. . . !" Ufer screamed. "The whole five years of Bo Schembechler and Woody Hayes on the toe of Super Toe. Will . . . he . . . do it? . . . It is snapped. It's spotted, it's kicked! It's end-over-end and it is . . . it is . . . it is . . . good! *(Instant horror.)* No good! Nooo goood. Oh, no, no, no. *(Measured tones of mourning.)* No, no. I can't believe we missed that field goal. And *(sob)* I just hurt in every ounce of *(sob)* my body."

In 1975 Ohio State won again, 21-14, scoring twice in the last 3 minutes, and in 1976 Ufer introduced his Bo George Patton Schembechler Scoring Horn, said to be the actual horn that General Patton had mounted on his

Jeep. Michigan won that one, 22-0, with Ufer's broadcast punctuated by blasts on the horn. He honked just as enthusiastically last year when Michigan won, 14-6. And last week, he tooted and shouted, "We'll shovel our way to Pasadena," as his beloved Wolverines won, 14-3.

Ufer says his mail runs 10 to 1 in his favor; after all, whoever hates him isn't going to tune in. His greatest non-admirer is Woody Hayes, whom Ufer calls Dr. StrangeHayes. It is said that Hayes once played a tape of Uferisms to get his team fired up before a Michigan game. Halfway through, he realized that his players were snickering because Ufer was ruthlessly lampooning him, and he rushed to turn it off. For the last nine years, Hayes has refused to acknowledge Ufer, let alone speak to him. "Why should I?" says Hayes. "He buried me in 1969."

27

CONTROVERSIAL TD GIVES TROJANS WIN

By WILLIAM N. WALLACE
Special to The New York Times

PASADENA, Calif., Jan. 1, 1979 — Southern California beat Michigan in the Rose Bowl today, 17-10, and projected itself into long-shot contention for the national title.

The Southern California claim is based on the victory over the co-champion of the Big Ten; on Alabama's defeat of Penn State in the Sugar Bowl, and on U.S.C.'s defeat of Alabama, 24-14, last September in Birmingham.

The Trojans won 11 of 12 games in a season in which no major team went undefeated. U.S.C.'s only loss was to Arizona State, 20-7, in its fifth game.

John Robinson, the winning coach, cited his team as "one of the greatest in U.S.C.'s history," which covered a lot of ground. But "one of the greatest teams" had a lot of trouble with a Michigan squad that contested every inch of ground before a crowd of 105,629 on a clear, warm afternoon.

"It was an exceptionally physical game," said Robinson. "One much like the one here two years ago."

Leach's Third Rose Bowl Defeat

Robinson was bringing up the fact that two years ago another Michigan team had lost another Rose Bowl game to Southern California with the same Wolverine quarterback, Rick Leach.

This was Leach's third straight Rose Bowl game and third defeat. Michigan teams have lost the last five times they played against the Pacific Coast champion — 1970, 1972, 1977, 1978 and 1979. The Big Ten representatives have lost this final postseason game to the Pacific 8 (now Pacific 10) champion every year since 1975, and the last victory was Ohio State over Southern California in 1974.

Leach gave it everything he had, and earned the plaudits of Robinson, who described the left-hander from Flint, Mich., as "one of the greatest players I've seen in my career." Two years ago the Michigan offense was widely criticized because it came without a passing attack, but today Leach was throwing passes throughout the game.

His first and last attempts of the 10 he attempted in the first half were thrown wildly and intercepted by Trojan defenders, setting up a touchdown and a field goal. Leach completed only two passes in the first two quarters but had a hot hand in the last two, with eight completions of 11 attempts for 109 yards and one touchdown.

Escapes Five Trojan Defenders

The scoring pass, the only touchdown of the second half, came midway through the third quarter and it was a beauty, thrown on the run while Leach was escaping five Trojan defenders. He fired a bullet 30 yards downfield to Roosevelt Smith, who completed a 44-yard touchdown play.

But Michigan never had any kind of a scoring threat thereafter as the Southern California running backs, especially all-American Charles White, ground out the yards. They were difficult yards because the Michigan defense, led by linebacker Ron Simpkins, played so well.

White scored what became the winning touchdown in the second quarter. But did he score? The U.S.C. tailback dived over left guard from the Michigan 3, losing the football somewhere along the way. Had he fumbled before he crossed the goal line? The head linesman, Gilbert Marchman, was emphatic in stating that White had the football in crossing the plane of the goal line.

The reruns of the play as recorded by television cameras provided considerable doubt, but the camera angles did not duplicate the line of sight of the head linesman standing on one far end of the scrimmage line. The umpire, Don Mason, standing 5 yards in the end zone, signaled a fumble, but the referee, Paul Kamanski, stuck with Marchman's decision. Marchman, however, was not in a good spot to see the ball breaking away from White's grasp.

The Michigan coach, Bo Schembechler, complained only mildly and said he was in no position to see what happened. "But White did fumble," he said. "There's no doubt about that."

Jerry Meter, the Michigan defensive end, recovered.

Michigan, which finished its season with 10 victories and losses only to Michigan State and Southern California, gained more yards than U.S.C., 236-157. But the Trojan kicking game was so good that the Wolverines could not run back punts or kickoffs to give Leach a decent launching pad.

His U.S.C. counterpart, Paul McDonald, also a left-handed passer, was a less conspicuous performer as he handed the ball to White and tried only nine passes. One was good for the game's first touchdown, a 9-yard toss to the tight end, Hoby Brenner.

White, a junior who has already erased most of the Trojan rushing records of such luminaries as O. J. Simpson and Anthony Davis, was a workhorse. He carried 32 times for 120 yards and was hit hard by Simpkins and other Wolverines every time.

This was the 65th Rose Bowl game, and one to be remembered for White's phantom touchdown, for Michigan's third straight loss, and for Southern California's pretentions to the national championship.

The Wolverines were the fifth team of the top 15 in the writers' and broadcasters' poll that the Trojans had defeated. The others were Alabama, No. 2 behind Penn State until today; Michigan State, the Big Ten cochampion with Michigan and ranked No. 12; Notre Dame, No. 10, and the University of California, Los Angeles, No. 15.

"What more could anyone ask of a team?" asked Robinson.

SCORE BY PERIODS

Southern Cal 7	0	0	10	—	17
Michigan 0	3	0	7	—	10

28

BUCKEYES DEFEAT MICHIGAN, GAIN ROSE BOWL BERTH

By GORDON S. WHITE JR.
Special to The New York Times

ANN ARBOR, Mich., Nov. 17, 1979 — Ohio State played its way into the Rose Bowl for the first time in four years today on a blocked kick in the fourth quarter that gave the Buckeyes an 18-15 victory over Michigan.

Ohio State, which completed its regular season undefeated and untied, trailed by 15-12 early in the final period, then executed the block play just as coaches draw it on a blackboard.

Jim Laughlin charged in from the left and slammed the ball and the kicker, Bryan Virgil, to the ground. Todd Bell, a junior linebacker, picked up the bouncing ball at the Michigan 20-yard line and ran into the end zone for the winning score.

The play was not a fluke; it was designed as a punt block with a 10-man rush and it worked, to the chagrin of the majority of the crowd of 106,255, the largest ever to see a regular-season college game.

Thus the Buckeyes, who played their first season in 29 years under a coach other than Woody Hayes, achieved a perfect record for the new coach, Earle Bruce. It was their first undefeated and untied regular season since 1975, when Hayes led them to the Rose Bowl, where they lost to the University of California, Los Angeles. Bruce was a former assistant under Hayes at Ohio State before becoming head coach at Iowa State, where he stayed for six years.

Michigan announced later that it had accepted a bid to play in the Gator Bowl on Dec. 28 in Jacksonville, Fla. The opponent of the 8-3 Wolverines, in their 11th season under coach Bo Schembechler, will be North Carolina.

Ohio State's triumph ended three years of frustration against Michigan in the season finale that has decided the Big Ten title and Rose Bowl visitor for more than a decade. Hayes' last three teams did not score a touchdown against Michigan, which went to the Rose Bowl by beating Ohio State in 1976, 1977 and 1979, only to lose there each New Year's Day.

String Is Broken

When Art Schlichter, Ohio State's fine sophomore quarterback, threw a 19-yard touchdown pass to Chuck Hunter for a 12-7 Buckeye lead halfway through the third period, it ended a string of 15 quarters during which Ohio State had failed to cross the Wolverine goal line.

Ohio State, which took a 3-0 lead in the second period on Vlade Janakievski's 23-yard field goal, trailed at halftime, 7-6, and had to rally twice to win. Two long Wolverine passes helped to counter the powerful Buckeye offense, which outplayed Michigan most of the time with 432 yards gained to 298.

The Buckeyes moved well until they got close. Then the Wolverine defense would prevent disaster.

Coach Gambles Early

Even if it had lost, Ohio State would still have gone to the Rose Bowl, since Purdue beat Indiana today. However, the Buckeyes took the situation into their hands by blocking the punt.

Coach Schembechler made a couple of early gambles that appeared to hurt Michigan. He started a freshman quarterback, Rich Hewlett; then, after little progress had been made, sent in John Wangler, who had started the four previous games.

Wangler took over after the first of Janakievski's two field goals. On his sixth play, he connected with a freshman wide receiver, Anthony Carter, for a 59-yard touchdown pass. Virgil's conversion kick gave Michigan a 7-3 lead, and after Janakievski's second field goal with 11 seconds to go in the half, the Wolverines left the field with a surprising 7-6 advantage.

Stopped With Foot to Go

Michigan might have held a 10-0 lead at the half and eventually gained a tie or better had the coach decided against trying a field goal on fourth down and about a foot to go for a touchdown in the first quarter. The Wolverines had got within striking distance when Mike Harden intercepted Schlichter's pass and returned the ball 13 yards to the Ohio State 31. Six plays later, Michigan was a foot away from the goal line.

Schembechler called for a run on fourth down, which lost 2 yards to the charging Ohio State defense. However, a tie would also have resulted in Ohio State's winning the Big Ten title and going to the Rose Bowl.

Michigan regained the lead at 10:12 when Wangler directed a long drive, marked by another long pass to Carter. This one was a 66-yarder to the Ohio State 19. Four plays later and after two offside penalties against Ohio State inside the 3, Roosevelt Smith barged into the end zone, bouncing a couple of times before falling over the line.

There was a moment of hesitation as one official held that the ball had not been carried in. But the touchdown was allowed, after which Smith ran up the middle for a 2-point conversion and a 15-12 lead.

Ohio State had attempted 2-point conversions after its touchdowns and failed each time.

10-Man Rush Is Set Up

Before the snap on the crucial punt, the Buckeyes moved four outside men quickly into the line to provide a 10-man rush. The two remaining outside men, moving in from 5 yards back, kept running forward as if blitzing a quarterback. Laughlin, a senior linebacker, was going in from the left flank and Mike D'Andrea, another senior linebacker, from the right.

They charged so fast that they crossed in front of Virgil as he kicked the ball. Laughlin was the middle man in the pile as both fell across Virgil and the ball bounced away to the right.

Bell, one of many Buckeyes trailing the initial charge, scooped up the ball and ran untouched into the end zone.

SCORE BY PERIODS

Ohio State 0	6	6	6	—	18
Michigan 0	7	8	0	—	15

29

WOLVERINES RISE TO OCCASION AGAINST OHIO STATE

By JAMES TUITE
Special to The New York Times

COLUMBUS, Ohio, Nov. 22, 1980 — Not even the cheers of a record crowd of 88,827 could inspire the Ohio State football team to win another trip to the Rose Bowl today. Michigan's mighty defensive line throttled the Buckeyes, and its backs dominated the ball and orchestrated a 9-3 victory in the decisive Big Ten clash at Ohio Stadium.

The Wolverines scored only one touchdown, in the third quarter, but that was sufficient to decide the 77th meeting of these two Midwest powers. First-half field goals by Vlade Janakievski for Ohio State and Ali Haji-Sheikh for Michigan were the only other points in the game.

The hard-hitting Michigan defense even earned an assist on the touchdown. When Tony Jackson recovered a fumble on an Art Schlichter-Gary Williams pass, the Wolverines were able to move into scoring position with a 56-yard drive.

Butch Woolfolk was the hero of the 14-play thrust that moved Michigan from its 44 to within 13 yards of the Ohio State goal. There, John Wangler faked and passed over the middle to Anthony Carter.

"The touchdown was an automatic," Wangler said later. "I called it on the line of scrimmage. I saw them playing man-to-man coverage, and Anthony did a good job of getting open."

The Wolverines settled for 6 points when Haji-Sheikh's try for the extra point bounced back at him from the crossbar.

The Big Ten rivals canceled each other out with sterling line play through most of the game, though Michigan accumulated 23 first downs to 14 for the Buckeyes. That meant that it was up to the defense to do the rest — and it did.

Woolfolk achieved his eighth career game of more than 100 yards and became the 10th best rusher in Michigan history.

He crashed through the Ohio State line, which seemed to bend more in the waning moments; he took pitchouts, turned the ends and ground out important yardage with each play.

Wangler, meanwhile, added to the yardage that has stamped him as the second-most productive passer in Wolverine history. Carter, a sophomore who has already surpassed the Michigan record for touchdown receptions, continued to be his favorite target, catching four for 47 yards.

Michigan, which lost two of its first three contests, brought a seven-game winning streak into the game; Ohio State had a six-game streak. It set up a classic confrontation, one that the Buckeyes were favored to win because of a home-field advantage.

"In this series," said the Ohio State coach, Earle Bruce, "there is no home-field advantage."

Bo Schembechler, coach of the Wolverines, admitted that "this was not the prettiest offensive explosion I've ever seen, but I've enjoyed this more than all the rest.

"This team has come far beyond all our expectations," he went on. "They gave us up for dead earlier in the season, but we vowed to come back and win the Big Ten title. Our defense was unbelievable."

The Big Ten rivals played the first half like two angry elk with their horns locked in a standoff. The halftime score of 3-3 reflected the prowess of their defensive lines.

Ignore the fact that the Wolverines had an overwhelming edge in first downs through the first two quarters, 13 to 3; they were still not able to break through the Buckeye line when it counted most.

Ignore the fact that Michigan outrushed the Buckeyes by 40 yards; two interceptions of Wangler's passes offset that advantage.

And the traditional rivals were even as well with a field goal each, although Janakievski's 33-yard boot early in the second quarter took on some significance. Michigan had played though 15 previous quarters without yielding a point against some formidable rivals.

The Yugoslav kicker, who came to the United States 11 years ago, capped a seven-play, 42-yard drive that set the ball up on the Michigan 23.

The key play was a pass that Schlichter, leaning away from a tackler, snapped to Cal Murray for a 38-yard gain. This put the ball on the Michigan 16, but the powerful Wolverine line clobbered the Buckeye plungers and set the stage for Janakievski.

Haji-Sheikh came through late in the second quarter, this time with a 43-yard boot that brought the rivals even.

The half ended with Michigan trying to set up a field-goal situation for Haji-Skeikh that ended when his kick went wide. The effort was set up on a spate of passes from Wangler to Ricks, Carter and Dunaway.

SCORE BY PERIODS

Michigan 0	3	6	0	—	9
Ohio State 0	3	0	0	—	3

MICHIGAN STOMPS HUSKIES IN ROSE BOWL, 23-6

By MAL FLORENCE
Special to The Los Angeles Times

PASADENA, Calif., Jan. 1, 1981 — Michigan, whose coach Bo Schembechler was zero for bowls coming into today's, dominated Washington, 23-6, for only the Big Ten's second victory over the Pacific Coast representative in the last 12 Rose Bowls.

Michigan had lost five Rose Bowls, an Orange Bowl and a Gator Bowl in Schembechler's 12 seasons. But there were no thorns in the roses today because Washington couldn't contain Wolverine tailback Butch Woolfolk and all-America wide receiver Anthony Carter in the second half.

Fifth-ranked Michigan led at halftime, 7-6, but No. 16 Washington, behind the passing of quarterback Tom Flick, seemed the better team. The Huskies, however, squandered scoring chances, on one of which they were stopped at the Michigan 1-yard line.

The Huskies, who had upset the Wolverines, 27-20, in the 1978 Rose Bowl, couldn't get anything going in the second half. Coach Don James' team didn't have good field position and Michigan controlled the ball.

Woolfolk, a Big Ten sprint champion, was named player of the game. The hard-running, 6-foot-1, 207-pound tailback gained 182 yards on 26 carries, a 7-yard average, and scored a touchdown.

Carter, a 5-11, 155-pound sophomore, did not catch a pass in the first half. But he contributed key plays in setting up a field goal and on both touchdown drives in the second.

Carter caught five passes for 68 yards, including a 7-yard touchdown throw from quarterback John Wangler that provided the Wolverines with a 17-6 lead late in the third quarter. He also ran for 33 yards on four pitchouts.

Wangler was out in front all the way today. He completed 12 of 20 passes for 120 yards and the scoring throw to Carter.

Flick looked as if he would rival Wisconsin's Ron Vanderkelen as the most prolific passer in Rose Bowl history in the first half.

The Washington quarterback spread his passes around to four alternating wide receivers, his tight end and his backs and had the Michigan defense off balance. He completed 15 of 23 for 188 yards in that half. Nice figures, but no touchdowns. And he was only eight of 14 in the second half as Michigan's offense kept Flick off the field with its time-consuming drives.

Michigan (10-2) finished the season with an impressive statistic: not allowing a touchdown in more than 22 quarters dating back to an Oct. 25 game with Illinois.

Moreover, the swarming Wolverine defenders allowed only three touchdown passes this season.

The Wolverines drove 80, 84 and 62 yards for touchdowns and 75 yards for a field goal.

The 84-yard advance in the third quarter put Washington (9-3) away. Wangler and Carter kept the advance going with a 14-yard pass on second down and 11 at the Washington 37. Carter cut quickly over the middle to take Wangler's pass. Two plays later Wangler found Carter in the end zone for a 7-yard touchdown.

Michigan now was ahead, 17-6, and a 13-play, 62-yard touchdown drive in the fourth quarter wrapped it up with fullback Stan Edwards diving in from the 1.

The Huskies could have put pressure on the Wolverines and might have won if they had cashed in on scoring opportunities in the first half.

The most frustrating miss came in the first quarter when, in a scoreless game, Husky fullback Toussaint Tyler dived over the middle on fourth and goal from the Wolverine 1.

One official signaled a touchdown but quickly pulled his hands down. Another official signaled no score. The Huskies didn't openly complain about the ruling in the locker room afterward.

Flick said he thought Tyler scored. Tyler said he didn't have control of the ball while airborne.

The Huskies blew other scoring chances, too. The breakdown:

• On Washington's first series, a Michigan defender tipped a Flick pass into the hands of wide receiver Aaron Williams, who ran 52 yards to the Wolverine 23. But Washington tight end David Bayle was cited for offensive pass interference, nullifying the long gain.

• The Huskies got to the Wolverine 37 late in the first quarter, but Flick misfired on two passes to Williams and Washington punted.

• Early in the second quarter, the Huskies had second and 6 at the Wolverine 25. But Flick was blitzed and threw a hurried pass that was intercepted by defensive back Brian Carpenter.

• With Washington trailing, 7-3, and time running out in the first half, Flick put on a big-league passing show. He completed seven straight as the Huskies moved from their 10 to the Michigan 19. With 17 seconds remaining, Flick threw a 9-yard sideline pass to tailback Kyle Stevens. It seemed Stevens had gotten out of bounds but an official ruled differently. So, with the clock still running, Flick rushed a pass to the end zone, it was incomplete and there was just time for Chuck Nelson to kick his second field goal.

• On Washington's first drive in the second quarter, Stevens fumbled after a 2-yard gain to the Michigan 22. Center Mike Reilly picked the ball out of the air and ran into the end zone. But an official had called the play dead before Stevens lost the ball.

SCORE BY PERIODS

Michigan 0	7	10	6	—	23
Washington 0	6	0	0	—	6

31

BO'S THE NAME

By DOUGLAS LOONEY
Sports Illustrated

NEW YORK, Sept. 14, 1981 — On a recent soft, warm evening at Glenn (Bo) Schembechler's home in Ann Arbor, dinner is being prepared. Bo is cooking chicken on the charcoal grill out back, alternating his attention between his task and hollering at his wife, Millie, who's fixing the rest of the meal in the kitchen. "The chicken is done, goddam it," Bo bellows. "Hurry up. I'll be bitterly disappointed if I overcook this chicken just because you can't get organized in there. Damn, the chicken is just right *now*, Mil, hurry up."

Millie, to her enormous credit, ignores the wordstorm blowing through the screen door. She is one of the few people in the U.S. who would dare. "I'm not afraid of him," she says, against a high-decibel backdrop of continuing advice and abuse from Bo, chicken cooker and card-carrying expert on all matters. "Well, I'm not afraid of him *anymore*." In truth, most everyone else isn't afraid of him any less. Coming upon Bo at his worst equates with meeting a hurricane in full force — at his best he's about like a tornado just getting organized. You don't explain Bo; you take shelter. However, there is much speculation that the 52-year-old University of Michigan football coach, who has put together a team poised to make a serious run at the national championship — *if* it can get past powerful Notre Dame on Sept. 19 — has mellowed. I have *not* mellowed, goddam it," he says.

But he has, in subtle ways. One old buddy, Gerald R. Ford, the center on Michigan's 1932 and 1933 national championship teams, who lived for a spell in downtown Washington, D.C., says, "Bo has relaxed a little. Frankly, I think he's a more effective coach when he's less tense." But the mere mention of his mellowing sets Schembechler off, and he goes out of his way to prove it isn't so.

For example, when linebacker Mike Boren walked into Bo's office recently, Mike opened his mouth but Bo spoke first, of course.

"Look at your hair."

"I was born with it like this."

"Naw, you got it all pushed up. You weren't born with it like that. It wasn't even like that when I met you. Get a haircut."

"Bo, it's only a half-inch long."

"Get a haircut. How much do you weigh?"

"Oh, 218, but I've been sick."

"You were 218 and sick last time you were in here."

"I'm a sick person."

"Get unsick."

Nothing is moderate about Bo. He has a firm view on everything. "If I make a mistake," he says, "I'm going to make it aggressively. I don't believe in sleeping on a decision." It is as impossible for Schembechler to hold his tongue as it is for the ocean to skip just one high tide.

He has two favorite expressions. The first is, "That would have killed an ordinary man." He uses that to refer to almost every bad thing that happens to him. Not long ago he was knocked down on the football field. Everyone held his breath until Bo hopped up and said, "That would have killed an ordinary man." The other is, "Got it?" Every time Bo talks to you, you have to acknowledge you got it, got it?

"I'm gonna tell you something, got it?" asks Bo.

Yup.

"Pay attention, got it?"

Yup. Got it, got it, got it, got it.

As the evening turns dark and even more gorgeous and serene around the Colonial-style house, its master only gets more rambunctious. Millie serves dessert, and after one bite, Bo says, "I've had pecan pie all over the world, and I want to tell you, Mil, this doesn't measure up." Millie immediately rises to her own defense, citing the balky oven with the erratic temperature control, distractions . . . .

"It's terrible," interrupts Bo. "That's all. Look, nobody can eat it."

"But, Bo," says Millie, "I got the recipe from the cookbook Barbara Dooley (wife of Georgia football coach Vince) sent me. It's Extra Rich Georgia Pecan Pie with molasses. I did. . . ."

Bo interrupts, of course. "See, the problem is the ingredients aren't any good. Then you messed up cooking it. That's that. Got it?"

The subject is closed. And Bo is right, it did happen to be less than great pecan pie. But heck, it was Barbara Dooley's fault, and she was 600 miles away. The point is, this is classic Bo Schembechler. He talks straight ahead; no matter what the circumstances, he says exactly what's on his mind; he makes judgments on everything; he is secure in every way; he dominates everywhere and everybody. All of which makes him, remarkable as it sounds, a good guy up close. A really good guy.

"It must be great to feel as confident as he does," says Millie, "but he truly is a good person. All I have to do is what Bo's mother told me. She said, 'Handling him is easy. Just remember that when he loses a game, don't talk to him.' And he does hurt so bad when he loses one those dumb football games."

O.K., from a distance, Bo comes on like a yahoo. And that's Bo's public image. He has had horrible problems with the press, which has this nasty habit of wanting to talk to him when he loses, his mother's advice notwithstanding. But even if the media's timing were better, it probably wouldn't make much difference, because Bo hates the press. Not just a little. A lot. The Voice of Michigan Football, Bob Ufer, says he has tried to get Schembechler to be nicer to the media. "But he told me," says Ufer, " 'Bob, if I win I don't need the press, and if I lose they can't help me.' "

Ufer defends Schembechler, whose record at Michigan over 12 years is 114-21-3; Bo's teams have won the Big Ten championship twice and tied for it seven times. Says Ufer, "Bo has two categories of things in life: what matters and what doesn't matter. What matters is football. What doesn't matter is everything else. Bo is the kind of guy who is so dedicated that he doesn't realize how he's coming off."

Woody Hayes, the former Ohio State coach and noted expert on press relations, says of Bo, "He's a hothead, like me. If you get along with most of the press, I think you have to be a little bit crooked." Bobby Knight, coach of the N.C.A.A.-champion Indiana basketball team, who has had some problems with the press himself, snorts, "Bad press relations aren't always the coach's fault, you know. You've heard those dumb questions at press conferences. Hell, *you've* asked some of them." Not surprisingly, these three supercoaches — Woody, Bo and Bobby — account for 84.5% of all problems members of their profession have had with the press.

The whys and wherefores are difficult and always different. "It's because most writers aren't worth a damn," says Bo helpfully. So while some coaches like to go out and drink with sports writers, Bo would prefer to break out in warts.

Like in 1973, when Ohio State and Michigan both finished the regular season 10-0-1. Even though the Buckeyes had gone to the Rose Bowl the previous year, the Big Ten athletic directors voted to send them again. Bo was more than a little sore. So sore, and so outspoken, in fact, that the conference adopted a coaches' code of conduct and put Bo — actually, put Bo's mouth — on probation for two years. It meant nothing, of course, because the conference would never have disciplined either Hayes or Schembechler, only the other, non-imperial, coaches. Bo never did say he was sorry for his outbursts. "Sorry for what?" he said years later. "Telling the truth?"

Until a couple of years ago, he would routinely storm out of press conferences, kick reporters out of the sessions ("Don't be offended," says one of Bo's friends. "He'd kick Millie out, too."), make himself unavailable and order his players not to talk. Talking very softly once at a press conference, he was asked to speak up. "I'm speaking as loudly as I can," said Bo softly — and arrogantly. And in a memorable set-to on Oct. 1, 1979, Schembechler gave an absolutely unnecessary push to a publicity-seeking college newspaper reporter.

Yet, too much is read into all this. As Don Canham, the athletic director at Michigan, says, "Bo is oblivious to life." That, though, is his appeal. The world clearly would be a better place if more people cared as much about their pursuits as Bo does about his. Canham, who had the genius to hire Bo, stretched his feet across the desk the other day and reflected on his coach.

"Bo is a delightful guy with a heck of a sense of humor," said Canham. "He also has a heck of a temper. I guess a lot of people do think of him throwing his hat and kicking dirt and screaming at the officials. But I've found that when he gets mad, it's time to get mad. And while he has a short fuse, he also has a short memory. The only danger with his temper is that he will do something dumb. I don't think he will." Something dumb would be, to give a purely hypothetical illustration, for him to slug an opposing middle guard in the face during a bowl game. But nobody would do that.

Former Michigan President Robben Fleming once took Bo out to lunch and asked him, "Do you really have to get on the officials the way you do?" Schembechler had no real response. He says now, "I didn't try to justify it. I think he was right. But the only way I know to get their attention is to yell. How else do you do it? I'm open to ideas."

Canham, a huckster in all the best senses of the word (he has filled Michigan Stadium with an average of 104,186 fans the last 33 games in a row), says his relationship with Bo was established from the start. Just after he had hired Bo, Canham told him, "Schembechler, if we have any trouble, it's going to be your fault — and I'm going to win." Indeed, not long ago Bo appeared in Canham's office, pounding and popping off about some injustice. Canham listened to the ranting and then said, "Schembechler, this is all your fault," and got up and walked out. When Canham returned to his office, Bo was gone and nothing else was said about the subject.

But Canham also has one other technique he used with Bo: "I give him everything he wants." Bo's salary is $60,000, and he earns another $50,000 or so from television and other appearances. But back in 1969 when he started coaching in Ann Arbor, Bo told Millie to buy as fancy a house as she wanted. Heck, go clear on up to $40,000 if need be, he said — a fortune to the Schembechlers then. Millie promptly bought a four-bedroom house for $58,000. Bo groused, "If I don't win, we're in deep and dire trouble." Unlike some coaches who want more than their prowess in the won-lost column warrants, Bo doesn't want much.

Except perfection. *Perfection.* Put Schembechler in the center of Camelot and he would spot a loose downspout. In 1975, the morning after an unthinkable tie with Baylor, he called in equipment manager Jon Falk. Bo was furious. "Why did Mike Kenn have a jersey with a bad number?" he steamed. A bad number in this case was one that was crinkled instead of smooth.

"I didn't think you would notice," said Falk.

"I notice *everything,*" said Bo. "Now, if you want to manage the goddam equipment, get busy and manage the goddam equipment."

Defensive coordinator Bill McCartney says of Bo, "Nobody calls to excellence more than he does. He forces every guy to measure up every time. He will never turn his head. I've got the feeling he's just reaching his peak." McCartney can even find a Biblical verse in defense of Bo's clamorous tongue. In a well-thumbed Bible. McCartney turns quickly to Proverbs 28:23 and reads, "He who rebukes a man will in the end gain more favor than he who has a flattering tongue."

If that be true, Bo has gained enormous favor. That's because there's no satisfying the man. Walking past the practice field last summer, Schembechler spotted defensive lineman Dave Meredith working out.

"Why don't I ever see you here?" Schembechler asked.

"I'm here four hours a day. What do you want?"

"Oh, six hours, maybe eight."

And Schembechler strolled on. Actually, he would prefer not eight hours, but maybe 10 or 12 or 14. Or, ideally, 24. Just after Schembechler arrived in Ann Arbor, Joe Falls, a Detroit sports columnist, wrote that the coach's idea of a perfect day would be "eight hours of meetings, eight hours of movies and eight hours of practice." Everything Bo does is precise, correct — which is why the prospect of overcooked chicken will worry him so much more than it does the rest of us. These days, for example, when he leaves the office, he goes home; when he leaves home, he goes to the office. At other times of the year, he leaves home, goes recruiting and then comes home. Bo doesn't stop at bars for drinks with the boys.

Obviously, when you're a winner like Bo, there are plenty of people who want to be your friend. But Bo doesn't really want friends. Or, more precisely, a few friends might be O.K., but he doesn't have time for them. Or, more precisely, doesn't want to have time for them. Over the July 4 weekend, he and Millie did get away for a few days to visit some friends on Indiana's Lake Wawasee, but he wasn't all that keen on going. Right before leaving, he went back and picked up something to take with him "just in case." It was the film of last year's Wisconsin-Michigan State game. "You never know," he said. "It might rain." As it turned out, it didn't rain, but he did study the film. Got it?

Bo's best friend is Joe Hayden, chairman of the board of The Midland Company in Cincinnati. Their friendship also involves business deals. Says Hayden, "Bo doesn't go out of his way to seek close friends. But the image he projects is so different from how he really is. He's well-rounded, and I don't mean his physique. I don't know why he keeps coaching, other than the thrill of the hunt, but I do know that one time I told him, 'As long as you get up in the morning and are in a hurry to get to work, you've got the right job.' Bo smiled and said, 'I've still got the right job.' "

Just before his quadruple bypass surgery in 1976, Bo called Hayden from the hospital. "Joe, is everything O.K. for Millie and the kids (there are four sons, ranging in age from 11 to 26) in case of, uh, stark disaster?"

"What do you mean, stark disaster?"

"You dumb son of a bitch. If something in there stops going ticky tick, it's stark disaster for Glenn Schembechler."

"It's all O.K."

"Good. Good-bye."

Schembechler will on rare occasions make an attack on relaxing and watch a video cassette of a movie on his television at home, sometimes with Falk. One night this summer was typical of the way things generally go. Falk picked up a selection of films for Bo's approval. Over dinner at Bimbo's Casa Di Roma — where for a guy who makes important snap decisions on everything, Bo sure had a helluva time trying to decide whether to have meatballs or Italian sausage on his spaghetti — he also was deciding which film they would watch that evening. "Caddyshack" was a candidate because it lasted less than two hours. "Urban Cowboy" was out because it had that Travolta character in it. "Heaven Can Wait" involved football, so that was nixed — this was to be relaxation. Falk lobbied for "Being There." The clerk at the tape store had made a sneering reference to Michigan's sometimes less than exciting brand of football when he said of "Being There," "It's kind of dull for the 15 minutes, but Bo ought to be used to that." "Being There" was selected. Bo promptly went to sleep in his recliner during the first five minutes of the film, awoke at its end, and said "That is the worst move I've ever seen." Got it?

Yet — in this bit of an example of the new Bo — he felt he *should* watch the movie, though not so deep down inside that he wouldn't much rather have watched game films. By himself. Still, he wanted to be hospitable, and he knew that's what he should do. But he couldn't resist asking a visitor at one point, "How long are you going to stay around here?" The visitor said, "About three months, and then I'll go home and get clean clothes and be back." Schembechler doubled over in laughter. He's trying to be more human, honest, but damn, it's hard. Millie does give him pretty good marks in this endeavor. She says, "He has had so much success that now he knows what he has to get done and that he can do it by being nice to people."

So much success. Ahhhhh, yes. "Schembechler," says Bobby Knight, "is the best coach coaching anything in college sports." Southern California coach John Robinson, a Bo buddy, says, "I'd love to have a son play for him. He'd come out of there a much better person." Jerry Ford says, "He's a helluva man, isn't he? The two things I think of with Bo are strength and success. And then, underneath the surface is a very, very compassionate man." Woody Hayes professes great admiration, although he does add softly, "Bo is the second best in the country. I have to say the first is that old man down at Alabama."

Bo wins, wins, wins, 88.8% of the time in the Big Ten. Eleven of his 12 Michigan teams have ended the season ranked in the nation's top 10. During the 1970's, the Wolverines were 96-10-3 in the regular season, best of any team in the country. For the same decade, the Wolverines were also first in rushing defense, first in total defense, first in scoring defense. Indeed, bringing the story up to date, nobody has scored a touchdown against the Michigan defense in 22 quarters. Schembechler's record of 154-38-6 in 18 years as a head coach, including five at Miami of Ohio, gives him the fourth-best winning percentage among all active coaches, behind Barry Switzer, Robinson and Joe Paterno.

One oft-repeated knock on Bo is that he doesn't pass. In truth, he has, and for sure he will this year with Anthony Carter, a certified game-breaker at wide receiver, on the loose. But quarterback coach Gary Moeller explains the Bo philosophy thusly: "You run the ball first, and if you are successful, you keep running it." Michigan has been successful running, and as Robinson notes, "Passing teams generally don't win." Further, Dan Devine says, accurately, "Every winning coach has been called too conservative."

Probably contributing most to this year's sunny outlook is the fact that Michigan at last won a Rose Bowl, whipping Washington last January, 23-6, after seven straight bowl losses. Former Notre Dame coach Ara Parseghian thinks the notion that Bo couldn't win the big one was a bum rap. "Most guys don't ever get in position to play in the big one," says Parseghian. "Just getting there is a big accomplishment." Still, not winning The Big One cast a pall over Bo — you can ignore the fact he says it didn't, got it? — all these years. Defensive coordinator McCartney says, "Bo's solution to everything is to work harder, but we kept losing the bowl games, and the people of Michigan became so exasperated with us."

There were always reasons and excuses, but Michigan kept getting beat. "How I feel about losing depends on how I lose," says Schembechler. "If we were just not good enough, fine." But Bo can think of only one time his team wasn't good enough — in the 1976 Orange Bowl, when the Wolverines lost to Oklahoma, 14-6. And he thinks he should have won that game. "Anytime you get within a touchdown, you're good enough to win," he says. Perhaps the importance of the 1981 Rose win is best illustrated by the positioning of a team picture celebrating the win. It's right by the door of Bo's office. You can't leave without seeing it, unless you choose to go out the window. And Bo can have that effect on people.

Now Bo has won everything in coaching — conference titles, a bowl game, Coach of the Year (1969) — except a national championship. You can ignore the fact that Bo says it's not important, got it? Parseghian, who goes way back with Bo and had him on his staff at Northwestern, says, "Sure it bothers him, just as it bothers Paterno. They have both been so close, but it has escaped them."

That's why the Sept. 19 game against Notre Dame in Ann Arbor looms so big. "It's the biggest non-conference game on our schedule," says Bo, which, taken at face value, means that later games with Northwestern and Illinois are bigger. And bears don't live in the woods. What the Notre Dame game really is, is the biggest game of Bo's career. Indeed, Schembechler is at the helm of an extremely talented team, and this would seem to be the year. But Notre Dame is a tough nut, with outstanding players recruited by former coach Devine and guided by the new, fiery Gerry Faust. At his ease during the summer, Bo laughed about a conversation he'd had with the irrepressibly religious Faust. "He even God-blessed me," said Bo.

But Bo's jesting was probably a defense mechanism. He is steadfast in his contention that "I don't lust after national championships; I lust after Big Ten championships." And to underscore that point, he insists that ridding himself of the Rose Bowl-loser image last year was a tremendous relief, but after the victory he still felt there "was nothing like beating Ohio State."

Ohio State and Michigan are always linked because for years they've been the only schools in the conference that have played superior football. Further, the Woody-Bo Show made that annual confrontation bigger than life. Perhaps too big, because — as in the Super Bowl and a few other spectacles — the players were so on edge that their performances weren't always splendid. Only now, with Woody three years out of coaching, is Bo emerging as his own man after a near lifetime of being linked with Hayes.

It all traces back to Miami of Ohio, where Bo played for Woody. At a reunion of Miami players last summer, Hayes recalled a 28-0 victory he coached over Cincinnati in 1950. "We scored four touchdowns," he said, "and would have had five if a certain overeager tackle hadn't been offsides." That tackle was Schembechler. But once you have played for a coach, he's always the coach and you're always the player. At this same reunion, Hayes was organizing things — surprise — and suddenly looked over at Bo standing across the way. "Bo," he said "you sit right here." Bo sat. And one suspects that if Woody had said, "Bo, run through that wall," Schembechler would have done that, too, without question.

Bo was an assistant under Hayes at Ohio State in 1951 and then again from 1958 to 1962. They were, although both vigorously deny it, two damn peas in a damn pod. In football meeting rooms, they even threw chairs at each other.

"No, no," says Hayes when asked about the flying furniture. "We just argued to beat hell."

But you didn't throw chairs at each other?

"Oh, well, sometimes we threw chairs . . . but not at each other."

Just sort of a case in which the two of you were in the same room when chairs were thrown?

"Yeah, that's right."

So what's the big deal? Of course they threw chairs at each other. Why wouldn't they? Don't bulls lock horns in the field? Since his days as an assistant Bo's been called "Little Woody." And there were distressing signs

117

that the nickname fit. In fact, Dick Larkins, the former Ohio State athletic director, once advised Canham, "Don't hire Schembechler. You'll end up with him just like we have with Woody. You'll never be comfortable with him." But Woody would tear up yard markers; Bo didn't. Woody hit a TV cameraman; Bo didn't. Woody hit an opposing player; Bo didn't. A Bo watcher says, "I think he was learning something all along. He thought, and thinks, that Woody was a great coach, but he was telling himself not to copy some of the old man's mannerisms."

To this day, Schembechler speaks of Hayes with reverence. "I'm a Woody Hayes man," he says. "I believe in him, I respect him, and I always will." Indeed, after Hayes' slugging of the Clemson player in the Gator Bowl, Bo arranged a meeting with his mentor/rival at a midway point between Columbus and Ann Arbor. He hoped to get Hayes to apologize publicly. Sadly, Bo at his most persuasive couldn't get Woody to say those two little words that would have made all the difference: "I'm sorry." Subsequently, Woody admitted to the conversation, but snorted, "Bo isn't always right."

Hayes and Schembechler were, then, the greatest of friends and the bitterest of rivals. They loved each other and they hated each other. They were a study in contradictions. "We respected one another so damn much," says Hayes. "Now that doesn't mean I didn't get so mad at him that I wanted to kick him in the, uh, groin." And for his part, Schembechler says, "You beat Woody and you beat the best. It's always best to beat the coach you have the most respect for."

The fact is, Schembechler is emerging now as King of the Mountain only because Woody is gone. Never mind that in the 10 games in which the two faced each other, Bo's teams won five, Hayes' four, and they tied once. Bo was Little Woody, got it? But that was yesterday.

Today Bo — he will deny this, too — is enjoying life a little more. He's stopping to smell the roses. His heart attack and the subsequent bypass may have put things in perspective. He yammers incessantly to his players about the value of education, but he has learned to kid them a little.

The phone rings and it's defensive tackle Winfred Carraway. "Wouldn't you like to work around here for $4 an hour?" Bo asks. "Why not? What? Well, until you get a degree, $4 an hour is all you're worth. How are your grades? Come on, if you got all A's and B's, you coach and I'll play defensive tackle."

His other favorite theme is honesty. He talks constantly about his honesty and that of Michigan, especially in regard to recruiting. Indeed, there has never been a hint of scandal or irregularity since Bo came to Michigan.

"There won't be, either," he says.

What Bo really likes is to be out on the field with the players and to talk on the phone with other coaches. The nuts and bolts of the profession are his loves. One of his assistant coaches, Jerry Hanlon, says, "Bo is learning to live with imperfections. So he enjoys being around his staff, he really does. A lot of us think he calls meetings just for that purpose, to be with us." Says quarterback coach Moeller, "Bo understands that the bad part about coaching is if you don't win, you won't be coaching." And that would be awful, for Bo simply loves coaching, got it?

Sitting in his family room one evening (on the wall is a cartoon of a wife who has just bashed her husband of the head with a frying pan, and she's telling the police, "When he said he had the whole football season on videotape, something inside me snapped"), Bo was feeling reflective. "I love to win," he said. "Love it. Football is just too hard and too tough if you're not successful. This isn't recreation, and the sport isn't for everybody. Soccer is a great game, too; it's just that by junior high, it's time to play football. Anyway, I just don't want to expend all this time and effort and come up short, got it? I love college because you have to make do with what you've got. I may want a better player, but I can't trade for one or pick up a free agent, so I'll coach the hell out of the guy because he *has* to play — and because he's mine. Sure, I know I've got a lousy temper, but sometimes it can make you compete better. But I'm smart enough to know you have to learn to control it. It's just when things aren't right, I react aggressively. And I'm a disciplinarian. At meetings, the players sit up straight, have both feet on the floor and don't wear any hats. They get in early at night, too. Why shouldn't they? You tell me — does anything good ever happen after 11 p.m.? I guess my philosophy is I want to do what I'm doing better than anyone else in the country. But the problem is I'm just an average guy, got it? But aren't we all? What I've learned is there are not nearly as many bad guys or super guys out there as you think. Just a bunch of average guys." He falls silent, thinking. A penny for your thoughts, Bo.

Because he loves the boys and the good old boys (former quarterback John Wangler says, "Once you're a part of Michigan football, he makes sure you always are. The older you get, the more you appreciate Bo."), he loves the good old stories. He tells of Carter showing up as a freshman and one of the coaches marveling, "My God, look at him run and catch." Later that same day, Carter ran and caught a plane back home to Riviera Beach, Fla. Bo caught up with him by phone. "I didn't think he was gone for good," Bo says. "He just needed to go home for a little reinforcement from his family and friends. And the reinforcement he got was, 'Get your ass back up there right now.' " Carter did.

From this shaky beginning, Bo and Carter have developed a close relationship. That's mostly because Schembechler is in awe of Carter's talents. "I just don't know what else I can say about him, got it?" says Bo.

That's understandable. Just about one of every three passes Carter catches goes for a touchdown (21 TDs in 68 receptions in only two years). He was the first Michigan sophomore since 1925 to be named an all-America; he's the first Michigan sophomore ever voted m.v.p. by his teammates. Indeed there is increasing speculation that Carter, a junior this season (Bo calls him "the finest receiver in the nation"), may turn out to be the best player Michigan has ever had.

Carter generally escapes Bo's acerbic tongue — and even Millie finds that remarkable. "He gets on me sometimes," says Carter, "but the other players say he gets on them more." That's probably true because when you meet Bo's standard of perfection, you have just exceeded the world standard, and therefore it's time for the screaming to stop. "It has been a great pleasure to play for Bo," says Carter.

Schembechler sees the qualities he admires most surfacing every day in Carter. His attitude is superior, he's single-minded, he's great in practice, he's interested in team rather than personal goals, he's fast, he's tough, his hands are terrific, he keeps his mouth shut and, most of all, he's Bo's. "Nobody can allow Carter to have single coverage," says Schembechler. He smiles when he says that, because teams must sometimes allow Anthony single coverage, or some other Wolverine, left unattended, will do them in.

Thus both coach and player know better than anyone that Carter is the heart and, more important, the soul of this football team. With such responsibility, it's no surprise that Carter chooses his words carefully when asked to evaluate Michigan's chances. "I hope we'll be able to compete,' he says.

Former players often drop by to see Bo, and he makes time for each of them. "All the players embellish the hell out of the stories," says Schembechler. "They say I was the toughest, meanest bastard that ever lived. I know that isn't true."

Yet Bo inspires extravagant tales because he can be so outrageous and because he is *sooooooo* competitive. Former linebacker Mel Owens, the No. 1 draft pick last spring of the L.A. Rams, shakes his head and says, "Every day Bo is fired up, every day. He's feisty and he goes after it." Once, on a quiet social outing, Bo and two other guys climbed on bikes for a peaceful ride through the countryside. No sooner was everybody rolling than Bo said, "Let's race." Another time, on Canham's boat for a pleasure cruise on Lake Erie, everybody was relaxed except Bo, who was trying to make sure the boat was *exactly* on course. Never mind that nobody had a course planned.

And Bo can now laugh at himself, which he does, recalling the night before the 1975 Northwestern game. Northwestern is a college football power on the order of most any high school you'd care to name. Sitting in his hotel room looking at films, Bo suddenly bolted upright. "Goddam, Northwestern is good and we aren't ready," he said. "I am sitting on an upset." Whereupon he raged through the hotel, clicking off TV's, screaming, berating, threatening, kicking ass and taking names. He finally returned to his hotel room, spent. Next day, Michigan won, 69-0. Got it?

32

MICHIGAN PUTS END TO IRISH ECSTASY

By JOHN FEINSTEIN
Special to The Washington Post

ANN ARBOR, Mich., Sept. 19, 1981 — After nine months of ecstasy inspired by its evangelical new coach, Notre Dame returned to reality today and found itself up against an angry, wounded Michigan football team.

The Wolverines, stunned by Wisconsin a week ago, came into Michigan Stadium smarting from a brutal week of practice, determined not to go through the agony again. The result was a dominating 25-7 Michigan victory over the country's No. 1-ranked team before 105,888, the third largest crowd in Michigan history.

"No one wanted to have to face another week like this past one," said tailback Butch Woolfolk, who rushed for 139 yards on 23 carries. "We had a lot to make up for today. Last year, last week, everything."

Last year Notre Dame beat Michigan, 29-27, on a 51-yard field goal on the last play of the game. Last week, Wisconsin shocked Michigan, then the No. 1 team, 21-14. Today, Woolfolk, Anthony Carter (two touchdowns) and sophomore quarterback Steve Smith, last week's goat, made sure the past would not ruin a perfect fall afternoon.

"Michigan just played great ball the whole day," said coach Gerry Faust, whose first Notre Dame loss also was his first in 34 games, dating back to a 1977 defeat at Moeller High School in Cincinnati. "You can't let your defense stay on the field as long as we did and not expect them to bend, break, sooner or later."

Notre Dame's defense finally broke because the offense never gave it a breather. Until their touchdown in the fourth quarter, which came with Michigan leading, 25-0, the Irish had crossed the 50 once. They had one first down in the second and third quarters. By game's end, 11th-ranked Michigan had gained 407 yards, Notre Dame 213, and much of that after it had ceased being a contest.

"We came back from the poorest performance I can remember at Michigan," coach Bo Schembechler said. "I think this re-establishes us as a good football team."

From the beginning, the Wolverines established themselves this afternoon. They took the opening kickoff and moved from their 12 to the Notre Dame 14 before stalling. A 31-yard field-goal attempt by Ali Haji-Sheikh was wide and many in the crowd cringed. But there was no panic on the Michigan sideline.

"We felt coming in that we could move the ball on their defense," said Smith, who was three for 18 passing with three interceptions in his debut a week ago. "When we moved the ball right away, we knew we were going to get it going sooner or later."

First though, Notre Dame had its brief moment. On their second series, the Irish, behind quarterback Tim Koegel, pushed the ball downfield to a first down at the 6. But two running plays and Koegel's slip produced fourth down at the 8 and placekicker Harry Oliver came in.

Faust, however, was not thinking field goal. When holder Dave Condeni, a Moeller graduate, took the snap, he stood up, took two steps and threw to Tony Hunter, another Moeller alumnus.

If Condeni had put the ball in Hunter's arms, he could have trotted into the end zone. Instead, Condeni seemed to aim for the hovering blimp and Hunter had to make a spectacular catch. But he landed on his back at the 4 and Michigan took over.

"The play was wide open," Faust said. "If we execute, it's a great play. But we didn't so I'll probably get 50 letters this week. I guess that's just part of being Notre Dame coach."

What happened the rest of the game is rarely a part of being Notre Dame coach.

Early in the second quarter, Schembechler stepped out of character to try a flanker reverse option pass. But Carter, whose talent lies in his thoroughbred legs and his soft hands, not in his arm, was tackled for an 11-yard loss. The Wolverines faced third and 20 at their 29. So Carter went back to doing what he does best.

"We'd been running the ball a whole lot and lots of times when we run, I just jog off the line of scrimmage," he said. "After a while, the halfback starts leaning back, relaxing a little."

Recovering from his bout with an attempted pass, Carter jogged off the line a few steps, then took off. Cornerback Stacy Toran stayed close but safety Rod Bone, who was supposed to help Toran deep, did not.

Carter got past Toran and Bone was not there to help. Smith finally was on target and Carter was gone, 71 yards for a touchdown and a 7-0 Michigan lead with 12:08 left in the half.

"That was so important for me after last week," said Smith. "I mean, I finally threw a good pass. I was embarrassed after Wisconsin, we all were. Getting that one just helped my confidence a lot."

It also let the Michigan defense know it was going to get some support and it began to shut down the Irish, three plays and out. It was still 7-0 at halftime, but Michigan looked ready to take over.

In the third quarter, it did. The debacle began for Notre Dame when Faust tried a halfback option pass, Hunter throwing to Dean Masztak. Hunter fared no better than the other non-quarterback passers of this game, under-throwing the ball into the arms of safety Keith Bostic at the Michigan 48.

From there, Michigan went 52 yards in 12 plays, the last a 16-yard Smith-to-Carter pass. Defender John Krimm, diving for Carter, missed everything as Carter stopped suddenly, then jogged in for his 24th touchdown in 26 college games. Even with a missed extra point, it was 13-0, Michigan.

"That was the turning point there," Smith said. "After that we weren't just holding on, we were looking to roll."

They did. Another Notre Dame punt preceded a 58-yard, eight-play drive, this one capped by a 1-yard waltz by backup tailback Lawrence Ricks. Finally, after another three-and-out series for the Irish, the Wolverines drove 53 yards. Smith scored on a 6-yard run and the rout was complete with 12:42 left.

Only Koegel's 8-yard pass to Hunter made the final score semi-respectable.

"They just did everything right and we did everything wrong," said Krimm, who covered Carter most of the day, although not on the 71-yard play. "Last year, the momentum went back and forth. This year, they got it and we never got it back."

Faust maintained his smile and his optimism through it all, even though his daughter Julie Marie burst into tears when she walked into the locker room.

"I'm not used to losing like this," Faust said. "But these things occur. Days like this happen and, if you survive them, you're very lucky. If not, you end up like we did today."

Score By Periods

Michigan 0	7	12	6	—	25
Notre Dame 0	0	0	7	—	7

33

BUCKEYES BEAT MICHIGAN, BUT IOWA IS IN ROSE BOWL

By **MALCOLM MORAN**
Special to The New York Times

ANN ARBOR, Mich., Nov. 21, 1981 — With Woody Hayes watching from on high, Art Schlichter, the quarterback who had brought the pass back to Ohio State football, beat Michigan with a run today in the last two and one-half minutes.

Playing his last regular-season game, Schlichter avoided three Wolverines on a 6-yard run that gave Ohio State a 14-9 victory at Michigan Stadium. With Michigan forced to worry about the possibility of a pass, a possibility that rarely existed when Hayes was the coach, Schlichter moved outside and reached the right corner of the end zone before a fourth Wolverine, the defensive back Brian Carpenter, could get to him.

But Schlichter's big moment and coach Earle Bruce's most rewarding victory did not guarantee a trip to the Rose Bowl. Iowa became the Big Ten representative with its victory over Michigan State. Ohio State and Iowa each played eight conference games, and the other teams played nine. The Buckeyes and Hawkeyes both finished with 6-2 conference records. Since the teams did not meet this year, the tie was settled on the basis of Ohio State's having made the more recent trip to Pasadena.

So the Buckeyes were left with a bittersweet feeling; they won here for the third time in the last four games, and sent Michigan, which would have gone to the Rose Bowl with a victory, to the Bluebonnet Bowl. This was the first time since 1967 that the Ohio State-Michigan winner did not go to Pasadena. Ohio State accepted a bid to play Navy in the Liberty Bowl in Memphis Dec. 30.

The Buckeyes had waited for the news from Iowa City while they dressed after the game. "Last I heard," Bruce said, "it was 16-0." No, someone said. 16-7. Bruce's eyes bugged. His face tightened. He sank almost to his knees. "Come on, Michigan State," he said. "I'd give anything for that."

"Is Iowa winning?" Schlichter wanted to know. Told that it was, the quarterback sneered.

Schlichter is considered the best quarterback in Ohio State history, but he faced the possibility of losing to Michigan for the third time in his four years. There was the crowd of 106,043, second largest in Michigan history, to deal with, and more significantly, there was the cold and wind. The temperature was 33 degrees at the start, and the wind gusted up to 28 miles an hour.

During the game, Schlichter took a shot to the stomach that sent him slowly to the sidelines, and he jammed a finger on his throwing hand when it hit a helmet. He was intercepted twice, once on an overthrown pass that was tipped, and again when he misread a receiver's route.

But he completed 12 of 24 passes for 131 yards, and scored two touchdowns when Michigan could not score any. He went straight ahead for a 1-yard score that put the Buckeyes ahead, 7-3, at the start of the second quarter and led to cheering in the press box. The noise came from where Hayes sat.

Hayes, the former coach who had come to the game at Bruce's invitation and talked to the team earlier this week, was standing and smiling before an announcement was repeated: No cheering in the press box.

The Ohio State defense, which had been criticized much of the season, stopped Michigan four times inside the 10-yard line. The first three times, the Wolverines had to settle for field goals of 19, 26 and 23 yards by Ali Haji-Sheikh. The last two kicks, in the third quarter, gave Michigan a 9-7 lead.

Early in the fourth quarter, after the Buckeye kicker, Bob Atha, had missed a 40-yard field-goal attempt, Michigan drove 69 yards to the Ohio State 8. But on third and goal, Steve Smith's pass to the tight end Craig Dunaway was tipped by the cornerback Shaun Gayle and intercepted in the end zone by the safety Kevin Ball with 8:32 to go.

Starting a drive at the 20, with the wind at his back, Schlichter completed four of five passes for 38 yards. On third and 1 from the Michigan 30, he dived ahead for the first down and fumbled, but Joe Lukens, a guard, fell on the ball and the Buckeyes still had their chance.

Tim Spencer, the tailback, carried the next three times for 23 yards to the 8. On third and goal, Bruce called for "play pass 21," a fake to the tailback off tackle, followed by an option for Schlichter to throw or run. Schlichter later said he thought he had changed 65 percent of Bruce's plays at the line of scrimmage, but he did not change that one.

"It's a play that had been open every time, but this time the Wolves knew," said John Frank, the tight end who caught seven passes for 68 yards.

And suddenly, things went wrong.

As Schlichter rolled to his right, Frank was covered, and three Michigan players — Carlton Rose, Keith Bostic and Mike Hammerstein — were closing in, with two others not far away. Schlichter said he was going to stay safely inside and not risk losing the chance for a field goal, when suddenly he spotted room to run outside.

"I almost threw the ball," he said, "but I thought it would be too much of a chance. So I moved on out and jitterbugged a little bit."

SCORE BY PERIODS

Ohio State 0	7	0	7	—	14
Michigan 3	0	6	0	—	9

34

OHIO STATE STUNS MICHIGAN, 24-14

By THE ASSOCIATED PRESS
The Atlanta Journal-Constitution

COLUMBUS, Ohio, Nov. 20, 1982 — Ohio State football coach Earle Bruce says it's a big disappointment that the Buckeyes are not playing in the Rose Bowl after beating Big Ten Conference champion Michigan, 24-14, on national television Saturday.

"It's bad, but I don't feel bad for myself," Bruce said. "I feel bad for the players.

"There's nothing we can do about it. We knew the schedule coming in," he said after the Buckeyes had scored their first touchdown at home against the 13th-ranked Wolverines in a decade.

The bitter rivals both suffered one conference loss, but Michigan played one more game to win the Rose Bowl berth against the Pac-10 Conference champion on New Year's Day. Immediately after the game, Ohio State accepted a bid to play in the Holiday Bowl on Dec. 17 in San Diego.

Meanwhile, Michigan coach Bo Schembechler accused Ohio State linebacker Marcus Marek of simulating the offensive cadence of Wolverine quarterback Steve Smith during the game. Schembechler said Marek shouted signals at the same time as Smith, leading to confusion for the offense.

Smith fumbled a snap at the Ohio State 7 early in the game as the Wolverines were driving for an apparent touchdown. It was one of six Michigan turnovers.

"It's a violation of the rules," Schembechler said. "The officials should call an unsportsmanlike-conduct penalty on the basis of what happened. It cost us a fumble at the 7-yard line."

Marek, a senior linebacker who was playing in his fourth game against Michigan, denied calling cadence Saturday.

"I didn't do it," Marek said. "On the first fumble, I don't remember saying anything. I wasn't even near the ball."

Schembechler and his players took the defeat hard.

"We just gave them the game," Schembechler said. "We handed it to them. We didn't just lose. We gave it away."

The Michigan locker room was solemn. Some of the key Wolverine players refused to discuss the defeat.

All-America flanker Anthony Carter, whose fourth-quarter fumble set up Ohio State's winning touchdown, stood with his face toward his locker, ignoring questions from reporters. A Michigan coach approached Carter and told the media, "Leave him alone."

The Buckeye attack was spearheaded by tailback Tim Spencer, who scored two touchdowns.

Score By Periods

Ohio State 0	14	0	10	—	24
Michigan 7	0	7	0	—	14

35

ALL THE WAY ON EVERY PLAY

By JOHN PAPANEK
Sports Illustrated

NEW YORK, Nov. 22, 1982 — The days are growing cold and windy in Ann Arbor, and this year more than ever Michigan coach Bo Schembechler is feeling the chill. Literally, because Anthony Carter's career with the Wolverines is coming to an end. Schembechler has another Rose Bowl team — his seventh in 14 years — but he won't ever have another Carter. Of that he's sure. So for the time being Schembechler is making the most of what he has got. On his angriest mornings the very mention of Carter's name will dissolve a Schembechler scowl into a beaming smile of the sort usually seen only on the faces of proud fathers, and he'll say, bet on it, "Anthony? Ahhh, isn't Anthony cute?"

Such an appraisal from Michigan's meanest man may come as a surprise — until one meets Carter. By golly, he *is* cute — and soft and warm and shy and funny. He is, in fact, one of those rare athletes who captivates admirers with his talent and turns them into idolators with his personality. And there is nothing illusory about Carter. He's the real thing, both on and off the field.

It would be difficult to ignore the Hope Diamond in a heap of pebbles. And so is Carter difficult to ignore in a Michigan football uniform — about as difficult to ignore as he is to defend against. He wears the number "1" on his back and covers his broomstick calves with long white stockings that seem to heighten his Bambiesque aspect, which is derived from being a shade under 6 feet tall and weighing a wispy 165 pounds. But it is what he does once the ball is snapped — what he has done since his days as a high school sensation in Riviera Beach, Fla., through his years at Michigan — that commands absolute attention. Watch him. You *have* to watch him.

Every time he runs a pass route, every time he positions himself to return a punt or kickoff, every time he reverses field and streaks around behind the quarterback to receive the football, Carter is a threat to score a touchdown. *Every* time. Consider: It's Oct. 27, 1979, Carter's freshman year at Michigan. The Wolverines, with a 6-1 record, 4-0 in the Big Ten, are tied, 21-21, with Indiana. There are 6 seconds left to play and Michigan is 45 yards from the Hoosier goal line. Carter brings in from the bench what has to be the game's final play. He's painfully shy, a lonely kid from Florida, unhappy in the North, who rarely speaks, even to his teammates. He calls out the play, 66 Post, and then shocks quarterback John Wangler by saying, "Hey, Johnny. Throw the ball to me. I'm going to be open."

Wangler remembers Ralph Clayton, then a senior and Michigan's leading receiver, raising his eyebrows on the other side of the huddle. "I couldn't believe A. C. said that," says Wangler, now a Wolverine graduate assistant coach. "But as soon as he did, I was going with Anthony all the way."

Seconds later, Carter, sprinting left to right, meets Wangler's pass in a seam over the middle at the Hoosier 25. Never shifting speeds, he makes a one-step cutback to his left to say good-bye to one defender and a quick shake back to the right to lose another. He crosses the goal line a few microseconds after the clock has run out of numbers. Michigan wins, 27-21. "I still don't believe it happened," says Carter now. "But I know it did."

Segue ahead to last Saturday. It's Carter's last home game. Victory over Purdue means Michigan goes to the Rose Bowl again. Early in the first quarter Carter pulls in a 48-yard pass, splitting two defenders as he runs the remaining 9 yards for a TD. In the last quarter he scores on a 62-yard pass play. In between he throws in a catch for a 2-point conversion. Thus Carter breaks the 42-year-old Michigan scoring record held by the sainted Tom Harmon, 244 points to 237, and earns a thunderous ovation from the Ann Arbor crowd of 105,281 as Michigan wins, 52-21.

The voice and the face — soft and appealing — fit in with the playing style of the man who outscored Harmon, although some of the freshman shyness remains. "You had to know him when he first got here," says Schembechler. "He had such a complex. I don't think he could trust anyone." Carter has made great strides, even if he still occasionally slips into the dialect of rural black Florida. He might say gooder for better or feets for feet. He also admits, with tongue in cheek, to being a bad speller.

"When I sign autographs for kids," he says, "I always ask them to spell their names. Even kids named Dick." Can he spell touchdown? "Yes. That's TD, isn't it?" Despite the self-deprecation and the occasional verbal fumble, Carter can hack it in the classroom reasonably well. Majoring in recreation, he has a bit better than a C average. And he has promised Schembechler he'll graduate next year.

131

Forget the word average, though, when you turn to Carter on the field. There have been four seasons' worth of incredible catches — that's Bo's word, incredible. What's more, there have been catches and kick returns and reverses and even passes thrown. And Carter has excelled for a coach who has lived by the run and has not had a superior passing quarterback to make the best use of Carter's talents. His 149 receptions over four seasons, with two games to go, this Saturday at Ohio State and New Year's Day in Pasadena, work out to a scant 3.23 per game and leave him far behind Howard Twilley's N.C.A.A. career record of 261 set at Tulsa in 1963-65. But Carter's total of 33 touchdown catches (excluding bowl games) is just one short of Elmo Wright's N.C.A.A. record set at Houston in 1968-70. Do some arithmetic and consider this staggering statistic: Including bowl games, in which Carter has caught four TD passes, nearly one of every four passes to him has meant 6 points for the Wolverines.

"He has the ability to score a touchdown anytime he touches the ball," says Notre Dame coach Gerry Faust, who was awed on Sept. 18 when Carter, though hobbled by a groin injury, returned a punt 72 yards for a touchdown against the Irish. Catching passes, running reverses and returning kicks, Carter has averaged 18.2 yards each time he has touched the ball, bettering by nearly 3 yards the N.C.A.A. record set by Arizona's Theo Bell in 1972-75.

One can only wonder what kind of numbers Carter would have amassed had he been given the opportunity to play on a team with a passer like Stanford's John Elway. "I suspect he would have broken every pass-receiving record in the book," says Iowa coach Hayden Fry. But Schembechler — and many others, it might be pointed out — argues that Michigan's offense is a perfect complement to Carter's talents. "Every play he makes for us is a big one," says Bo, "because teams that overload on Anthony are giving up the run. Teams overload on him anyway, and he still beats them."

Just how good is Carter? "I don't know that I'm gooder than a lot of receivers in the country," he says. He does know that he loves, no, *yearns* to handle the ball, and he makes the most of every opportunity.

In a playful mood one day, Carter said to Schembechler, "Bo, I think I'll forget about pro football and become a coach like you. Only I'm not going to have any running plays in my book. Only passes. And maybe a few end-arounds."

"Don't come *here* looking for a job when you're fired, Snake," said Bo. Carter pranced away laughing.

Before his junior season, Carter met Elway at a preseason gathering

132

of Playboy magazine all-Americas at Lake Geneva, Wis. Elway took Carter's hand and said, "A. C., gee, I sure wish you and I could hook up."

"John," said Carter wistfully, "so do I. So do I."

"Elway is going to win the Super Bowl for the team that drafts him," says Dick Steinberg, director of player development for the New England Patriots. "But he's the only one in the draft who'll be able to do that. Then come the guys you know are winners. Carter's one." Some, but hardly all, of the N.F.L. people are concerned about Carter's size, which could mean the difference between his being a low first-round pick and a high second-rounder. Grambling's Trumaine Johnson and Arkansas' Gary Anderson, both of whom are bigger, and Tennessee's Willie Gault, a world-class hurdler, could be chosen ahead of Carter.

Still, many scouts feel that in the N.F.L., with receivers protected from contact once they're 5 yards downfield, Carter will be even tougher to cover than he is in college. Says Tim Rooney, a Detroit Lions scout, "I'll compare him favorably right now with John Jefferson and James Lofton, and they're the best. Anthony's no more than 10 or 15 pounds lighter than Lynn Swann, and he has the same great hands and great moves and acrobatic flair — and more pure speed. I'll say this. If you're not going to draft Carter, you'd better draft somebody who can cover him."

"There are two things that set Anthony apart from every other receiver I've even seen," says Wangler. "One is that he runs a 4.4 40, but he can run 4.4 *sideways*. The other thing is his ability to position himself to make the catch, no matter where the ball is thrown. You just throw it, there's Anthony, always open and gliding into it." *Always open*. And this despite repeated muggings by opponents who have had Carter's picture pinned to their lockers for four years and game plans concocted especially to cope with him. Nothing has stopped him because there are so many things he can do. "He can take the ball on the sweep, or run the reverse, or cut up-field, or cut across the short zones," says Fry.

"If you want a single-word capsulization of Carter," says U.C.L.A. coach Terry Donahue, "you spell it p-h-e-n-o-m-e-n-a-l. In caps." Adds Purdue's Leon Burtnett, "We've tried double and triple coverage, and he still catches passes."

How? Carter gives a cute shrug. "Maybe it's this hook I have on my finger," he says smiling, holding up a meanly misshapen index finger on his left hand, the result of a high school football injury.

How does any superior receiver — a Swann, a Jefferson, a Lofton, yes, a Carter — catch balls lesser men can't handle? Carter's hands are of normal size by human — forget football — standards. The ball may come speeding at him like a bullet, yet there is no sense of impact when it meets his hands, nor is there any extraneous movement in his transition from receiver to ballcarrier. It is a physical puzzle that would confound Einstein. Carter says that in four years he has dropped only seven balls he should have caught, none of them in crucial situations. "Just sometimes when I'm lazy. Lackadaisy," he says.

"Truthfully, some of the things I do amaze me. I look at films and say, 'How did I do that?' I look awkward. Knock-kneeded. Both my feets be off the ground. I know it can't be true, but it shows up on the film like that."

Carter realizes that his one weakness is a tendency to cut his routes a bit shorter than he is supposed to. He has his reasons for this. For one thing, he doesn't trust current quarterback Steve Smith's arm the way he trusted Wangler's. But mostly, he says, "It's 'cause I want the ball early. I'm out there wanting to yell at him, 'Give me the ball! I'm open! Now! Here! Give it to me now!' "

"He has that sense," says Schembechler. "He knows where everybody on the field is. I don't know how. And after he catches the ball" — Bo says this with maximum emphasis — "he's the best receiver I've *ever* seen in the open field."

Off the field you'd never take Carter for a guy who is shortly sure to become Michigan's second three-time football all-America (Bennie Oosterbaan was the first, 1925-1927). He doesn't mix into Ann Arbor's social whirl, has virtually no friends outside the football team and is one of the least likely candidates around for Big Man on Campus. "The guys on the team call me the 'Hermit,' " he says. A typical Carter evening consists of study and viewing the likes of "That's Incredible!", "Benny Hill" and "The Three Stooges" on the tube. "And then I'm into bed. Every night," he says.

Carter gets along especially well with children. He enjoys the one day a week he works with handicapped youngsters at Ann Arbor's High Point School as part of the requirement for a course in special education.

Being the sixth in a family of eight children tends to give one the patience to do such work. His mother, Manita, who works as a chambermaid in a Palm Beach hotel, raised that brood all alone. Anthony was a bit of a problem to Manita at one time, skipping school to hang out at the Jiffy Pool Hall — "Jiffy University we called it," he says — until she sat him down one day. "I scared him up," she says. "Told him if he didn't go to school I'd put him in a children's home."

By the time he was in the ninth grade, Carter was on the Sun Coast High varsity football team, and soon word of his deeds spread through

Florida and beyond. He scored 54 touchdowns in four years and the recruiters came in droves, hustling the not very worldly Carter with outrageous promises. Shirley Burgess, the dean of students at Sun Coast, helped him sort out the blatantly bogus from the merely enthusiastic and urged him to "go someplace where they'll like you as a person and not just a football player." That pared the list down quickly, and Michigan emerged as the winner, beating out Florida State and Texas.

Thus began the father-son relationship between Schembechler and Carter, one that nearly ended when Carter fled for home only three days after he arrived in Ann Arbor. "That was the funniest story of all," says Schembechler. "I had him on the phone and said, 'Now Anthony, you're not going to leave here without talking to me, are you?' 'Oh no, Coach. I'm not going to do anything without talking to you.' So I hung up the phone and the next thing I know he's in Florida! So I got him on the phone down there and said, 'You promised me you'd talk to me before you left here.' Anthony said, 'Oh yeah. I'm going to talk to you. I'm not going to do *anything* before I talk to you.' " Schembechler convulses in laughter telling the story. "Oh, he's beautiful, isn't he? Isn't he cute?"

Carter was on campus three days later, and since then Schembechler has personally monitored practically every move he has made. And when Carter does something Schembechler doesn't like, Schembechler lets him know about it in Bo-speak, which is to say, as bluntly as possible. The coach worries most about agents, crawling — in Schembechler's view — from under every rock, looking for an opportunity to get Carter's signature on the nearest dotted line. If any are trying, they are surely out-of-towners, because everyone who knows anything about Michigan football knows better than to trespass on Schembechler's lawn. The other day former President and Michigan center Gerald Ford showed up at the Wolverines' practice field. A photographer asked for permission to pose Ford with a fellow Michigan m.v.p. named Carter. "Christ," said Colonel Bob Barrett, Ford's aide, "he's on Bo's turf now. The President wouldn't go to the bathroom here without asking Bo's permission."

Schembechler is fiercely protective of Carter — whom the Michigan players have nicknamed Little Schemmy — and as with any father whose son is growing up too quickly, sometimes the relationship gets a little strained. Schembechler loudly disapproves, for instance, of Carter's year-old romantic relationship with Ortancis Thomas, a 32-year-old city councilwoman in Riviera Beach. Carter shrugs and says, "I didn't pick Bo's wife, Millie, for him."

Schembechler says that he's going to have "a lot of work to do" when the season is over, preparing Carter for life outside the nest. He intends to send Carter out as pure as he was when he arrived. Schembechler smiles when he says, "I've kept Anthony in poverty."

And just like a boy anxious to be a man, Carter says, "Sometimes Bo treats me like I'm still a freshman. He's got to learn that little Anthony has grown up."

Schembechler will. But letting go won't be made any easier by the fact that Carter's name will be engraved in memory alongside those of Harmon, Oosterbaan and Ron Kramer. As he thinks about Michigan football without Carter, Schembechler gazes skyward and then back toward earth. A beatific smile crumbles into his surliest General Patton scowl, and he says, "Replace Anthony? Hell! You can't replace Anthony!"

Bill McCarthy *(right)* served as an assistant to Bo Schembechler for 8 seasons (1974-81) before leaving to become head coach at Colorado.

Garland Rivers (13) reaches high for an interception attempt against Notre Dame in 1981.

Ohio State coach Earle Bruce *(left)* and Bo Schembechler were great rivals during the late 1970's and on through the mid-1980's.

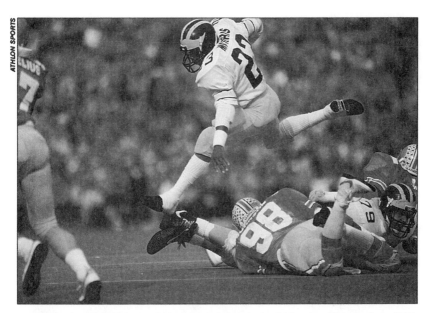

Jamie Morris (23) hurdles an Ohio State defender in the Wolverines' 27–17 win in 1985.

After Michigan defeating Nebraska, 27–23, in the 1986 Fiesta Bowl, Bo Schembechler enjoys a victory ride.

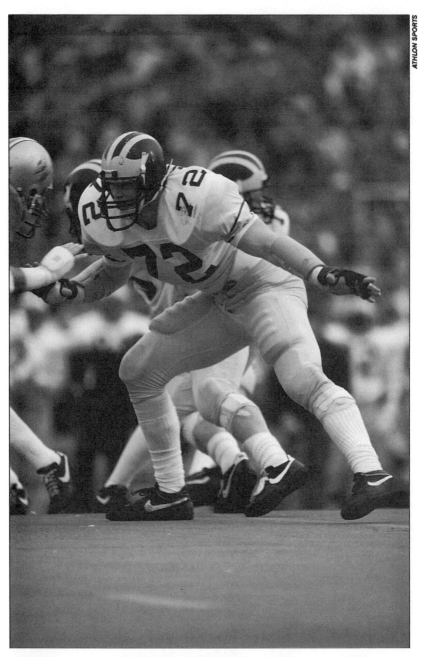

John Elliott was a two-time all-America lineman for the Wolverines in 1986-87.

Gary Moeller *(left)*, a longtime Schembechler assistant, signals in a play from the sidelines in 1986.

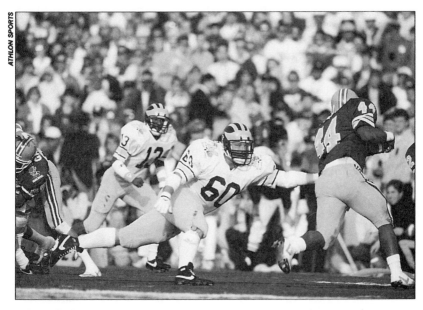

Mark Messner (60), a Michigan two-time all-America defensive tackle (in 1987-88), attempts to corral an Arizona State running back in the 1987 Rose Bowl.

Jim Harbaugh (4) earned all-America honors at quarterback in 1986. He later became the quarterback for the Chicago Bears and the Indianapolis Colts of the N.F.L.

Jamie Morris' great speed and shifty moves made him an elusive target for opposing defenses.

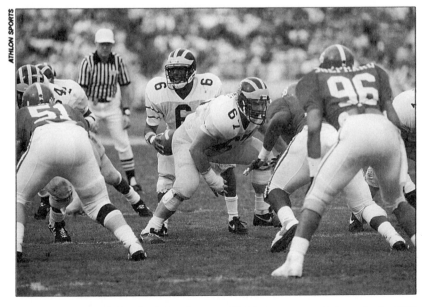

Demetrius Brown (6) led the Wolverines to a 27–24 victory over Alabama in the 1988 Hall of Fame Bowl.

Greg Strepenak (75), a two-time all-America in 1990-91, was rarely knocked around by defensive lineman.

36

U.C.L.A. JOLTS SMITH, WOLVERINES

By **MICHAEL WILBON**
Special to The Washington Post

PASADENA, Calif., Jan. 1, 1983 — When this 69th Rose Bowl is relived and recounted, two plays will be remembered as contributing most to U.C.L.A.'s 24-14 victory over Michigan today.

With 7 minutes left in the second quarter and Michigan trailing by 7 points, Wolverine starting quarterback Steve Smith was knocked from the game with a separated right shoulder by a tackle at the end of his 8-yard run.

In came seldom-used backup David Hall, and out went most of Michigan's offensive plans. "Dave Hall has never really played," Bo Schembechler, the Michigan coach, said. "You yank this kid off the bench and tell him, 'Go win the Rose Bowl.' It's hard to do."

The other key play was electrifying. It came with 8 minutes to play. The Wolverines had just stopped U.C.L.A.'s Kevin Nelson for no gain on fourth and goal from the 1 to get the ball back, trailing, 17-7.

On second and 9 from his 2-yard line, Hall dropped into the end zone, looking for all-America receiver Anthony Carter. Hall saw Carter, but not Blanchard Montgomery, the gambling inside linebacker.

Montgomery stepped in front of Carter at the 11, intercepted the pass and ran it in for the touchdown. That gave the No. 5-ranked Bruins a 24-7 lead. Even though 19th-ranked Michigan would score again, with 5:20 left, on a 4-yard pass from Hall to Dan Rice, the game was out of reach.

"That was definitely the turning point of the game," said U.C.L.A. safety Don Rogers. "The quarterback didn't see Blanchard and he made the play of the game."

There were other good plays made by other good players. U.C.L.A. quarterback Tom Ramsey completed 18 of 25 passes for 162 yards. Michigan tailback Lawrence Ricks rushed 23 times for 96 yards. Hall, the backup quarterback, completed 13 of 24 passes for 155 yards and two touchdowns. Rogers stopped a second-quarter Michigan drive by intercepting a pass from Smith inside the 15. U.C.L.A.'s Mike Durden recovered a punt-return fumble by Carter, which led to a Bruin field goal just before halftime.

But as Terry Donahue said, moments after coaching his first Rose Bowl game, "There were three key points in this game: our second touchdown drive, the loss of Steve Smith to Michigan and Blanchard Montgomery's interception."

Donahue felt his team's 80-yard drive in the third quarter deserved special mention because it followed a 45-yard drive by Michigan that cut U.C.L.A.'s lead to 10-7. Michigan had run seven straight plays, then scored on a fourth and goal, 1-yard pass from Hall to tight end Craig Dunaway.

Ramsey, who had completed his first seven passes but then cooled down, got comfortable again. Ramsey completed a third-down pass to Jojo Townsell to keep the drive alive at the Bruin 31 and several plays later ran 15 yards to the Michigan 37. Four plays later, tailback Danny Andrews took it in from the 9, boosting U.C.L.A.'s margin to 17-7 with 12 seconds left in the third quarter.

"That," said Donahue, "was the drive of the game."

But Donahue didn't want to downplay how drastically the game changed when Michigan's Smith went out.

"It's very difficult to weigh the loss of Smith, to their offense and to Anthony Carter," Donahue said. "It would be like us trying to play without Tom Ramsey. The second-string quarterback is not the option-type quarterback. And when a Michigan team doesn't have that threat, it's easier to defend against, quite frankly."

Schembechler, who lost his sixth Rose Bowl in seven tries, didn't want to blame the loss on the injury to Smith. But he, too, knew the significance.

"Losing him took away a lot of our offense," Schembechler said. "We were planning to roll Smith, bootleg him, option him. Smith runs that team. Nobody else has run it for two years. Hall gets about 25 to 33 percent of the practice time. When Steve went out, we were out of the option and the bootleg, out of all the roll stuff."

Michigan's running game also was off form. The Wolverines average about 240 yards per game rushing, but ran for only 142 today. Part of that was because strong tackle Rich Stenger, a 6-foot-7, 260-pound senior who opens large holes for Ricks and the other Wolverine backs, left with a knee injury on the second play of the game.

The other part was because U.C.L.A.'s defense was very, very good. Cornerback Lupe Sanchez, Montgomery and Rogers played the run well.

"Our defense deserves a standing ovation," said Montgomery.

"Our defense has been pretty much underrated most of the year," said Rogers, co-player of the game with Ramsey.

Montgomery said he had "dropped back 6 or 8 yards" on the play that would produce his interception-touchdown. "When (Hall) threw it, I was wondering whether or not I could jump high enough to catch it. The next thing I knew, I was running into the end zone."

Schembechler talked about his team's turnovers. The Wolverines had three interceptions and one fumble. "We had four turnovers and didn't get any from U.C.L.A." he said.

So, while Big Ten champion Michigan went back to the Midwest, pondering yet another Rose Bowl defeat, Pac-10 champion U.C.L.A. celebrated its first Rose Bowl victory since 1976, on its home field.

"This is the pinnacle of college success," said Donahue, even though his team will not end ranked No. 1 or 2 in the final polls, which will be released Sunday.

U.C.L.A.'s victory also served another purpose. Michigan defeated U.C.L.A. New Year's Eve, 1981, in the Bluebonnet Bowl. U.C.L.A. defeated Michigan, for the first time ever, Sept. 25 in Ann Arbor.

"I'm just happy," said Rogers, "that we broke the tie."

SCORE BY PERIODS

U.C.L.A. 7	3	7	7	—	24
Michigan 0	0	7	7	—	14

37

SMITH IS HERO IN WIN
OVER BUCKEYES

By GORDON S. WHITE Jr.
Special to The New York Times

ANN ARBOR, Mich. Nov. 19, 1983 — Steve Smith, Michigan's senior quarterback, made up for a lot of past mistakes today when he threw for two touchdowns and ran for another to lead the Wolverines to a 24-21 victory over Ohio State and into the Sugar Bowl game on Jan. 2.

Smith had been blamed quite a bit for Michigan's losses to the Buckeyes in 1982 (24-14) and 1981 (14-9). But this time the Michigan quarterback excelled before 106,115 fans in Michigan Stadium. The result left Michigan with a 9-2 record and a berth against Auburn in the Sugar Bowl game while Ohio State (8-3) earned a trip to the Fiesta Bowl game against Pittsburgh on Jan. 2.

Bo Schembechler, the Michigan coach, wearing a rare and very broad smile after the game, said: "I think this was a personal triumph for Steve Smith. It proves he is one of the best quarterbacks in the country. The kid's been playing hurt. To tell you the truth, this is the first time this season that we played all right. It's really the only time he didn't have problems."

It was a big day for Smith, who passed for 207 yards and had no interceptions this time whereas he was intercepted on crucial plays in the last two years against Ohio State. He also ran for 44 yards.

Smith had played much of the season with a shoulder harness on his right — passing — arm. This was the result of bruises to a shoulder that was separated earlier in his career at Michigan. Today's game was the third this year he played without the harness.

This game is the regular-season finale and traditionally the biggest game every year for these teams, but it was not quite a usual year for either. For only the second time in the last 16 years neither one is going to the Rose Bowl as representative of the Big Ten Conference in that richest of all bowl games.

Illinois won the Big Ten title and the Rose Bowl spot this season after beating both Michigan and Ohio State during the season. Michigan finished second in the Big Ten with an 8-1 record to 9-0 for the Illini. Ohio State finished 6-3 in the league.

Michigan was trailing Ohio State, 14-10, late in the third period when the game turned on a pass interception by the Wolverines' Brad Cochran and a fumble recovery by the Wolverines' Mike Hammerstein on a trick play that backfired for Ohio State. Each of these turnovers started Michigan to a touchdown and led to victory before the largest crowd to watch a college football game this season.

Schembechler said: "You cannot turn the ball over against them much and win. We turned the ball over nine times in the last two years against them and what happened? Today we capitalized on the turnovers and that was the difference in the game."

Following Cochran's interception of the pass by Mike Tomczak at the Michigan 48, the Michigan cornerback returned the ball to the Buckeyes' 29. Cochran had another pass interception late in the fourth period to stop another Ohio State drive.

Seven plays after the first Cochran theft, Smith went in easily from the 1 on the option play right to get the score to 17-14 for Michigan with 12 minutes 8 seconds to play.

Following the fumble recovery by Hammerstein, a defensive tackle, at the Michigan 39, it took the Wolverines eight plays to score. The touchdown came on an 8-yard, near-perfect pass play from Smith to a tight end, Eric Kattus, with about 7 minutes left. Smith had looked right for a couple of seconds, then suddenly turned back to his left and threw to Kattus, who was unguarded at the 2.

Ohio State, which had just driven 41 yards and was trailing by 3 points, attempted a "fake fumble" on the play in which Michigan recovered. This is the same play Nebraska tried with success against Oklahoma four years ago even though Oklahoma won.

On the play, Tomczak took the snap and then simply put the ball on the ground and turned away as if to give a handoff or run. A pulling guard was supposed to pick up the ball and run with it because the offense is allowed to advance a fumble.

Earle Bruce, the Ohio State coach, said: "We ran it all week in practice and it looked like a million dollars, but today nobody picked up the ball."

Instead, Hammerstein fell on it.

Ohio State pulled to 24-21 when it scored a touchdown with 1:52 left on a 32-yard pass from Tomczak to Cedric Anderson. But it was not enough.

Michigan's Bob Bergeron had opened the scoring with a 26-yard field goal at 8:14 of the first period.

Five minutes later, Michigan scored on a 67-yard pass play from Smith to Triando Markray.

Keith Byars, Ohio State's fine sophomore tailback who ran for 115 yards, scored from the 1 midway in the second period and on a 19-yard run midway in the third for the 14-10 Buckeye lead. With those scores, Byars set a Big Ten season record of 19 touchdowns and another conference record of 110 points in a season.

Score By Periods

Michigan 10	0	0	14	—	24
Ohio State 0	7	7	7	—	21

38

TIGERS SET BACK MICHIGAN 9-7

By ROY S. JOHNSON
Special to The New York Times

NEW ORLEANS, Jan. 2, 1984 — For Auburn's coach, Pat Dye, and his players, the easy part is over. Behind three field goals by Al Del Greco, the last one a 19-yarder with 23 seconds left, Auburn defeated Michigan, 9-7, in the 50th Sugar Bowl game tonight.

Now comes the hard part: waiting for the results of the final news agency polls, which will be released Tuesday.

Auburn came into the game ranked third in the polls. Combined with the upsets of top-ranked Nebraska in the Orange Bowl and No. 2 Texas in the Cotton Bowl, Dye said that his team now deserved the final No. 1 ranking.

'Cut and Dried'

"It's cut and dried," Dye said. "If there's going to be a national title in America, and have any credibility, there's no way Auburn shouldn't be No. 1."

Dye, whose team finished the season with an 11-1 record, bases his belief on the difficulty of the Tigers' schedule.

"I just happened to have this with me," Dye said, before reciting a list of the winning percentages of the opponents of the nation's top-ranked teams.

Dye said the opponents of Miami, which stunned Nebraska, 31-30, in the Orange Bowl, went 55-52-3 for a percentage of .514. Nebraska's opponents were 63-56-3, .528; Michigan's were 60-48-2, or .555; Texas' opponents were 63-43-5, .590.

Eight of the Tigers's 12 opponents this season appeared in bowl games. All told, the opponents had a record of 75-32-3, or a percentage of .695.

"I don't know what you've got to do to win the national championship," Dye said. "But you can check into the history of college football, and no one's played a harder schedule than we have."

In the last computed ranking conducted by The New York Times, Auburn was No. 1. The final computer ranking will be announced Tuesday.

For most of the time tonight, Auburn struggled against a good Michigan defense. The Tigers committed an uncharacteristic four turnovers — three fumbles and a rare interception of a Randy Campbell pass — and trailed by a point, 7-6, when they received the ball on their 38 with 7:44 remaining.

Until that point, the Michigan defense had given yardage to the talented Tiger runners — Bo Jackson, Lionel James and fullback Tommy Agee — but had not allowed a touchdown.

In that final drive, Agee (16 carries for 93 yards) broke two runs of 11 yards each and one of 7; James (18 carries, 83 yards) converted a fourth down with a 3-yard effort; and Jackson (the game's most valuable player with 130 yards on 22 carries) had five runs, the final one a 6-yard scamper over the left side that put the ball on the 2 with only 23 seconds remaining.

One Bad Kick in Four Years

Essentially the kick, which was placed slightly to the left of the goal posts, was an extra point for Del Greco, a senior. For him, that was almost automatic. In four years he has missed only 1 of 111 extra points.

After a Wolverine timeout, Del Greco placed the ball through the uprights. "I waited a long time for a chance to do something like that," he said after the game.

The Wolverines had two final plays — two passes of 22 and 38 yards from the quarterback Steve Smith to the flanker Vince Bean and the tailback Rick Rogers, respectively — before the final gun.

Rogers was the Wolverines' leading rusher here with 86 yards on 17 carries.

Campbell Intercepted

"The way we won tonight was more meaningful and will mean more down the line than if we'd won by a large margin," said Dye, whose team won its first Southeastern Conference title in 26 years. "The lessons they learned will supplant what might have been learned in a rout."

For Michigan's Bo Schembechler, whose team fell to 9-3, the loss was a disheartening one. His team, led by its defense, dominated the first half. On the Tigers' first possession of the night, Brad Cochran, a Wolverine defensive back, picked off a short Campbell pass on the Michigan 30-yard line and returned it 7 yards.

The interception was only the fourth of the year against Campbell.

That play sparked the Wolverines' only scoring drive — a nine-play, 63-yard march that ended with a sweeping touchdown run by Smith, who sliced through two defenders at the goal line to complete a 6-yard run with 7:30 left in the opening period.

The biggest plays of the drive were a 19-yard pass from Smith to the split end Triando Markray, who became a starter only late in the year, and a 20-yard run through the left side by the tailback Rick Rogers.

The Tigers' sole scoring threat in the first half was a 58-yard run by Jackson — that ended with a 36-yard field-goal attempt by Del Greco that sailed wide to the left.

The Wolverines' defense relied on quickness against the Tigers' triple-option wishbone offense in the first half. So in the second half, the Tigers altered their strategy, attacking Michigan with misdirection plays that caused the quick Michigan defense to overreact and commit itself.

"They hurt us with the counter," said Mike Mallory, a Michigan linebacker. "We seemed to be looking for the option. They caught us off guard."

For the Michigan offense, the second half was filled with frustration. The Wolverines failed to gain a first down in the half, and were assessed several key penalties and had a failed fourth-down attempt to stall drives.

"This is a tough loss," said Schembechler. "We expected to win." he said after the game.

Score By Periods

Auburn............	0	0	3	6 —	9
Michigan	7	0	0	0 —	7

39

MICHIGAN INTERCEPTIONS HALT KOSAR & CO.

By PETER ALFANO
Special to The New York Times

ANN ARBOR, Mich., Sept. 8, 1984 — Sometimes, a good quarterback can make the job easier for an opposing defense. A good quarterback is arrogant and defiant, the type of athlete who doesn't like to make concessions. In little more than one full season, Bernie Kosar of the University of Miami has become that kind of quarterback. Today, it cost him for the first time.

His strong arm and swagger were confronted by a Michigan defense that gave Kosar his most frustrating day in a brief but spectacular college career. The Wolverines opened their season with a 22-14 victory against Miami, and ended the Hurricanes' 13-game winning streak — the longest in the nation.

Kosar was intercepted six times, which he said had never happened even when he played touch football. He also fumbled once and was sacked three times by an aggressive defense that was counting on the fact that Kosar might be reading his press clippings too closely.

"Everything has been Bernie, Bernie, Bernie, and I guess he didn't want to feel he couldn't get those passes in there," said Rodney Lyles, a linebacker who intercepted three passes. "Bernie gambles a lot and it's been working. He's been on a roll. But I was surprised that he kept trying to throw over me. I guess it became a challenge to him."

Kosar led the Hurricanes to the nation's top ranking as a freshman last season. There was more success in the first two games this year as Miami defeated Auburn and Florida, and was ranked No. 1 in the country. Kosar already was being touted as a Heisman Trophy favorite when the Hurricanes arrived here.

Lyles helped make it a race again. He is a 6-foot-3, 226-pound senior who was moved this season from inside linebacker, where his duties were to rush the passer and protect against the run, to the outside, in order to take advantage of his height and quickness.

He is from Miami, and had committed to going to school there four years ago, when he changed his mind and came to Michigan. "I guess," he said smiling, "I always wanted to go away to school."

Defense has been the backbone of Bo Schembechler's teams here for 15 years and this season is not expected to be any different. The coach did promise more diversity on offense this season, though, and felt it would be necessary to throw the ball well against high-scoring teams like Miami.

But not too often. And for one day at least, it was a victory for conservatism over the daring young passer who had played as if he already belonged in the pros.

"I've never been this bad, anywhere, anytime," Kosar said. "It was terrible. It's the sickest feeling I've ever had."

Kosar completed 16 of 38 passes for 228 yards and two touchdowns. but as late as midway through the fourth quarter, he made the Wolverines and their fans rather nervous when he showed that quick-strike ability that a consummate passer possesses.

Trailing by 19-7 and facing a fourth down and 10 from the Michigan 4-yard line, Kosar rolled out to his left, scrambled, then fired a touchdown pass to Stanley Shakespeare. The conversion narrowed the deficit to 19-14 and there was still 6:25 remaining in the game.

"You just can't go to sleep on him out there," Lyles said.

Lyles certainly didn't. The next two times Miami had the ball, he made interceptions. In both instances he was defending against the wide receivers Shakespeare and Eddie Brown.

In addition to his interceptions, Lyles stopped a Miami drive early in the first quarter when he hit the running back Darryl Oliver, stripping him of the ball. Michigan's Tim Anderson recovered the fumble, setting up the first score of the game.

The Wolverines drove 54 yards in nine plays, mostly on the ground. Jim Harbaugh, a first-time starter at quarterback, completed two passes in the drive which was culminated when the fullback Bob Perryman ran 6 yards for a touchdown. The conversion was missed. After Miami regained the lead in the third quarter, Harbaugh, who completed 11 of 21 passes for 163 yards, coolly led Michigan on an 80-yard drive, Perryman again scoring, this time from 3 yards out.

Score By Periods

Michigan	6	0	6	10 —	22
Miami	0	0	7	7 —	14

40

OHIO STATE TAKES TITLE BY 21-6 OVER WOLVERINES

By THE ASSOCIATED PRESS
The New York Times

COLUMBUS, Ohio, Nov. 17, 1984 — Mike Tomczak's key third-down passes in the fourth quarter and Keith Byars' three touchdowns led Ohio State to a 21-6 victory over Michigan for the Big Ten Conference title and the Rose Bowl berth.

Moments after the final gun, portions of the largest Ohio Stadium crowd in history — 90,286 — streamed onto the field. However, campus police circled both goal posts to keep the fans from tearing them down.

The Buckeyes, 9-2 over all and 7-2 in the conference, will face Southern Cal in the Rose Bowl on New Year's Day.

The loss dropped Michigan to a 6-5 record over all, the worst season in Bo Schembechler's 16 as coach. Michigan wound up 5-4 in the Big Ten.

Tomczak connected on two long third-down passes to flanker Mike Lanese and split end Cris Carter to keep the deciding touchdown drive alive in the final quarter.

Byars, the nation's leader in rushing, scoring and all-purpose running this season, went 1 yard to help give Ohio State a 7-0 lead in the first quarter. His second score led to a 14-6 lead with 6 minutes 8 seconds to play. Less than 2 minutes later, the 235-pound junior ran 2 yards for his 22d touchdown of the season.

Byars, limited to fewer than 100 yards rushing for the second time in 1984, ran 28 times for 93 yards. That left him with 1,647 yards this season, falling short of the league and the school single-season mark of 1,695 by Archie Griffin in 1974.

Michigan dominated the third quarter and missed a chance to take a 9-7 lead when Bob Bergeron missed his third field-goal attempt from 37 yards. Earlier, Bergeron had made field goals of 37 and 45 yards, cutting Ohio State's margin to 7-6.

The Buckeyes, the first team in 88 years to win the Big Ten despite two conference defeats, built a 7-3 halftime lead on Byars' first score, capping a 61-yard drive with 4:47 remaining in the first quarter.

Michigan, thwarted by an interception in the end zone on the fourth play of the second quarter, took advantage of Lanese's fumble with 17 seconds left in the half. Brad Cochran recovered the fumble on Lanese's attempted punt return at the Ohio State 9. Zurbrugg threw an incompletion and was sacked by safety Terry White. Bergeron then made his 37-yard field goal on the last play of the first half.

SCORE BY PERIODS

Ohio State 7	0	14	0	—	21
Michigan 0	3	3	0	—	6

41

MICHIGAN DOWNS NOTRE DAME, 20-12

By **MALCOLM MORAN**
Special to The New York Times

ANN ARBOR, Mich., Sept. 14, 1985 — Steve Beuerlein did not have his throwing shoulder cut open for this. An inch of bone was removed from the clavicle of his right shoulder less than five months before today, the day the quarterback wanted to help point Notre Dame's football program in the right direction after four years of frustration.

And for much of this afternoon, against the Michigan Wolverines at Michigan Stadium, Beuerlein was right where he wanted to be. Eleven times, the junior took the snap from center at or within the Michigan 15-yard line. Ten of those times Beuerlein handed the ball to Allen Pinkett. The last time Beuerlein was tackled for a loss.

Not once did the Notre Dame offense cross the goal line. When the conservative Irish approach was undermined by errors, Michigan was able to come from behind for a 20-12 victory. And Notre Dame was left with the what-might-have-beens that have characterized Gerry Faust's four years as the head coach.

He Wanted the Ball

Pinkett, the senior tailback, gained 89 yards on 22 carries. But of those rushes from the 15-yard line on in, three resulted in losses and one was stopped for no gain. The 10 carries from close range produced an average gain of 1.2 yards.

"I want the ball in those situations," Pinkett said. "That's what they brought me to this school for. There were a few blocking mistakes. A few missed assignments, which is typical of an opening game. I can even think of three or four mistakes I made. Nobody's perfect."

Beuerlein completed 11 of 23 passes for 160 yards. His only attempt from inside the 15 came in the final 2 minutes, when the Irish were scrambling for a touchdown and 2-point conversion that would have tied the score. He was tackled for an 11-yard loss, the sixth and final Michigan sack of the afternoon.

"It gets frustrating sometimes," Beuerlein said of the coaching strategy. "All I can say is, they have their reasons. I don't want to point fingers. They obviously thought we could pound it in. A lot of guys didn't understand it. But the coaches have been around a lot longer than we have.

"I can understand the coaches have confidence in our running game," Beuerlein said. "But there were a lot of times when I thought, a lot of people thought, we should have thrown the ball. It's not something I have any control over."

Reflections by Faust

"If I had a chance to do it over, I'd call a different play," Faust said. "If it had worked, I'd call that play."

After losing 20 of the 46 games in the Faust era, his team was beginning the fifth year of his five-year contract on national television and before a crowd of 105,523, the 61st consecutive six-figure crowd to watch the Wolverines at home. What better place than Michigan Stadium — "the Big House," Pinkett called it — to regain the success the Irish followers have grown to expect?

For a half, the plan was working. John Carney, who tied a Notre Dame record with four field goals, made kicks of 34, 41 and 47 yards in the first half to give the Irish a 9-3 lead.

But the Irish were knocked back on their heels, and the pace changed completely, when Alonzo Jefferson failed to control the kickoff at the start of the second half. Dieter Heren recovered for Michigan at the Irish 14, and three plays later Jim Harbaugh, the senior quarterback, ran 10 yards on a draw play to put the Wolverines ahead, 10-9.

The Irish took advantage of a fumbled punt to set up Carney's 25-yard field goal for a 12-10 lead. But a roughing-the-passer penalty against Notre Dame extended a Michigan drive after an incompletion on a third-down-and-7 situation. Three plays after the penalty, Gerald White went off left guard for the 3-yard touchdown that put Michigan ahead to stay with 1:12 to go in the third quarter.

A pass-interference penalty against Marv Spence, the junior Irish cornerback, led to a 23-yard field goal by Michigan freshman Mike Gillette for an 8-point lead.

There once was a time when a victory over Notre Dame provided a measure of excellence. Today? "It means we're decent," said Bo Schembechler, the Michigan coach. "We're not the dog people think we are."

Score By Periods
| Michigan | .... 0 | 3 | 14 | 3 | — | 20 |
| Notre Dame | .... 3 | 6 | 3 | 0 | — | 12 |

42

MICHIGAN SHATTERS OHIO STATE HOPES

By MICHAEL JANOFSKY
Special to The New York Times

ANN ARBOR, Mich., Nov. 23, 1985 — With 106,102 fans in Michigan Stadium cheering as if a bid to the Rose Bowl were at stake, Michigan defeated Ohio State today, 27-17, to win a berth instead in the Fiesta Bowl to play Nebraska. The winner of this game was denied a trip to the Rose Bowl earlier when Iowa defeated Minnesota, 31-9, to win the conference championship.

Michigan's victory gave the Wolverines second place with a 6-1-1 conference record and an overall 9-1-1 record. Ohio State, which will go to the Citrus Bowl to play Brigham Young, finished 8-3 and 5-3. Iowa won the conference with a 7-1 record.

"We're runner-up in the conference, and some people may think we're the second-best team," Bo Schembechler, the Michigan coach, said. "But it's not so much wins and losses that always count, but the type of group you're working with. This group seemed to work, have fun and are a great bunch."

For Michigan fans, the victory highlighted a festive day that ended with swarms of youngsters from the fourth-largest crowd in the stadium's history tearing down the goal posts at the north end of the field.

In between, the Wolverines got a fine performance from the senior quarterback Jim Harbaugh, who threw for three touchdowns, completed 16 of 19 passes for 230 yards and set Michigan single-season records for most touchdown passes, 18, and most passing yards, 1,913.

His performance and 110 yards of rushing by Gerald White offset Michigan's worst defensive performance of the season. The Buckeyes, who were playing the Wolverines for the 82d time and 43d time here, scored two touchdowns and a field goal, to account for more points than any other team had scored on Michigan in 10 previous games this season. Also, the Wolverines had given up only three previous touchdowns, and never more than one in a game.

One of the Buckeyes' touchdowns was particularly scary to the Wolverines, who were leading at the time, 20-10, early in the final period. Jim Karsatos, the Ohio State quarterback, moved the Buckeyes 80 yards for a score, finishing the drive with a 36-yard pass to Cris Carter, who outjumped two defenders in the end zone for the ball.

But the euphoria on the Ohio State sideline faded quickly. After the kickoff, White ran for 3 of his 110 yards to open Michigan's next series, before Harbaugh, reading a blitz, connected with John Kolesar, a freshman wide receiver, for a 77-yard scoring pass to put the game out of reach.

"We got a real break when the score got to 20-17," said Earle Bruce, the Ohio State coach. "I thought only a big play could beat us, and it did. It was too big of a play."

SCORE BY PERIODS

Michigan 3	7	10	7	—	27
Ohio State 0	10	0	7	—	17

43

MICHIGAN RALLIES TO WIN OVER CORNHUSKERS

By THE ASSOCIATED PRESS
The New York Times

TEMPE, Ariz., Jan. 1, 1986 — Michigan turned two third-quarter Nebraska fumbles into 1-yard touchdown runs by Gerald White and Jim Harbaugh and rallied to beat the Cornhuskers, 27-23, in the Sunkist Fiesta Bowl game today.

Behind by 14-3 at halftime, the Wolverines, ranked fifth in both news-agency polls, scored twice in a 2 minute 14 second span to spark a 24-point third period that led to the victory. Michigan wound up with a 10-1-1 record, losing to Iowa by 2 points and tying Illinois. Nebraska, ranked sixth by the United Press International poll and seventh by The Associated Press, finished with a 9-3 mark.

The linebacker Jeff Akers' recovery of a fumble by Doug DuBose, the Nebraska I-back, at the Cornhuskers' 21-yard line set up White's 1-yard dive 2:03 into the third quarter. On the next series, the Nebraska quarterback McCathorn Clayton's fumble was recovered by the Michigan tackle Mark Messner at the Cornhusker 38. Harbaugh scored on a quarterback sneak five plays later.

David Arnold's blocked punt was recovered by Michigan at the Nebraska 6-yard line and it set up Pat Moons' 19-yard field goal for a 20-14 Wolverines lead with 6:42 left in the third period. Harbaugh's 2-yard run 4:49 later made it 27-14.

Coach Bo Schembechler said the Michigan defense was the key.

"The third quarter won the game for us," he said. "We came out for the second half, and we knew we had to get the ball back. Fortunately, we got the turnovers."

In the fourth quarter, Nebraska closed the gap to 27-23 on a 1-yard sneak by Steve Taylor, a backup quarterback, with 2:29 remaining in the game. Then the Cornhuskers earned a safety with 1:22 left when the Michigan punter Monte Robbins intentionally stepped out of the end zone rather than risk having a punt blocked or giving the Cornhuskers good field position.

Cornerback Garland Rivers' end zone interception with 29 seconds left sealed the Michigan victory.

The Cornhuskers got all their first-half points on two touchdowns by DuBose, who was a questionable starter because of a bruised left shoulder. Clayton's 5-yard pass to DuBose 38 seconds into the second quarter put Nebraska ahead by 7-3 and DuBose's 3-yard run with 3:55 left in the first half made it 14-3.

It marked the first time this season that Michigan had allowed two touchdowns in one half. The Wolverines, ranked first nationally in scoring defense and second in overall defense, had given up only five previous touchdowns, only two through the air.

Michigan's Jamie Morris earned the game's outstanding offensive player award by rushing for 156 yards on 22 carries.

SCORE BY PERIODS

Michigan	3	0	24	0 —	27
Nebraska	0	14	0	9 —	23

44

MICHIGAN EDGES IRISH IN THRILLER

By MALCOLM MORAN
Special to The New York Times

SOUTH BEND, Ind., Sept. 13, 1986 — He would stop pacing the sidelines whenever something went wrong, and a lot of things went wrong.

In the days and weeks and months before his first game as Notre Dame's 25th football coach, Lou Holtz never questioned whether something bad would happen. His concern was what would follow for a group that had grown accustomed to disappointment.

At the end of a gripping afternoon at Notre Dame Stadium today, after John Carney's 45-yard field goal attempt failed with 13 seconds to play and third-ranked Michigan's 24-23 victory seemed assured, Holtz strode toward his kicker, held up his right hand, and repeatedly bent his index finger toward his face.

Holtz held Carney's neck in the crook of his left elbow and patted his helmet with his right hand. "I told him that he's made some great ones in the past and he'll make some great ones in the future," Holtz said. "He shouldn't feel bad at all about it."

The thought applied to his team. "I think the fight is back in Notre Dame," said Robert Banks, the senior defensive tackle, a converted linebacker who was part of 12 tackles, three for losses.

Can a team omitted from the preseason rankings break into the top 20 by losing its first game? The Irish lost a fumble at the Michigan 7-yard line. They allowed an interception in the Wolverine end zone. They watched a windblown kickoff take an odd bounce into Michigan hands at the Notre Dame 27 in the third quarter following Jamie Morris' 1-yard touchdown. When the recovery led directly to a 27-yard touchdown pass from Jim Harbaugh to Morris — his third score of the game, six seconds after the previous one — Notre Dame was faced with a 24-14 deficit.

Still, the Irish created a chance to win. Notre Dame gained 455 yards against a unit that allowed an average of 253.6 last season. Steve Beuerlein, the once-maligned senior quarterback, completed 21 of 33 passes for 263 yards and a touchdown.

Holtz replaced inertia with initiative, apprehension with imagination. His offense lined up in an I-formation, a wishbone, with running backs split, with a single back, with two tight ends and the I-formation, and with two tight ends and a wishbone. "A couple of times I made up my own pattern," said Tim Brown, a junior flanker who was also used as a running back. "They let me do that. Just get open."

Brown led the Notre Dame rushers with 65 yards — including a 3-yard score — and caught a 32-yard pass. Mark Green, a sophomore tailback who gained a total of 64 yards last season, rushed for 57, scored on a 1-yard dive and caught six passes for 79 yards. The strategy was in striking contrast to the ideas of Gerry Faust's five years as coach, the last four with Allen Pinkett at tailback. "Pinkett right, Pinkett left, Pinkett up and middle," Brown remembered. "And punt the ball."

Today, the Irish did not punt once. "I don't recall a team never punting against Michigan," said Bo Schembechler, the Michigan coach.

"We had so much confidence, we were craving for an opportunity to get back out there," Beuerlein said.

Trailing by 10 points, the Irish drove from their 34 to the Michigan 3. On first down, Beuerlein faked a handoff up the middle, held the ball up and pushed a shot-put-style pass ahead to Joel Williams, the tight end, to make the score 24-20. But Carney, who had made 48 of 51 point-after kicks in his career to that point, was wide to the left with his kick, and the Irish needed more than a field goal to tie.

The Wolverines were forced to punt. Notre Dame drove to the 7. On third down, a pass to Williams in the back of the end zone was called incomplete when he was judged to be out of bounds. Carney made a 25-yard field goal, and the Irish were within a point with 4 minutes 26 seconds to go.

Michigan, which had now been forced to punt three straight times, faced a third down with 6 yards to go at the 22. Harbaugh, the senior who completed 15 of 23 passes for 239 yards, threw to John Kolesar, the sophomore flanker, for a 38-yard gain. But four plays later, Bob Perryman fumbled, Wes Pritchett recovered at the Irish 26, the crowd was frantic and Notre Dame had its last chance.

Beuerlein found Alvin Miller over the middle for 33 yards to the Michigan 26, and two plays later, hit Milt Jackson for 16 more to the 29. A shovel pass moved the ball to the 28. "I really had the script written out," Holtz said. "If we were going to win the game, we'd come from behind in the second half."

Score By Periods

Michigan 7	3	14	0	—	24
Notre Dame 7	7	6	3	—	23

45

MICHIGAN VICTOR ON LAST PLAY

By PHIL BERGER
Special to The New York Times

ANN ARBOR, Mich., Oct. 18, 1986 — Mike Gillette booted a 34-yard field goal on the last play of the game today to give undefeated Michigan a 20-17 victory over Iowa in a showdown of Big Ten powers.

As Gillette's kick sailed through the uprights, Wolverine fans in the Michigan Stadium crowd of 105,879 raced onto the field, unfurling white streamers.

For the Michigan faithful, the victory was a sweet reversal of the Wolverine-Hawkeye contest of a season before. In that game, Rob Houghlin of Iowa kicked a 29-yard field goal on the final play with Michigan leading by 10-9.

This year the roles were reversed, and Iowa did its best to compound the pressure. As Gillette, a 6-foot-1-inch, 185-pound sophomore from St. Joseph, Mich., was lining up the crucial field goal with 5 seconds remaining, the Hawkeyes called a time-out, trying to upset him.

The strategy didn't work.

"You're not going to fluster him," said Bo Schembechler, the Michigan coach. "He is the cockiest guy that ever lived."

Gillette's kick hit dead-center, and it gave Michigan, ranked fourth, its sixth victory of the season without a loss. Iowa, ranked eighth, dropped to 5-1. Michigan had a chance late in the game to win on a field goal from 27 yards, a shorter distance than Gillette's game-winning kick.

Pat Moons, who specializes in short-distance field goals for the Wolverines, missed that kick with 6 minutes 11 seconds left.

Gillette said afterward that when Moons missed his kick, Schembechler advised him that he would get the next chance at a field goal.

"Right then," Gillette said, "I set my mind to working to get ready."

Gillette claimed he never saw the ball cross through the goal posts because he had been knocked to the ground.

"But I knew it was good as soon as I hit it," he said.

Gillette's winning field goal was the payoff on a comeback by Michigan, which trailed at the half, 10-3.

Gillette was responsible for the only Michigan score of the first half, a 53-yard field goal, the longest in the school's history.

The Wolverine attack was stymied by Iowa's defense until the second half. "I couldn't understand what we were doing," Schembechler said. "It was almost as if we didn't practice last week."

But down the stretch, the Wolverine offense got going, sparked by the quarterback, Jim Harbaugh, and the fullback, Gerald White.

Harbaugh, a 6-3, 207-pound senior, completed 17 of 28 passes for 215 yards. His 25-yard pass to White tied the game, 10-10, at 9:35 of the third quarter.

White gave the Wolverines a 17-10 lead in the third period when, with the ball at the Iowa 10, he burst through the Hawkeye line and carried a pair of defenders across the goal line for the touchdown.

But Iowa came back. Dwight Sistrunk, a defensive back, intercepted a Harbaugh pass at the Michigan 40 and returned it to the 19. On a third and 6, Mark Vlasic, the quarterback who took over from Tom Poholsky in the second half, hit Robert Smith, a wingback, with a 15-yard touchdown pass to tie the game at 17-17 with 11:15 left.

After Moons missed his field goal, Iowa took over at its 20-yard line and drove to the Michigan 43. Then, on an option play, Vlasic tossed a lateral to Richard Bass, who never could get a grip on the ball.

Andy Moeller, a Michigan linebacker, recovered at the Michigan 49 with 1:57 left.

With White, Jamie Morris and Bob Perryman carrying, the Wolverines took the ball down to the 17, setting up the final play of the game.

SCORE BY PERIODS

Michigan	3	0	14	3 —	20
Iowa	7	3	0	7 —	17

46

THE SHOE WAS ON THE OTHER FOOT

By RICK REILLY
Sports Illustrated

NEW YORK, Oct. 27, 1986 — The college football year is only half spent, and most of the hardware has already been sent to the engravers. You give the Heisman to Miami's Vinny Testaverde. The truth is, the guy is so good maybe you give him last year's, too. You give the Butkus to Oklahoma's Brian (Did I Say That?) Bosworth. You give a Rose Bowl jacket to America's favorite curmudgeon, Bo Schembechler. You give the Coach of the Year plaque to Iowa's hayseed genius, Hayden Fry. Finally, you give a gold '57 Chevy hubcap to the Big Ten, which, just for nostalgia's sake, staged a big game on Saturday without lawyers, expectorations, in-house investigating committees or misplaced handguns.

Proved it can be damned entertaining, too. Just on story line alone, No. 5 Michigan's 20-17 victory over No. 7 Iowa — won by Mike Gillette's close-shave 34-yard field goal as the clock struck midnight — rated at least three bags of popcorn. There was the Rose Bowl race to consider; there was a nip of revenge in the air; and there was even a bit of coaching melodrama.

Stage left was Fry, one of the game's brightest and best, but still playing the Beaver to Michigan's and Ohio State's Wally and Eddie. "Seems like it's awful hard for a newcomer to get any recognition in this league," said Fry before the game. "I guess people think we're doin' it with tricks. They think I'm some kind of magical medicine man." It's a complex that's going around the complex. Said one of Fry's assistants, "Just once I would like to hear Bo say, 'You know, those guys have built a damn good program down there.' "

Even in the face of two Rose Bowl trips inside of five years, two straight wins over Schembechler going into last week's game and the news that The Des Moines Register thinks he would make a fine governor, Fry still seems to crave Schembechler's acceptance. Indeed, from his Photograys to his gum-chewing to his bulldog competitiveness (he once painted the visiting locker room at Kinnick Stadium pink), Fry resembles nobody as much as Schembechler himself. Nobody wants an invitation to light up in the back room with the Big Two more than Fry, just as nobody wanted Woody Hayes' acceptance more than the young Schembechler.

Stage right is Schembechler, who mostly just pats Fry on the head. "He *does* have a good program," Schembechler says. "They can play with anybody in the country. It's just that . . . well, it's that other stuff that I don't think is necessary." What Schembechler doesn't cotton to is Fry's fondness for mind games, like being overly morose about injury reports. Before the game Fry lamented that 15 players on his two-deep roster were laid up and that, all told, 43 had some kind of ailment. Bo scoffed. "Last year he had some guys in intensive care before the game and then, next thing you know, they're out there making tackles," said Schembechler. Of those 15 mortally wounded Hawkeyes, 14 played in Ann Arbor on Saturday.

Nor did it set too well with Schembechler when, after Iowa beat Michigan State earlier this month, Fry predicted that the Spartans would win the rest of their games. He knew full well that their next date was with Michigan. The Wolverines won, 27-6. "He wasn't too accurate there," says Bo. After losing badly to U.C.L.A. in last season's Rose Bowl, Fry said that Michigan couldn't hold a candle to U.C.L.A. Says Schembechler, "If I had been run through, passed over and blown out like that, I would have found something to say, too. Besides, at the time he was saying that, we were beating Nebraska."

Still, like it or not, even Schembechler must be coming to appreciate the full value of a large order of Fry. Three of the last four Michigan-Iowa games have been decided by three points or less. That the most recent one was close shows the grandeur of the Xanadu that Fry has built in Iowa City. This is a man who lost three first-round 1986 N.F.L. draft picks; 11 starters from 1985 altogether; two quarterbacks to injuries in (honest) the first three games; his all-conference defensive tackle, Jeff Drost, indefinitely; his star fullback, David Hudson, for two games; and nearly his mind, trying to fend off rumors that had him hightailing it to the University of Texas. He's not. Nonetheless, his Hawkeyes were 5-0 going into Saturday, and he gave Bo all he wanted. More than he wanted.

"We shoulda been up 13 to 3 at the half [instead of 10-3]," said Fry. "No, 17-3 it shoulda been." And might have been, too, were he not so loyal to the fourth-string sophomore quarterback, Tom Poholsky, who was overeager and whose receivers were thus mostly overthrown. Poholsky failed to come up with any points in an unheard-of fit of Michigan untidiness — three turnovers in the second quarter. Only the Hawks' first-drive TD and a 29-yard field goal were listed on the scoreboard against Gillette's school-record 53-yarder for Michigan.

At halftime Schembechler largely overlooked his team's good fortune. "Of the 15 minutes in the locker room," said Michigan quarterback Jim Harbaugh, who suffered two lost fumbles and an interception in the first half alone, "Bo was probably yelling 10. . . . He was definitely not a happy camper."

The mood at Camp Winonenow brightened considerably when Harbaugh directed the first two drives after intermission for touchdowns, both of which were punctuated by the theretofore unheralded senior fullback, Gerald White. He scored on a 25-yard pass to make it 10-10 and then on a give up the middle from 10 yards out to put the Wolverines ahead 17-10.

That's when Fry unwrapped his No. 1 quarterback, Mark Vlasic. He's known to his teammates as Pickle, perhaps not so much because of his last name but because, like the Vlasic Stork, he usually delivers. Until Vlasic's shoulder separated against Texas-El Paso on Sept. 27, only one quarterback in the country outranked Harbaugh in passing efficiency, and that was the Pickle himself.

With Vlasic running the show — he completed four of four passes — Iowa was liquid again. When Harbaugh was intercepted at the Michigan 40 by Dwight Sistrunk (nephew of Otis Sistrunk) early in the fourth quarter, Vlasic made good, finding Robert Smith on a third-down scramble for a touchdown: 17-17.

Back came Harbaugh, who's nothing if not persistent. He drove the Wolverines nearly 80 yards to the Iowa 2, only to be caught from behind on a third-down rollout by cornerback Ken Sims. On came wedge-shot specialist Pat Moons for a 27-yard attempt. A funny thing happened: Moons missed.

Back came Vlasic, leading Iowa to the Michigan 43 with two minutes remaining. Then, faced with a third-and-one, the Hawkeyes did a strange thing. They called their first option run of the afternoon. Good call, because the play set up perfectly, with Vlasic pitching to fullback Richard Bass, who had acres of artificial turf in his immediate future. Except that a funny thing happened: The ball bounced Bass-akwards off his hands and into Michigan's.

Back came Harbaugh with 1:57 left, screening and flat-passing and generally hoarding the ball until he handed it over to Moons' sudden and probably permanent all-yardages replacement, Gillette. His third field-goal attempt of the year would be a 34-yarder with five seconds showing on the clock, precious little wind in the air and even less coming and going out of the lungs of 105,879 fans at Michigan Stadium.

And that's when it started to get eerie. Hadn't we seen this last year: both teams 5-0 and ranked in the Top 10; the Rose Bowl in the ante; the game coming down to a forgotten sort, a kicker unable to hear the screams of thousands for the pounding of his own heart? "I did; I thought of last year," said Gillette. And who couldn't? *Iowa's 1 versus Michigan's 2 . . . an endless drizzle . . . two seconds to go . . . Iowa's kicker, Rob Houghtlin . . . the weight of the farm belt on his shoulder pads . . . the 29-yard try . . . the referee's raised arms . . . the locusts descending on him . . . Iowa, 12-10. . . .*

"I wasn't scared," said Gillette, whom Schembechler calls "the cockiest kid who ever lived." "I just wanted to show people that I could go out and do the same thing that Houghtlin did to us."

On the sideline Harbaugh envisioned nirvana. "Just standing there, I was planning my run out onto the field," he said, "how it would feel to jump on that pile, just like we saw Iowa do last year. Hey, man, they took *Pasadena* away from us."

The snap . . .

Gillette: "Last night at the hotel I envisioned how it would happen 15 or 20 times, seeing it go through."

The crackle . . .

Schembechler: "I knew nothing would ruffle that kid."

The pop . . . the raised arms . . . the locusts . . . Michigan, 20-17.

How 'bout that?

Boja vu.

47

MICHIGAN DEFEATS BUCKEYES, GATHERS ROSES

By LONNIE WHEELER
Special to The New York Times

COLUMBUS, Ohio, Nov. 22, 1986 — Back East, Joe Morris might have thought he was watching Giant game films. There was Morris, shooting through the holes, straining for the extra yards, making touchdowns, carrying the team on his abbreviated back. Only this Morris was wearing Michigan colors. His name was Jamie, and he is going to the Rose Bowl.

That was resolved today when the Wolverines came from behind to bump Ohio State, 26-24. Both teams finished with 7-1 records in the Big Ten, but Michigan will go to the Rose Bowl by virtue of today's victory. The Buckeyes will play in the Cotton Bowl, having missed out on the preferred invitation when Matt Frantz hooked a 46-yard field goal attempt with 1 minute 6 seconds to play.

"I visualized that this was going to be my game," said the 5-foot-7, 180-pound Morris, who gained 210 yards on 29 carries and scored twice. "I called my mom Thursday, and she told me Joe was going to be watching. I said, 'Ma, this is the game.' "

For Morris, the younger brother of the Giants' running back, it was the biggest and best game of his burgeoning career. It was on his second-half running — 19 carries for 148 clutch yards — that today's game turned. "That," said Morris, "is why I came to Michigan."

Morris, a junior who was the Massachusetts 100-meter high school champion, brought Michigan, 10-1, back from a 14-6 halftime deficit with a battery of big plays. First, he beat an Ohio State defender with a stunning fake for a 4-yard touchdown. Then he slipped a tackle, made a move and raced 52 yards into Buckeye territory, setting up his own twisting, pulling 8-yard touchdown for Michigan's first lead, 19-17.

When Michigan scored early in the fourth quarter on a 7-yard run by Thomas Wilcher, it led by 9 and looked secure in its bid to return to the Rose Bowl for the first time since Jan. 1, 1983.

But Ohio State came back on a 17-yard touchdown pass from Jim Karsatos to Cris Carter, then recovered Thomas Wilcher's fumble at its 38-yard line with 3:17 remaining. Karsatos and Carter brought the Buckeyes within field-goal range, but, on fourth and 2, Frantz's miss to the left brought a collective groan from the record crowd of 90,674. The Buckeyes, who had won nine in a row, slipped to 9-3.

Victory 'Guaranteed'

Michigan's victory had been "guaranteed" early in the week by Jim Harbaugh, who passed for 261 yards. But early in the game, it appeared that Harbaugh's bold prediction had aroused the Buckeyes.

"I'd have said it myself if I had any guts," said coach Bo Schembechler of Michigan.

Ohio State had posted Harbaugh's remarks all over its practice facility, and the home team came out with a cause. Bucking its up-the-middle tradition, Ohio State scored touchdowns the first two times it had the ball.

After Jamie Holland had taken the opening kickoff into Michigan territory, the Buckeyes went immediately for the open spaces. Vince Workman, a tailback, found room on a pass and a run and Carter got the Buckeyes close with another catch from Karsatos. Then Carter, the Buckeyes' leading career receiver with still another year to play, caught a looping 4-yard throw for a touchdown.

Michigan registered a field goal, but then Ohio State accomplished something uncommon in its low-shouldered history. It scored a second straight time without the fullback even touching the ball. The touchdown came when Workman, a sophomore, took a pitch from Karsatos, got a block from Carter on the corner and cut back to the inside for a 46-yard run.

"Ohio State's two quick scores really shook us," said Schembechler, who surpassed Fielding Yost to become the Wolverines' victory leader with 166. Schembechler is now 166-39-4 at Michigan and 206-56-7 over all.

"I couldn't believe our defense wouldn't tighten," he said. "I can't remember a year in the Michigan-Ohio State rivalry when there were so many yards and so many big plays. It was so unlike this game." Michigan had 529 total yards and Ohio State had 358.

Since the Michigan-Ohio State game was moved to the final week of the season in 1944, the rivals have played 18 times for the championship of the conference. Each has won eight, with two ties.

Score By Periods

Michigan 3	3	13	7	—	26
Ohio State 14	0	3	7	—	24

48

ARIZONA STATE WINS, SIXTH IN ROW IN ROSE FOR PAC-10

By GORDON S. WHITE Jr.
Special to The New York Times

PASADENA, Calif., Jan 1., 1987 — Well before Arizona State switched from the Western Athletic Conference to the more prestigious Pacific 10 in 1978, the Pac-10 had gained dominance over the Big Ten in their annual Rose Bowl match. In its first Rose Bowl appearance, Arizona State carried on the tradition of its league today.

After trailing Michigan, 15-3, early in the second period, the Sun Devils scored a touchdown on their last drive of the first half and on the first drive of the second half to gain a 22-15 triumph over the Wolverines before 103,168 fans.

Jeff Van Raaphorst, the Arizona State quarterback who was voted the most valuable player of this 73d Rose Bowl, tossed short passes to his flanker, Bruce Hill, for both Sun Devil touchdowns. Ken Bostrom kicked three field goals to tie a Rose Bowl game record as the Pac-10 champion beat the Big Ten champion for the sixth straight year and for the 16th time in the last 18 years. The Big Ten trails in the series, 22-19.

Strong Defense

The fast and swarming Arizona State defense shut down Michigan completely after the Wolverines got their second touchdown early in the second period. When Robby Boyd of Arizona State intercepted Jim Harbaugh's pass with just a minute left, the Sun Devils nailed down the biggest football victory in the history of the Tempe, Ariz., university.

Arizona State, ranked among the nation's top 10 teams, finished its year with a 10-1-1 record while coach Bo Schembechler's Wolverines, ranked among the top five before today, ended at 11-2. This marked the seventh time in eight Rose Bowl tries a Schembechler Michigan team had lost. He has a 3-11 bowl record in his 18 seasons at Michigan.

"We come out here every year and get beaten by 7 points," Schembechler said. "We do it every year."

When Van Raaphorst accepted the m.v.p. award, he said, "I'm glad I had the opportunity my dad never had."

The senior Arizona State quarterback, who completed 16 of 36 passes for 193 yards and two touchdowns without an interception, is the son of Dick Van Raaphorst, who was Ohio State's placekicker in 1961 when the Buckeyes won the Big Ten title. But the Ohio State faculty, citing "overemphasis" on football, voted against allowing the Buckeyes a trip to the 1962 Rose Bowl.

Arizona State, in only its second year under coach John Cooper, settled down after being jarred by the two early Michigan scores and played so well for the last two and a half quarters that Michigan rarely had the ball long enough to make an impression. In the second half, Michigan had possession for less than 10 minutes.

"You can't do much without the football," Schembechler said.

"We coach to protect the football," Cooper said.

No Turnovers

Arizona State, which turned the ball over only 15 times during the regular season, didn't give it up once today. The Devils intercepted Harbaugh three times after his two touchdown aerials.

The Sun Devils seemed to be in trouble when Michigan had to punt from deep in its territory late in the second quarter. The Devils took a fair catch on their 40 with 3 minutes 59 seconds left in the half. This was five minutes after Bostrom had kicked his second field goal, cutting the Arizona State deficit to 15-6.

Out of the shotgun formation, which he used well all game, Van Raaphorst flipped a short screen pass to his tailback, Darryl Harris, on the third play after the punt. With good escort blocking, Harris made a gain of 19 yards on the screen pass. He was the game's leading rusher with 109 yards and added 34 receiving.

Van Raaphorst ran for another 10 on the next play. Then Van Raaphorst connected with Hill for 15 yards to get the ball to the Michigan 5. Two plays later it was at the 4.

That's when Van Raaphorst connected with Hill, who was deep in the end zone, for the first Arizona State touchdown, just 29 seconds before the half ended. Bostrom's extra point made the intermission score 15-13, for Michigan.

But the momentum had swung Arizona State's way.

The Sun Devils took the second-half kickoff and started a drive from their 20. In 15 time-consuming plays, they went the distance.

Van Raaphorst, however, missed on a 2-point conversion pass, so the score remained 19-15 until Bostrom's final field goal, which came 44 seconds into the final quarter.

Harbaugh directed a 66-yard touchdown drive in eight plays on the first series of the game. Jamie Morris, the tailback whose brother Joe runs for the Giants, ran the ball in for the score from the 18.

In a surprise play after the touchdown, Schembechler had his place-kicker, Mike Gillette, throw a pass to Gerald White for 2 points. The snap from center went directly to Gillette, a former high school quarterback.

Harbaugh came back with another good drive of 58 yards in nine plays that ended when he went over from the 2, giving Michigan a 15-3 lead.

From then on Arizona State shut down Michigan and Morris, who gained 1,039 yards in the regular season. He rushed for only 47 yards today, only 4 in the second half.

SCORE BY PERIODS

Arizona State......... 0	13	6	3	—	22
Michigan 8	7	0	0	—	15

49

BRUCE FIRES LAST SHOT, BEATS MICHIGAN

By BOB LOGAN
Special to The Chicago Tribune

ANN ARBOR, Mich., Nov. 21, 1987 — Who's that man standing in the unemployment line wearing a brown suit and a mile-wide grin?

Why, it's Earle Bruce, the former Ohio State coach. Unceremoniously booted out by O.S.U. President Edward H. Jennings to start this week, Bruce finished it Saturday by riding out of Michigan Stadium on the shoulders of his triumphant Buckeyes.

Ohio State's emotion-packed 23-20 upset of Michigan ended a sad chapter in Buckeye football history on a happy note. It was all the sweeter because the winners trailed, 13-0, before they stopped battling their own feelings and started pummeling the Wolverines.

Despite the loss, Michigan (5-3 in the Big 10, 7-4 overall) accepted a bid to the All-American Bowl on Jan. 2 in Tampa against next week's Auburn-Alabama loser.

The Buckeyes (4-4 in the Big Ten, 6-4-1 overall) go home with their pride intact. The stunned silence among departing Wolverine fans in the throng of 106,031 was punctuated by joyous whoops from O.S.U. players.

"I saw President Jennings on campus yesterday," said Matt Frantz, who kicked the winning field goal with 5:18 left. "He told me if our defense wanted to get pumped up, they should imagine his face on the ball whenever Michigan had it.

"We deserve a bowl trip as a payoff for all the effort we put into a tough season. The coaches told us to think of Michigan as our bowl game."

Frantz, whose missed field goal against Michigan last year kept the Buckeyes out of the Rose Bowl, called his shot this time before booting the decisive 26-yarder.

The Buckeyes showed where they stood, coming onto the field wearing white headbands with "Earle" in red letters. Tackle Joe Staysniak had them printed up and passed them out at Saturday's team breakfast. They didn't have much effect until linebacker Chris Spielman's halftime pep talk.

"We were nervous in the first half," Spielman said later. "All we had to do was come out and play better football."

It was much better — almost letter perfect. Outgained by 192 yards in the first half, the Buckeyes turned the game around on one third-quarter play.

The defense forced a punt, and quarterback Tom Tupa dropped back from his 30 on first down. Everett Ross was covered deep, so tailback Carlos Snow took Tupa's outlet flip on the left sideline behind Allen Bishop, outran John Milligan, reversed his field to evade Doug Mallory's desperate leap at the Michigan 30 and cruised in for a 70-yard TD.

When Frantz converted, the Buckeyes led, 14-13. They were flying too high to be shot down after that, even though Michigan tied it at 20-20 late in the third period.

"I'm so proud of this team," Spielman said. "We watched the coach go through everything they put on him this week, and we came through for him today.

"Earle Bruce is a true Buckeye. We gave game balls to him and Rick Bay (O.S.U. athletic director who quit when Bruce was fired) for their integrity and motivation.

"This helps ease the pain. Bowl game? How can we play a football game without a coach?"

Bruce resisted media invitations to lash out at his bosses. A lawsuit has been filed by his lawyer against the university and Jennings, but Bruce wanted to put his players in the spotlight.

"This is one for the Buckeyes — God bless 'em," he said. "My stomach has been in a knot all week, trying to figure out how you leave all this. I guess I have to, but I don't like what the (O.S.U.) president and the trustees said about my character and integrity. If somebody's gonna judge me, their life had better be perfect."

Bruce Reportedly Sues Ohio State

COLUMBUS, Ohio — Ohio State football coach Earle Bruce, who was fired last week by university President Edward Jennings, reportedly has filed a $7.44 million suit against the university and Jennings.

The suit, filed late Friday in Franklin County Common Pleas Court by attorney John Zonak, charged that Bruce was wrongfully dismissed and was slandered by Jennings, radio station WTVN and television station WSYX reported.

"When you're hit hard, as a football coach, it hurts," Bruce said Saturday night. "But that doesn't mean you can't hit back."

Jennings told The Cleveland Plain Dealer following Ohio State's 23-20 victory over Michigan Saturday that he was unaware of the suit.

"I haven't heard anything," Jennings said. "If any litigation comes, we'll deal with it."

The suit asks for $448,800 in actual damages and other monetary losses, $2 million for violating Bruce's due process rights and $5 million compensatory and punitive damages from Jennings, according to Zonak.

Calls to Bruce and Zonak were not immediately returned.

SCORE BY PERIODS

Ohio State 0	7	13	3	—	23
Michigan 7	6	7	0	—	20

50

MICHIGAN QB ATONES FOR BAD DAY

By THE ASSOCIATED PRESS
The Chicago Tribune

TAMPA, Jan. 2, 1988 — Instead of getting even, Demetrius Brown got angry — and that made Michigan better than even against Alabama in the Hall of Fame Bowl Saturday.

Jamie Morris carried Michigan for three quarters with his running, but it took a 20-yard, fourth-down touchdown pass from Brown to John Kolesar with :50 left to give the Wolverines a 28–24 victory.

Through the first 55 minutes of the game, Brown had passed for only 21 yards.

"I was throwing lousy balls and was mad at myself, but the game wasn't over," said Brown, who found Kolesar in the left corner of the end zone less than three minutes after Alabama went ahead, 24–21, to complete a comeback from an 18-point deficit.

"I had to get it done," Brown said. "I visualized it in my mind."

Kolesar beat Alabama cornerback John Mangum and jumped high to catch the winning pass. It was his only reception, and the touchdown finished a six-play, 62-yard drive fueled by Brown's 31-yard pass to Greg McMurtry.

"Alabama played good defense, but you don't have any choice when it's fourth and 3," Kolesar said. "You just have to go and get it. You have to give credit to Demetrius, who threw a great pass, and to the line that gave him enough time."

Morris, Michigan's all-time leading rusher, gained a career-high 234 yards and scored three touchdowns.

The Wolverines (8-4) played without coach Bo Schembechler, who didn't make the trip after undergoing heart surgery last month in Ann Arbor, Mich. Offensive coordinator Gary Moeller coached in Schembechler's place.

"It's still Bo's team," said Moeller. "I talked to him (by telephone), and he said, 'You did a great job.' "

Brown directed the winning scoring drive after Alabama (7-5) took a 24-21 lead on Bobby Humphrey's 17-yard touchdown and Jeff Dunn's 2-point conversion pass to Clay Whitehurst. Michigan led, 21-3, in the third period before Alabama rallied.

Morris, who scored on runs of 14, 25 and 77 yards, dedicated his performance to Schembechler. "I cherish the moments that I had playing for Bo Schembechler," he said. "I learned a lot, not just about football, but about life. He's like a father to me."

SCORE BY PERIODS

Michigan	0	14	7	7 —	28
Alabama	3	0	6	15 —	24

51

MIAMI RALLIES TO WIN OVER WOLVERINES

By MALCOM MORAN
Special to The New York Times

ANN ARBOR, Mich., Sept. 17, 1988 — The list of places where the University of Miami has won football games during the past four seasons would trace a roadmap to dominance. The Hurricanes of Jimmy Johnson's brief but stunningly successful era as coach established credibility in Norman and South Bend. They earned hard-fought recruiting prestige with victories in Tallahassee and Gainesville. They won the school's second national championship of the decade.

But no Hurricane team had ever won here. And few teams, anywhere, have won a game quite like this.

Miami scored 17 points in the final 5 minutes 23 seconds to shock the University of Michigan, 31-30, and extend the longest winning streak in the nation to 14 games.

Carlos Huerta, a second-year freshman playing in the second game of his college career, kicked a 29-yard field goal with 43 seconds to play to preserve what just minutes before had been Miami's precarious top ranking in the national polls.

Until the final minutes, the warm afternoon had held a succession of Michigan celebrations and Miami frustrations. Steve Walsh, the Miami junior who has never lost a game as a starting quarterback, completed 24 of 45 passes for 335 yards and three touchdowns.

But for much of the game, Walsh was outpassed by Michael Taylor, a Michigan senior who had thrown for 230 yards in his career before today.

While Taylor nearly matched that total in one afternoon, Walsh was becoming a victim of the failures of his teammates. Walsh, who threw just seven interceptions all last season, had two today — on passes that caromed off the hands of receivers.

The second pass intercepted against Walsh, in the third quarter, led to Mike Gillette's third field goal of the game, a 29-yard kick that gave Michigan a 23-14 lead.

And when Michigan drove 68 yards at the start of the final period, with a 16-yard touchdown pass from Taylor to the junior Chris Calloway, giving the Wolverines a 30-14 lead with 10:32 remaining, Miami seemed certain to become the second team to lose the No. 1 ranking in a season that is just a few weeks old.

But just minutes after celebrating that 16-point lead, the maize-and-blue clad fans in the crowd of 105,834 at Michigan Stadium stood stunned at Miami's breathless comeback. Their Wolverines last lost the first two games in 1959, 10 years before Bo Schembechler became the coach.

Miami (2-0) won its 34th consecutive regular-season game and its 20th straight on the road. Its last regular-season road loss had been here, in the massive place known as the Big House, when Michigan defeated another No. 1-ranked Miami team by intercepting six Bernie Kosar passes in 1984.

Analytical Approach

When the same frustrations happened to another generation of Hurricanes, Walsh's analytical approach allowed him to look beyond his failures to see opportunities to succeed.

"You just hope the clock doesn't run too fast," he said. "We had already gone 90 yards and had an interception. Then we went 40 yards and had an interception. Then a guy's open, I miss him, and it's three and out. I knew if we got the ball we could make the plays."

Walsh threw a 7-yard touchdown pass to the sophomore tight end Rob Chudzinski, and added a 2-point conversion pass to the junior Dale Dawkins, to cut the lead to 8 points with 5:23 to go.

Michigan's offense had combined the power that has characterized the Schembechler era and Taylor's exciting improvisation. Taylor completed 16 of 24 passes for 214 yards and three touchdowns. Tony Boles, a junior running back, gained 129 yards in 33 carries behind a line that outweighed the Miami defensive line by an average of 32 pounds.

But with 5 minutes to go, in the sequence that could have stifled the Miami comeback, the Wolverines were forced to punt after three plays and the Hurricanes had their slim chance.

Miami took the ball with 3:45 to go at its 43. On fourth down, with a yard to go at the Michigan 48, Walsh threw a short pass over the middle to the senior fullback Cleveland Gary at the Michigan 35.

Gary avoided a group of Wolverine linebackers in his pass pattern, received the help of a block by Dawkins, and cut up the right sideline for a 48-yard touchdown to make the score 30-28.

Still, the Michigan lead seemed safe with 2:58 to go when Walsh's pass on the 2-point conversion attempt was intercepted by the senior defensive back David Arnold at the goal line.

But then Huerta, a non-scholarship player whose role last year was to chart plays, continued the sequence that stole a game.

Huerta to Rescue

Huerta replaced the junior Edgar Benes, who normally kicks off for the Hurricanes, and jammed an onsides kick into the artificial turf. The ball bounced once, twice and then took a third hop that bounded high into the air.

The Wolverines, who were placed on the defensive by the charging Hurricanes, did little more than watch Bobby Harden, a junior defensive back, leap for the ball at the Michigan 47 with 2:57 to play.

With Michigan blitzing on second down, Walsh threw a 14-yard pass to the senior receiver Andre Brown at the Michigan 33. On the next play, against another blitz, Gary powered 17 yards to the 16. With 2:38 to play, the Hurricanes were within Huerta's range.

Two short runs and one memorable kick later, Huerta was under an orange-and-green pile. "We have a lot of young players," Walsh said, "but they all aged two years today."

SCORE BY PERIODS

Miami	7	7	0	17	—	31
Michigan	3	17	3	7	—	30

52

MICHIGAN SQUANDERS LEAD TO BUCKEYES, RALLIES TO WIN

By THE ASSOCIATED PRESS
The Chicago Tribune

COLUMBUS, Ohio, Nov. 19, 1988 — It's not how you win, Michigan coach Bo Schembechler said, "it's how many you win."

Both Schembechler and Ohio State coach John Cooper credited their teams with great comebacks, but only Schembechler was left smiling.

The Wolverines blew a 20-0 halftime lead as the Buckeyes scored the first 24 points of the second half, then came back from two deficits in the fourth quarter for a 34-31 victory Saturday to win their 12th outright Big Ten title.

In the end, it took John Kolesar's 59-yard kickoff return to set up his own 41-yard touchdown catch to provide the winning points. Marc Spencer's last-minute interception sealed the outcome.

The lead changed hands four times and there were five scoring drives in the final quarter.

"Kolesar's big plays won it for us," Schembechler said. "He's a game-breaking guy. He was running possessed on the kickoff return. That was the first time we had run that kickoff-return play. He just made a great catch on that touchdown.

"Let's face it, we did all we can for TV. They must not have liked the first half."

Cooper said he told his players at halftime, "Hey, you're going to get embarrassed if you keep playing the way you're playing."

They didn't and they weren't. But the Buckeyes (4-6-1, 2-5-1) still saw a string of 21 straight winning seasons come to an end. It was Ohio State's worst finish since going 4-5 in 1966.

"We played a heck of a third and fourth quarter," said Ohio State linebacker John Sullivan. "It's human nature, I guess. Once you are in a corner, you get wild. We looked at each other and said, 'We can play better than this.' "

Leroy Hoard rushed for 158 yards on 23 carries and two TDs for

Michigan (8-2-1, 7-0-1). Tony Boles added 103 yards on 19 carries. Bill Matlock had two TDs for State. Carlos Snow rushed for 170 yards on 25 carries and a TD.

SCORE BY PERIODS

Michigan 10	10	0	14	—	34
Ohio State 0	0	14	17	—	31

53

MICHIGAN UPSETS TROJANS, 22-14

By GORDON S. WHITE Jr.
Special to The New York Times

PASADENA, Calif., Jan. 2, 1989 — Maybe, just maybe, the big pendulum of football fortunes is finally swinging toward the Big Ten in its long, frustrating Rose Bowl wars with the Pacific-10 Conference.

Bo Schembechler, probably the most frustrated of all Big Ten people, wants to think so after his Wolverines rallied for three second-half touchdowns to beat Southern California, 22-14, before 101,688 in the Rose Bowl today.

Leroy Hoard, a sophomore running back who scored the last two touchdowns and won the game's most valuable player award, led the rally with some spectacular runs and plunges, rushing for 113 of his 142 yards in the second half. He had runs of 61 yards and 31 yards to set up his own touchdowns, and made up considerably for the time he spent in Schembechler's often crowded doghouse this season.

This marked the second straight year that a Big Ten team had won the Rose Bowl game, with the Michigan victory coming 367 days after Michigan State beat Southern Cal, 20-17. Not since Illinois and Michigan won Rose Bowl games over Washington and Oregon State in 1964 and 1965 had the Big Ten put together successive victories.

A 92-Yard Drive

The deciding touchdown came on the first play of the final quarter when Hoard, the right halfback in the wishbone, went in for the first of his fourth-period touchdowns from the 1. This concluded a 92-yard drive in nine plays that included the 31-yard run by Hoard, during which he almost fell after gaining 10. Michigan failed on a 2-point attempt and held a 15-14 lead.

Hoard then broke a 61-yard run to set up his final score, which came on a fourth-down play from the 1 with 1 minute 52 seconds left. Michigan uses the wishbone only when in close and going for a touchdown.

Schembechler, who was coaching his ninth Michigan team in a Rose Bowl, came away with only the second triumph in those games. This was only the sixth Big Ten victory in the Rose Bowl in the 24 years since those successive triumphs. Schembechler, who has coached Michigan since 1969, said, "Last time we were here, we lost, and no matter how you add it up, this today beats losing." Michigan lost in 1987 to Arizona State.

Flushed with victory and the hero's spotlight, Hoard said: "I want to thank all the seniors. They got me through when I was in the doghouse.

"There was a misunderstanding between us," Hoard said, referring to Schembechler. "I'd go astray sometimes. A man gets after you, after you, and it's times like this when you see it pays off."

Wolverines Stall Early

Rodney Peete, Southern Cal's highly regarded scrambling quarterback, seemed destined for the hero's role as he scored two touchdowns in the first half and directed the Trojans on substantial drives. Michigan, meanwhile, was being stalled constantly and could only get a field goal by Mike Gillette in the first 30 minutes.

Michigan gained strength from a good drive of 65 yards to a touchdown on the first series of plays in the second half. Demetrius Brown, the Wolverines' southpaw quarterback, tossed a 6-yard touchdown pass to Chris Calloway.

Hoard's two big runs were stunning balancing acts. On the 31-yard run, he was hit at the line of scrimmage and got free. Then he nearly fell, stumbling near the right sideline. Yet he settled in his stride and added another 20 yards to the run.

Brown flipped a 22-yard pass to his tight end, Derrick Walker, to get the ball to the 2 before Hoard got his first touchdown. A few minutes later, after Michigan's defense stalled a good drive by Southern Cal at the Wolverines' 30, Hoard broke free for the really long run. It was on the first play after Quin Rodriguez missed a 47-yard field-goal attempt.

Junior Seau, a linebacker, had Hoard by the ankles 2 yards behind the line of scrimmage. But the Michigan back slipped away, found a big hole right of center and headed out. He was caught by Chris Hale, a cornerback, after carrying the ball 61 yards to the Trojan 9. Then, on fourth and goal from the 1, Hoard went right and just made it into the end zone.

Michigan (9-2-1) ended on a high note in a season that started with a low one at South Bend, Ind., when Notre Dame won, 19-17. Southern Cal finished at 10-2.

For Peete, it was a continuation of poor bowl-game efforts. Although he scored twice on short runs, the senior had his least productive game of the season with only 158 yards passing and two interceptions.

SCORE BY PERIODS

Michigan 3	0	6	13	—	22
Southern Cal 0	14	0	0	—	14

54

ISMAIL LEADS NOTRE DAME PAST MICHIGAN

By MALCOLM MORAN
Special to The New York Times

ANN ARBOR, Mich., Sept. 16, 1989 — They speak in the complex football language of the late 1980's at places like Notre Dame. They prepare for months for days such as this one, the first of several decisive meetings to determine the New Year's Day matchups and define the final outcome of the national college polls.

The Irish worried about the sudden absence of three significant starters, and four other first-team or second-team players, as a result of university probation, injury or a decision to leave.

But after all that advance effort and worry, the direction of the new season turned on one word.

"Middle," said Lou Holtz, the coach of the Fighting Irish.

Raghib Ismail, the slender Notre Dame sophomore called "Rocket," followed the plan and his blockers to take some fleeting steps into his school's long football history this afternoon.

Streak Ends for Michigan

His second-half kickoff returns of 88 and 92 yards, through the middle of the Wolverines, became the difference in a 24-19 victory over Michigan that strengthened Notre Dame's top ranking in the news agency polls. The Irish (2-0) extended the nation's longest major-college winning streak to 14 and ended Michigan's unbeaten streak at 10 games in its first game of the season.

"This won't ruin our season," said Michigan's coach, Bo Schembechler. But the Wolverines were not helped by two moments that stunned the crowd of 105,912 at Michigan Stadium and decided the 25th meeting of the two top-ranked teams in the 53-year history of The Associated Press poll of reporters and broadcasters.

Ismail's first score, a return at the start of the third quarter and the first touchdown against Michigan on a kickoff in 32 years, provided the Irish with a sudden 14-6 lead after the Wolverines had come within a point 25 seconds before halftime.

His second touchdown, with 12:46 to play in the fourth quarter, blunted an emotional Michigan comeback after the quarterback, Elvis Grbac, who entered his first college game as a replacement for the injured starter, Michael Taylor, had brought the Wolverines within 5 points on a 5-yard touchdown pass to the tight end Derrick Walker.

Ismail, a 5-foot-10-inch flanker who has run 40 yards in 4.28 seconds, led the country last season with an average of 36.1 yards per return. He returned two kickoffs for scores last year, both in a 43-point victory over lowly Rice.

"The only job I have to do is to make one person miss," Ismail said. "When everyone takes care of their blocking assignments and I make one person miss, we do pretty well."

Both times, Ismail took advantage of blocks by Rodney Culver, a 6-foot, 219-pound sophomore. He was not forced to break a tackle on the first return, and only briefly felt a Wolverine grab his legs on the second.

Ismail's 88-yard return was the first for a touchdown against Michigan since Ron Engel of Minnesota ran 95 yards on Oct. 26, 1957. His 92-yard return was believed to be the first time Michigan has allowed two kick-off returns for touchdowns in a game.

Only once, at the end of the first half, did Michigan attempt to keep the ball from Ismail, the lone deep returner, with a low, shorter kickoff. "We thought they were going to do that the whole game," Ismail said.

Michigan's failure to avoid Ismail, a decision Schembechler said was made to prevent the Irish from easily gaining good field position, will provide the latest debate among the followers of a program that has not been voted national champion since 1948.

The returns provided the Irish with a luxury they needed after a heavy early-afternoon rain left puddles on the artificial surface.

Tony Rice, the senior quarterback whose passing skills improved dramatically last season, completed just one of two throws, a 6-yard touchdown pass to the senior fullback Anthony Johnson, for a 7-0 lead.

While Rice was the second-leading Irish rusher with 79 yards, including a 24-yard run, a Michigan defense that concentrated on taking away the outside prevented Rice from becoming a decisive factor.

Ismail made that unnecessary. With the kickoff return unit twice providing a margin for error, Notre Dame was never placed in the position of having to take the offensive chances made necessary by playing from behind.

186

"We didn't do anything special," Holtz said. "With the weather, we did not open it up. We didn't want to give Michigan anything they didn't earn."

The gambles were forced upon the Wolverines. When Taylor, the only experienced Michigan quarterback, left the game with a bruised back early in the second half, the Wolverines were forced to call upon Grbac (pronounced GER-back), a sophomore who had never played in a college game.

He nearly became a hero. Grbac completed 17 of 21 passes for 134 yards and two touchdowns. He compensated for a rushing game that produced just 94 yards despite an average weight advantage of more than 40 pounds in the Michigan offensive line.

Grbac's 4-yard pass to the split end, Greg McMurtry, brought Michigan within 5 points with 4:08 to play. But with Johnson gaining the last of his 80 yards to maintain possession on a fourth-and-1 play with 1:58 to go, the Wolverines never had the ball with a chance to win.

Notre Dame became the first team in Schembechler's 21-season era to defeat the Wolverines in three consecutive years.

SCORE BY PERIODS

Notre Dame	0	7	10	7 —	24
Michigan	0	6	0	13 —	19

55

MICHIGAN KNOCKS OFF SPARTANS, 10-7

By ED SHERMAN
Special to The Chicago Tribune

EAST LANSING, Mich., Oct. 14, 1989 — Two down, six to go. Even after Michigan's 10-7 victory over Michigan State, Bo Schembechler, afflicted with tunnel vision, didn't see any light Saturday.

Michigan perhaps cleared its biggest obstacle in its attempt to repeat as Big Ten champion. But after the game, Schembechler had corn on his mind, not roses.

"Let's entertain thoughts of Iowa (Michigan's next opponent)," said the Wolverines coach when asked if the victory had him entertaining thoughts of the Rose Bowl. "What people have got to understand is that we still have to play Iowa and Illinois on the road and Ohio State at home. We've got the toughest schedule in the league. To say we've got the inside track. . . . Hey, we're only 2-0 (in the Big Ten), and we share the lead. We've got a long way to go."

Michigan (4-1 over all), though, made its job much easier by beating the Spartans, who definitely are the best 2-3 team in the country. Michigan State's three defeats have been to No. 1 Notre Dame, No. 2 Miami and now No. 5 Michigan by a total of 17 points.

Yet the Spartans showed their home crowd of 76,913 fans why they've played in only one Rose Bowl during the last 21 years, compared to nine for Michigan and Schembechler. The difference between going to the Rose Bowl and the Peach Bowl was defined clearly Saturday.

Michigan State made big mistakes. Michigan did not.

Michigan State kicker John Langloh had one field goal blocked in the first quarter, which helped set up a Michigan touchdown, and missed another attempt during a crucial point in the fourth quarter.

Michigan State gave Michigan 3 points in the second quarter when J.D. Carlson's woefully short field goal try from 46 yards was wiped out by a Spartans' offside. The penalty handed Michigan a first down and enabled Carlson to connect on his second attempt, this time from 35 yards. The kick gave Michigan a 10-0 lead, and ultimately, the difference in the game.

Need more examples? In the first quarter, Michigan put the ball in the end zone on fourth down from the Spartans' 1; Leroy Hoard ran in untouched. When faced with a similar situation in the fourth quarter, Michigan State's Blake Ezor ran into Wolverines safety Tripp Welborne far short of his destination.

"We've got to get the ball in from the 1, we can't kick the ball low, and we can't miss the field goal," said Michigan State coach George Perles, accurately wrapping up his team's failures.

"Too many mistakes," said Spartans linebacker Percy Snow. "We knew we couldn't make any mistakes if we wanted to beat them. No breaks, no missed opportunities. Damn, we just had too many mistakes."

Michigan State did have its chances. After looking dead in the first half, the Spartans essentially dominated the last 30 minutes.

However, in crunch time, Michigan State cracked in the fourth quarter. With the Spartans trailing, 10-0, with the ball on the Michigan 1-yard line and fourth down, Ezor attempted to drive in up the middle. Welborne and the Michigan defense made sure he didn't come close.

"Coach Carr (Lloyd, defensive coordinator) said they'll come out in a certain set in that situation," said Michigan safety Vada Murray. "J. J. Grant (Michigan's defensive captain) made the right call, and Tripp was right there."

The Spartans, though, didn't give up. They drove again, only to see Langloh miss a 34-yard field-goal attempt. Michigan State finally put the ball in the end zone on Dan Enos' 4-yard pass to Courtney Hawkins with 5 minutes 9 seconds remaining in the game.

But by then, the wasted opportunities had caught up with the Spartans.

"We didn't score points when we had the chance," Enos said. "We have the ball down there, but we didn't get it in."

Michigan received just enough offense from tailback Tony Boles, who rushed for 104 yards. Defensively, the Wolverines were led by Grant with 14 tackles. Grant, though, left the game in the fourth quarter with an injured knee.

It was the kind of game that left a Midwest-born-and-bred coach beaming.

"It was a nice, hard-hitting game," Schembechler said. "Nice and physical. A lot of good collisions. And the best team won. There's not much more you can say."

Save, perhaps, that the road to the Rose Bowl just got shorter for Michigan.

SCORE BY PERIODS

Michigan 7	3	0	0	—	10
Michigan State 0	0	0	7	—	7

56

MICHIGAN STRUGGLES AGAINST O.S.U. BUT CLINCHES ROSE BOWL BID

By DON PIERSON
Special to The Chicago Tribune

ANN ARBOR, Mich., Nov. 25, 1989 — With two interceptions in the fourth quarter, cornerback Todd Plate handed Michigan the Rose Bowl on a silver platter Saturday and gave Ohio State its lunch, 28-18.

Michigan touchdowns by Ohioan Jarrod Bunch came after both interceptions and kept Ohio State quarterback Greg Frey from burning the Wolverines with another fast finish.

After taking a 14-0 lead and fumbling away two other scoring opportunities in the first half, the Wolverines had to fight off the Buckeyes to earn their second consecutive Big Ten title. They did it by blocking field-goal and extra-point attempts and ordering a Maize-and-Blue Plate special for the fourth largest crowd in Michigan history — 106,137.

Michigan became the first Big Ten team to win back-to-back outright titles since Michigan State in 1965-66. No Big Ten team has won back-to-back Rose Bowls.

Coach Bo Schembechler sounded more thrilled about the former than the prospect for the latter. Michigan beat Southern Cal last year in Pasadena and will get a rematch.

"For me, the fun part is gone. Now I have to be a personality," Schembechler said.

He conceded his team had accomplished "something very special" in going undefeated in the Big Ten for two years and losing only three games — two to Notre Dame and one to Miami.

Ohio State, headed for the Hall of Fame Bowl in Tampa, had chances to pull an upset in the 29th Ohio State-Michigan game to decide the Big Ten title. Then Plate literally stepped in.

So did Leroy Hoard, filling his customary role this time of year.

Tailback Hoard gained 152 yards in 21 carries and scored a touchdown. His 40-yard burst, longest play of the day, set up the touchdown that made it 21-12 with 12:22 to play.

"One long run and I got beat up the rest of the game. Ask my body," Hoard said.

Hoard was subbing for injured tailback Tony Boles, and neither Ohio State nor U.S.C. can figure out why. Hoard was m.v.p. of the last Rose Bowl with 142 yards and got 128 last year against the Buckeyes.

"He ran well," Schembechler said. "But he fumbled the ball (once). It's the only thing I've held against Leroy."

Like Hoard, Plate was a sub who came through in a season of attrition for both teams. Playing for injured Lance Dottin, Plate knocked down an end-zone pass by Frey in the first half, forcing the Buckeyes to settle for a field goal.

Playing without top tailback Carlos Snow, Ohio State got 133 yards from sophomore Scottie Graham, who switched back and forth from fullback to tailback throughout the game.

With Ohio State closing in at 14-12, Plate benefited from an errant throw by Frey on the first play of the fourth quarter against the wind. The walk-on senior from Brooklyn, Mich., picked it off on the 47, and Hoard's run set up a 5-yard TD pass from quarterback Mike Taylor, another Ohioan, to fullback Bunch.

"There were a lot of momentum shifts," Schembechler said.

Ohio State grabbed it back with an 80-yard drive to make it 21-18 with 7:04 left. Safety Tripp Welborne blocked the extra-point attempt by Pat O'Morrow, fulfilling the prediction by Ohio State coach John Cooper that the kicking game would make a difference.

At 14-12, the Buckeyes fumbled the snap on a 2-point conversion try. They never were playing for a tie, but either PAT would have allowed them to go ahead by a late field goal. A 42-yard attempt by O'Morrow in the first half was blocked by safety Vada Murray, another Ohioan.

Hoard injured his left ankle on his 40-yarder and, without him, the Wolverines were forced to punt with 3:42 left. Plate got cramps on the return and missed Ohio State's first play from its 34.

When he returned, Plate was late in getting the defensive signal, but he saw Frey eyeing receiver Greg Beatty on a post pattern.

"I might have hit him before the ball got there, but I was going for the ball," Plate said.

He intercepted it cleanly and knocked teammate Murray into the hospital with a shoulder pad. Murray was removed carefully from the field but pronounced all right.

The interception came with 2:48 left at the Michigan 41. Taylor got an interference call against cornerback Vinnie Clark on third down and hit

Greg McMurtry on another third down before Bunch broke a 23-yarder into the end zone with 1:28 to play.

"It's hard to describe the feeling," Plate said. "I played on a 1-8 team in high school and didn't get many offers. I told my dad, 'If I'm going to walk on, I'm going to do it on a big level.'"

SCORE BY PERIODS

Michigan 7	7	0	14	—	28
Ohio State 0	3	9	6	—	18

57

SCHEMBECHLER WILL RETIRE AS MICHIGAN COACH

By JOE LAPOINTE
Special to The New York Times

ANN ARBOR, Mich., Dec. 13, 1989 — After more than two decades as one of America's most successful college football coaches, Glenn Edward (Bo) Schembechler of Michigan announced today that he would leave his job following the Jan. 1 Rose Bowl game against Southern Cal.

Schembechler will be succeeded by Gary Moeller, his top assistant for many years. Schembechler said he was also considering resigning as athletic director, a position he has had for two years.

"The toughest thing I've ever had to do is to give up my football team," Schembechler said as his voice cracked and his eyes grew misty at a news conference in Crisler Arena. "But I'm doing it. I'm a very happy man. If I shed a tear, it's not because I'm sad."

Schembechler, whose 234 victories are the most among active coaches in Division I-A and the fifth-highest total in football history, said that his health was fine but that he wanted to take things more cautiously after he had one major heart attack, one near heart attack and two bypass operations. The most recent surgery was two years ago.

'I'll Probably Miss It'

"I don't want to run my luck too far," Schembechler said. "I don't know how I'll react next fall when football season comes along. I'll probably miss it, but that's the way it goes."

Although the 60-year-old Schembechler has hinted frequently in recent years that he didn't want to grow old on the sidelines, his announcement jolted the fans and the sports community of the Great Lakes State, where Schembechler has been the transcendant sports personality since arriving from Miami of Ohio for the 1969 season.

"I can't imagine football Saturdays without Bo Schembechler," said Alissa Feldgus, a senior economics major from Philadelphia. "Bo is Michigan football."

Word of Schembechler's decision began to circulate around campus Monday night after Schembechler spoke to students in a sociology seminar. When a student asked Schembechler about the new coaches' offices in the new football building. Schembechler said he wouldn't be using the office.

"Bo is to Michigan what macaroni is to cheese," said Adam Schrager, a senior from Evanston, Ill. "He means more to the state than any particular individual and it's obvious from walking through campus that his leaving has had a tremendous impact at a time when students should be studying for finals."

Another Effect

Schembechler's announcement also created the possibility of a major side effect: that if the Wolverines beat Southern Cal in the Rose Bowl, they could be chosen as national champions for the first time in his career.

There is no tournament to determine a national champion. The two most widely acknowledged polls are conducted by the news agencies, The Associated Press poll of sportwriters and sportscasters and United Press International poll of coaches. The outspoken and sometimes bombastic Schembechler has friends and foes in both groups but is highly regarded in his profession.

Currently, both polls show Michigan ranked third, behind No. 1 Colorado and No. 2 Miami. If Colorado loses to No. 4 Notre Dame in the Orange Bowl and if Miami loses to No. 7 Alabama in the Sugar Bowl, Michigan could move up with a Rose Bowl victory.

"I've never dwelled on records," Schembechler said. "I've never worried if I've won the national championship, or if I'm the worst bowl coach in America."

In 21 seasons at Michigan, Schembechler has a record of 194-47-5. Including his six years at Miami, his record is 234-64-8. His highest finish in the polls was 1985, when his team was second by both A.P. and U.P.I.

Schembechler said he was reluctant to remain as athletic director because "I'd want to go to practice and I shouldn't do that. I don't want to be looking over Gary Moeller's shoulder." Schembechler said he enjoyed the athletic-director role "as long as I could coach football."

"He keeps telling me, 'You don't want me around, you don't want me around, you don't want me around,' " Moeller said.

Schembechler said he might take a larger role with the Detroit Tigers. He is currently on the board of directors. He has said, in the past, that he might want to be a football commentator.

"I love all sports," Schembechler said. "I love to be around sports. A lot of people have talked to me about a lot of things. I have to work. There is a great misconception that I am so narrow, that football is everything in my life."

Asked how he would like to be remembered, Schembechler said of himself: "He's a decent guy. He's honest. He worked hard and he knew a little football."

Bo Schembechler directs traffic on the playing field during his final game in the 1990
Rose Bowl against U.S.C.

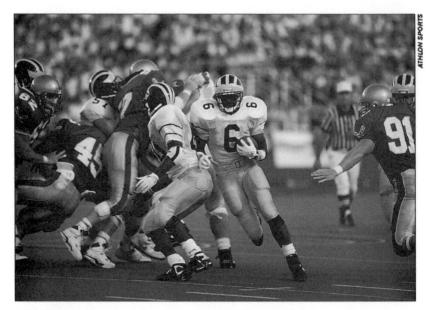

Tyrone Wheatley (6) cuts through traffic against Boston College in 1991. The Wolverines won, 35–13.

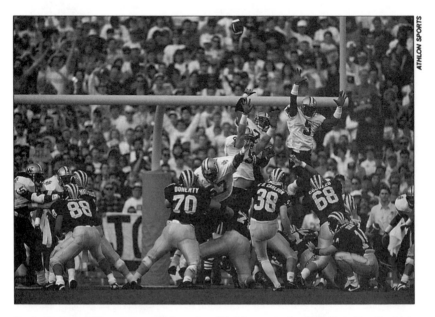

Justin Carlson (38) attempts a kick against Washington in the 1992 Rose Bowl, which was won by the Huskies, 34–14.

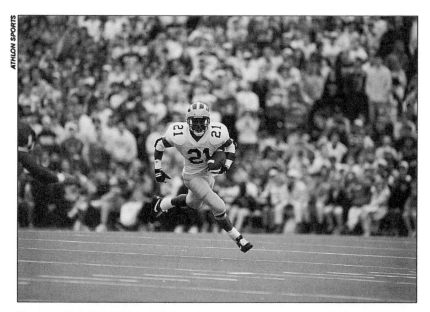

Desmond Howard (21) used skillful running and artful pass receiving to win The Heisman Memorial Trophy in 1991.

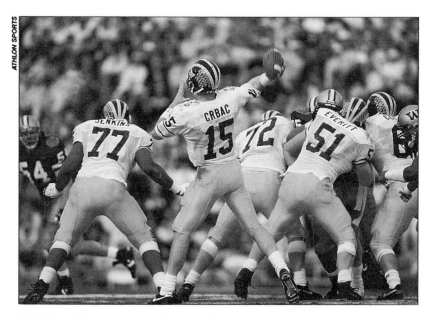

Elvis Grbac (15) was on the pitching end of the many long passes which allowed Desmond Howard to sparkle in 1990 and 1991.

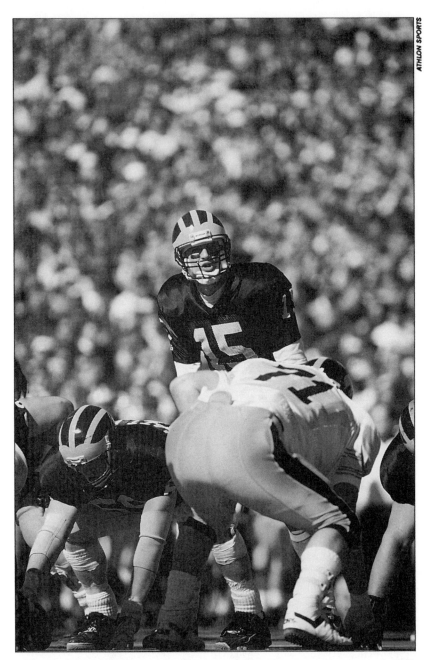

Elvis Grbac (15) quarterbacked the Wolverines to two Rose Bowl appearances in 1992 and 1993.

Entering the 1994 season, Tyrone Wheatley (6) was a leading candidate for The Heisman Memorial Trophy.

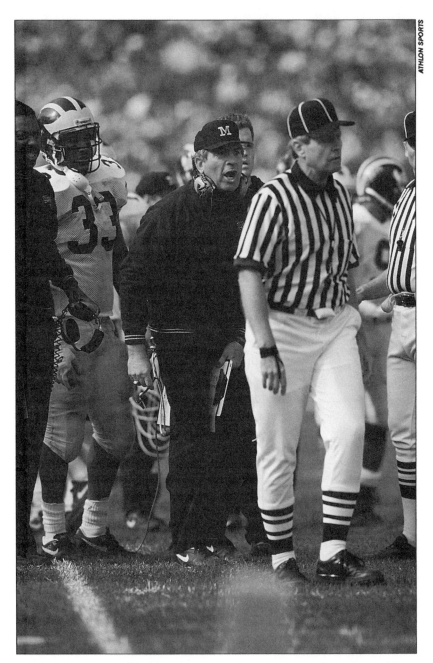

Gary Moeller succeeded Bo Schembechler in 1990 and has led the Wolverines to 2 Rose Bowl appearances in the past 4 seasons.

58

U.S.C. SPOILS SCHEMBECHLER'S EXIT

By MICHAEL MARTINEZ
Special to The New York Times

PASADENA, Calif., Jan. 1, 1990 — In his final game, Bo Schembechler refused to fade quietly into the landscape of old college football coaches. He joked and laughed tonight when the Rose Bowl was over, and then he walked away with a casual wave. But deep inside, where no one could see, there must have been a seeping anger.

Schembechler's retirement bash ended glumly when Southern California drove 75 yards in the final minutes to defeat Michigan, 17-10, and end the Wolverines' slim hope for a national championship. Then Schembechler issued his parting shot at the officiating, which might have cost his team a chance for a late — and possibly deciding — touchdown.

"One thing I won't miss in retirement," he said long after night had fallen, "is incompetent officiating."

The words left Schembechler's exit as something less than memorable. But the 60-year-old Michigan coach, who announced Dec. 13 that he was leaving his position after 21 seasons, had some cause for anger.

Questionable Holding Call

The Wolverines were called for holding on a late drive that appeared to put them in position to take their first lead. A fake punt resulted in a 24-yard run by Chris Stapleton, the Michigan punter, and would have put the Wolverines at the Trojans' 31-yard line.

The call negated the run, and then Schembechler, after hurling a play sheet, almost took a pratfall, losing his balance and nearly tripping over a cable. Michigan, which finished at 10-2, was assessed another penalty, this one for unsportsmanlike conduct on its volatile coach.

"It was the most unbelievable call I've ever seen," Schembechler said, "and it came in my final game. It was an absolutely ridiculous call. If I see the film and I'm wrong, I'll retract what I've said. But people who saw it in the press box said it was a ridiculous call."

What additionally bothered Schembechler was the fact the flag was thrown long after the apparent infraction by Bobby Abrams, who was blocking on the left side of the Michigan line, and that it was made by an official of the Pacific-10 Conference, Charles Czubin, the line judge.

Asked which official had made the call, Schembechler smiled slyly and answered, "The incompetent one." He also said he was initially told that the penalty was made for blocking below the waist, then changed to holding.

None of the game officials were made available after the game, but a Pac-10 official reported that Verle Sorgen, the supervisor of officials for the conference, said that Abrams was called for holding with both hands.

Schembechler, 2-8 in Rose Bowls, said he had always believed that the officiating crew should be neutral, coming from neither the Pac-10 nor the Big Ten. Asked about officiating in general, he said: "You want to know what my humble opinion is? The game has passed up all amateur officiating. They can't keep up. It's too fast."

Abrams answered questions quietly after he emerged from the Wolverines' locker room, saying: "I was shocked. I didn't know what they could call. I didn't hold the guy. It was just a bad call, I guess."

When the Trojans got the ball again, they made their best drive of the day, moving from their 25 to the deciding score. This was the key: Todd Marinovich, the redshirt-freshman quarterback who completed 22 of 31 passes, connected on a 20-yarder to John Jackson on a third-and-5 play to put the ball at the Michigan 24. Then Ricky Ervins, who rushed for 130 yards, did most of the remaining dirty work, carrying the final 14 with 1 minute 10 seconds to play.

"I told the guys in the huddle that we didn't need to get it all in one shot," Marinovich said. "We just needed to work our way down the field and use the clock."

Michigan, which was behind by 10-3 at the half, got 108 yards rushing by Leroy Hoard, who became the only player the last two seasons to gain at least 100 yards on the ground against Southern Cal. But by himself, he wasn't enough.

The Trojans, who finished the season at 9-2-1, won their first Rose Bowl since 1985. It was also the first for coach Larry Smith, whose team had lost the Rose Bowl each of the last two years and who is a former Schembechler assistant.

"It feels good to get a bowl victory," Smith said. "It's been a long time coming. There's no better feeling."

Then someone asked about Schembechler.

"We're losing one of the warhorses," Smith said, "one of the guys who did things the plain and simple way."

Smith had not spoken to his former mentor when the game was over, but he said he would find him later. And what would he say?

"What I'll tell him," Smith said, "is that I can't say I'm sorry, because you don't apologize for a win. But I'll tell him I'm sorry he's leaving."

SCORE BY PERIODS

Southern Cal 0	10	0	7	—	17
Michigan 0	3	7	0	—	10

59

A MOST APPROPRIATE EXIT

By **DOUGLAS S. LOONEY**
Sports Illustrated

NEW YORK, Jan. 8, 1990 — Bo Schembechler's glorious 21-year coaching career at Michigan ended on a fitting note at the Rose Bowl late Monday afternoon. He lost. Ranting, raving, raging, he lost, 17-10, to U.S.C. The defeat ran his Rose Bowl record to a horrid 2-8 and extended his overall bowl record to an awful 5-12. Near the end of the game, he threw a classic, out-of-control, Bo temper tantrum that contributed mightily to the loss.

With 5:24 left to play and the score tied, 10-10, Michigan had a fourth-and-two when Chris Stapleton ran a fake punt for 24 yards to the U.S.C. 30 and an apparent first down. But blocker Bobby Abrams was called for holding, thus nullifying the play and forcing Michigan to punt for real. Bo went bonkers, slamming his play sheet to the turf, and Michigan received a 15-yard penalty for unsportsmanlike conduct. The holding call and that memorable fit may have cost the Wolverines a chance to win. U.S.C. immediately began a 75-yard drive, which ended with tailback Ricky Ervins's 14-yard touchdown run.

Shortly before the game Schembechler said, "My bowl record is pathetic." Indeed, it would not have seemed right if Bo — with the most wins of any active major college coach with a 234-65-8 record — had gone out with a triumph at the scene of his most ignominious defeats. Bo just don't know bowls.

But Bo knows how to make a noisy exit. Since Dec. 13, when he made his surprise announcement that he did not feel he could push his twice-bypassed heart any further, Schembechler has been talking loud on a variety of issues. He complained bitterly when the presidents of the Big Ten universities voted to admit Penn State to the conference without discussing the matter with their athletic directors. "In the next five years the presidents will completely confuse the field of intercollegiate athletics," said Bo, who is, at least for now, Michigan's AD. About a possible national championship playoff, Schembechler warned, "It will kill the game." Of recruiting, he observed, "You start to feel like a pimp." It was as if Bo knew that he had to speak his mind fast, since the days during which he could command an audience were numbered.

Happily, though, Schembechler, 60, did know when to quit. And while some members of the public will remember him as the guy who threw childish tantrums on the sideline, his legacy is more positive. During Schembechler's tenure — a period rife with football scandals on other campuses — there was no scandal in Ann Arbor. And his teams invariably were solid winners: From 1970 to '74, Michigan was a remarkable 50-4-1.

In truth, Schembechler's final blowup was more like a curtain call: once more for old times' sake. Two days before the game, he said he wasn't sure how his resignation would affect the play of his Wolverines during the Rose Bowl. "Emotions can work both for you and against you," he mused. In the end, Bo's own emotional eruption worked against Michigan.

60

No. 1 IRISH ESCAPE MICHIGAN

By STEVE BERKOWITZ
Special to The Washington Post

SOUTH BEND, Ind., Sept. 15, 1990 — Like Lucy pulling the ball away from Charlie Brown, Notre Dame has done it again to Michigan.

Tonight the top-ranked Fighting Irish invited the fourth-ranked Wolverines to a 10-point lead midway through the third quarter. They then scored a pair of fourth-quarter touchdowns, the last on an 18-yard pass from Rick Mirer to sophomore flanker Adrian Jarrell with 1:40 to play, and defeated Michigan, 28-24, before a sellout crowd of 59,075 at Notre Dame Stadium.

It was Notre Dame's fourth consecutive victory over the Wolverines, who had not lost to the same opponent in four straight years since they lost to Purdue five times from 1962 to 1966.

"There are some senior kids hurt very, very badly," said Gary Moeller, who was making his debut as Michigan coach after replacing Bo Schembechler in January. "They wanted to win for themselves and they wanted to win for Michigan because we haven't done it in quite a while. It hurts."

Wolverines junior tailback Jon Vaughn fumbled on the game's second play — a turnover Notre Dame converted into a touchdown — but he came back to gain 201 yards on 22 carries, becoming the first player to reach the 200-yard rushing mark against Notre Dame since Penn State's Blair Thomas ran for 214 yards in 1987. Vaughn also caught 6 passes for 41 yards. As a team, Michigan rushed for 253 yards on 40 carries.

Said Notre Dame coach Lou Holtz: "I've never seen a team run the ball on Notre Dame like that . . . I don't know yet how we won this football game. I guess it's the luck of the Irish and the Lady on the Dome. Good things just seem to happen to us."

Mirer, in his first start for the Irish, was one of those things when it mattered most — in the fourth quarter. He completed 14 of 23 passes in the game for 165 yards, one interception and one touchdown. But in the final period, he was five of seven for 57 yards.

"I think he can play better," Holtz said, "but he competed well and did a very, very good job."

He keyed the final drive, 76 yards, with an excellent play on third down and 6 from Notre Dame's 28. Flushed out of the pocket, he scrambled a bit, then completed a 13-yard pass to split end Tony Smith.

The Fighting Irish did not face another third down the rest of the drive, which Mirer concluded by rolling to his right and splitting two defenders with his pass to Jarrell.

"It was a great win for us and a great win for me, too," Mirer said. "I'm glad it started this way, and I hope there are many more."

Michigan trailed, 14-10, at halftime, but its huge and veteran offensive line had begun asserting itself. The five starters, all of whom started last year, average 6-feet-5, 288 pounds. Behind them, Vaughn, who carried just 10 times all of last season, had 96 yards on 12 carries at intermission. As a team Michigan had 113 yards on 20 carries. In addition, quarterback Elvis Grbac was getting time to throw.

After holding Notre Dame on the first series of the second half, the Wolverines drove 85 yards in 11 plays for a go-ahead touchdown. Grbac passed to junior flanker Desmond Howard for 21 yards, to Vaughn for 10 and to Howard for 19. That put the ball on the the Fighting Irish 45. Fullback Jerrod Bunch, a 247-pound senior, bulled inside twice for 14 yards and Vaughn scampered twice for 27. On third and goal from the 1, senior tailback Alan Jefferson swept around left end for the score.

Notre Dame had too many players on the field for the extra point, and Michigan kicker J.D. Carlson used the 15-yard penalty on the kickoff to boot the ball through the end zone. On first down, Wolverines senior safety David Key jarred the ball from tailback Tony Brooks' grasp. Senior defensive tackle Mike Evans won a prolonged scrum, giving Michigan possession at the 26.

On the ensuing play, Grbac passed to Howard in the left flat. Junior cornerback Rod Smith rushed up to make the tackle, but Howard dodged him and sped down the sideline, past two more defensive backs, and into the waiting arms of Michigan students seated on the field behind the end zone. Just like that, the Wolverines were ahead, 24-14.

They held Notre Dame on four plays, and Vada Murray's 22-yard punt return gave them possession at their 38. They swiftly moved deep into Fighting Irish territory, and on fourth and 1 from the 19, sent Carlson out for a 36-yard field goal. He missed wide left with a little less than 3 minutes left in the third quarter.

The Fighting Irish took advantage — with a little bit of luck. On third

203

and 15 from their 15, Mirer fired a pass downfield that bounced off junior Raghib (Rocket) Ismail's hands and into those of freshman Lake Dawson. Dawson, who snagged the ball at midfield, carried it to Michigan's 40. Notre Dame continued to move, and with 13 minutes left in the game, fullback Rodney Culver dove for a 1-yard touchdown, making the score 24-21, Michigan.

Michigan came right back, however. Vaughn broke for runs of 22, 9 and 24 yards, and the Wolverines drove to a first down at Notre Dame's 11. But Grbac then short-armed a pass into the end zone, and senior linebacker Michael Stonebreaker intercepted.

Notre Dame drove from its 20 to Michigan's 35, but Mirer overthrew Tony Smith and Murray intercepted.

The Wolverines had to punt, however, and the Fighting Irish began their game-winning drive.

Notre Dame snuffed out Michigan's next drive when Reggie Brooks intercepted Grbac on the Irish 40 with 1:21 remaining. Michigan got the ball back with 15 seconds left on its own 29, but Grbac was unable to connect on two desperation passes.

On the game's second play, Vaughn burst through a hole on the left side, then fumbled without being touched. Notre Dame safety Greg Davis recovered at the Wolverines' 26-yard line, and the Fighting Irish didn't take long to move in front, 7-0.

Culver carried three times for 19 yards as they moved to the 2. Mirer, whose dropback passing ability is supposed to give Notre Dame's offense a decidedly different look, then did a suitably effective imitation of his predecessor, Tony Rice. He went down the line on an option play, cut back inside right end and sprinted to the corner of the end zone.

But the Wolverines went right back to Vaughn, and he provided the spark for a 56-yard drive that resulted in a field goal by Carlson with 7 minutes left in the first quarter. Vaughn handled the ball on the first three plays. He turned a screen pass into an 8-yard gain, then broke a quick-opener for 10 yards and a draw play for 19. Michigan converted a fourth down and 1 at Notre Dame's 31, but stalled thereafter.

Then came the moment everyone had been waiting for — a Michigan kickoff with Ismail in single safety. Even though Ismail returned 2 kickoffs for touchdowns against Michigan last year, Moeller had promised he would not have Carlson squib the ball and simply hand the Fighting Irish respectable field position. Sure enough, Carlson kicked the ball deep to the left side, and sure enough, Ismail nearly broke away. But just as the crowd drew in its breath for a roar, he was tripped at the 25.

Michigan's defense could not trip the Fighting Irish, though. They drove 75 yards in 11 plays for a 2-yard touchdown run by Tony Brooks. Linebacker Chris Hutchinson sacked Mirer for an 8-yard loss on the drive's first play, but senior tailback Ricky Watters made a diving catch for a 17-yard gain on third and 13.

SCORE BY PERIODS

Notre Dame	7	7	0	14 —	28
Michigan	3	7	14	0 —	24

61

IRISH'S MIRER COMES OF AGE

By MALCOLM MORAN
Special to The New York Times

SOUTH BEND, Ind., Sept. 16, 1990 — Late Saturday evening, somewhere along the way to Catholics vs. Convicts III, the football game between Notre Dame and Miami that has already inspired T-shirt sales five weeks before the Oct. 20 kickoff, the inhabitants of Notre Dame Stadium discovered this problem.

By the final minutes of the third quarter of the game against Michigan, the Irish had a change to make in order to preserve a No. 1 position that had just been bestowed upon them. The spoon-feeding of Rick Mirer had to be abandoned.

Notre Dame's first game with Mirer as its starting quarterback had deteriorated into a 10-point deficit. The creativity of Michigan's no-huddle offense that marked Gary Moeller's first game as its coach, combined with the power football that characterized the 21-season Bo Schembechler era, had created a sense of urgency for the Irish.

It was time to overlook the facts that Mirer had played a total of 36 minutes 3 seconds and had thrown 30 passes before Saturday night. "The plan was, 'Let everybody else play the game, and you just be the sophomore quarterback,' " said Tim Ryan, a senior offensive guard. "But things happened."

Wearing No. 3, the number Joe Montana once wore for the Irish, Mirer helped produce the kind of finish that made Montana famous. He completed his last five passes, including an 18-yard touchdown to Adrian Jarrell with 1 minute 40 seconds to play, for a 28-24 victory over the Wolverines and perhaps the beginning of his own era in the history of Notre Dame football.

The first touchdown pass of Mirer's college career ended a decisive drive on which 52 of the 76 yards came on passes. Notre Dame's fourth consecutive victory over Michigan was also the 18th straight Irish victory at Notre Dame Stadium, and the 15th in 16 games as a No. 1-ranked team in Lou Holtz's five seasons as coach.

Mirer completed 14 of 23 passes for 165 yards to help the Irish overcome the 201 rushing yards of the Michigan tailback, Jon Vaughn, the most against Notre Dame since Penn State's Blair Thomas gained 214 in 1987.

But more important, the urgency of the moment presented Mirer with a chance to demonstrate the sense of confidence necessary to succeed at a new level. "You can tell when someone has an air of confidence," Ryan said. "It flowed from him. It was like, 'We're going to go down there and score.' "

"When it came down to the time we were running out of time," Mirer said, "we had to get something going."

With less than 3 minutes to play in the third quarter, and Michigan's lead still at 10 after J.D. Carlson missed a 36-yard field-goal attempt, Notre Dame's faith in Mirer's passing skills led to a moment that began to change the game.

At that point, as Notre Dame faced a third and 15 from its 15, the previous seven Irish possessions had ended with five punts and two fumbles. But Mirer's pass for Raghib Ismail was deflected into the hands of the freshman Lake Dawson for a 45-yard gain to the Michigan 40. Ten plays later, Rodney Culver's 1-yard score, with 12:59 to go, reduced the Michigan lead to 3 points.

Mirer's only interception of the game, by Vada Murray at the Wolverines' 10-yard line with 7:57 to play, delayed the comeback. But after forcing a Michigan punt, the Irish began at their own 24 with 4:33 to go.

"You just play by instinct and ability," Mirer said. "People were in the right place at the right time. We had them on their heels."

62

OHIO STATE'S GAMBLE PAYS – FOR MICHIGAN

By BOB SAKAMOTO
The Chicago Tribune

COLUMBUS, Ohio, Nov. 24, 1990 — Ohio State had come to the brink of its football season Saturday when Buckeyes quarterback Greg Frey made his run for the roses.

It was fourth down and 1 on the Buckeyes' 29-yard line, and Ohio State and Michigan were deadlocked at 13 with 1 minute 47 seconds left. Only a victory would earn the Buckeyes a trip to the Rose Bowl. They needed Iowa to lose, and the Hawkeyes trailed Minnesota, 7-0, at the time.

If Iowa lost, Ohio State tied and Illinois won, the Illini would be Pasadena-bound. Who was Illinois playing? Northwestern.

The Buckeyes went for it.

Frey ran the option and was turned back inside by the penetration of Wolverine defensive tackle Chris Hutchinson. Middle guard T. J. Osman grabbed his ankles, teammates Mike Evans and Erik Knuth wrapped him up and Brian Townsend made certain Frey didn't fall forward.

The Wolverines then drove to the Buckeyes' 19, where J. D. Carlson kicked a 37-yard field goal with time elapsed for Michigan's 16-13 victory.

"If I go for a tie and Minnesota beats Iowa, then I couldn't face our football team," Ohio State coach John Cooper said. "I've been telling this football squad ever since the Indiana game that I really felt we had a chance to go ahead and win and go to the Rose Bowl. So why not go for broke?"

That critical play broke down mostly because the Buckeyes had the wrong offense in against the Wolverines' goal-line defense. They didn't have any timeouts left during which to make an adjustment.

That's because 90,054 howling partisans made such a ruckus in the third quarter that referee Tom Quinn issued two crowd warnings. Michigan quarterback Elvis Grbac still couldn't operate. On the third work stoppage, N.C.A.A. rules mandated Quinn call a timeout and charge it to the home team.

"As I reflect back, that really hurt us," O.S.U. cornerback Vinnie Clark said. "I can't really blame them because they're into the game, but it did hurt."

"They had the wrong offense in against our goal-line, six-man front," Wolverine linebacker Erick Anderson said. "It's tough to run an option against a six-man front because the linebackers can float free. But they had no timeouts left."

And now the 7-3-1 Buckeyes have nothing left except a consolation matchup with Air Force in the Liberty Bowl. The 8-3 Wolverines probably will face either Mississippi or Auburn in the Gator Bowl.

Carlson redeemed himself after missing from 38 yards with 4:16 left in the game.

Carlson is accustomed to kicking off artificial turf, although Ohio Stadium's grass didn't seem to bother him on 27- and 30-yard field goals in the second quarter. But he thwarted this one, kicking up a divot and renewing Ohio State's rosy aspirations.

"It's time to start saying your prayers," was Carlson's reaction after the first miss. "On that fourth and 1, I had my fingers crossed and everything. I was hoping. When the defense stuffed them, I knew I'd get another chance."

Jarrod Bunch ran for 2 yards, Jon Vaughn gained 7 and Ricky Powers added 5 onto his game-high total of 128 yards on 27 carries. Grbac lost 4 yards and called time with 0:03 showing on the clock.

"As I ran out there, my teammates had faith in me, and that helped," Carlson said. "All I heard were words of encouragement."

Michigan coach Gary Moeller labeled this a game ex-Buckeye coach Woody Hayes would have loved. A fired-up Ohio State defense led by 6-foot-6, 265-pound sophomore defensive end Alonzo Spellman, sophomore linebacker Steve Tovar (13 tackles) and senior safety Mark Pelini (11 tackles) twice stopped Michigan deep in Ohio State territory, forcing the Wolverines to settle for field goals.

"I expected our offense to play better than it did," Moeller said. "Give their defense credit."

Tim Williams booted a 33-yard field goal for O.S.U., and 44 seconds before halftime, Frey connected with Jeff Graham on a 12-yard touchdown pass.

The 10-6 halftime lead was extended to 13-6 early in the third quarter on a Williams 43-yard field goal. Derrick Alexander ran the ensuing kickoff back 48 yards to the Buckeye 38. Michigan then ran the ball until Grbac hit Desmond Howard with a 12-yard touchdown pass to tie the game.

SCORE BY PERIODS

Michigan 0	6	7	3	—	16
Ohio State 3	7	3	0	—	13

63

A DARING MICHIGAN DOWNS THE IRISH

By MALCOLM MORAN
Special to The New York Times

ANN ARBOR, Mich., Sept. 14, 1991 — The words of the prophet are no longer written on the subway walls. They are conceived by entrepreneurs, silk-screened onto T-shirts, and sold by the dozens. And at Michigan Stadium, these were the words that were placed on sale today: "You Da Man, Desmond."

And the price of the T-shirt is going up by the quarter.

With what once was a 17-point Michigan lead over Notre Dame all but gone, and with the Wolverines facing the nervous push-and-shove business of a fourth-and-1 at the Irish 25 with just over 9 minutes to play, Desmond Howard turned the most daring decision of the afternoon into its most breathtaking moment.

Streaking up the right sideline, Howard, having beaten Irish defensive backs Greg Davis and Jeff Burris, threw himself forward in the end zone, stretched parallel to the ground, extended his arms, gripped Elvis Grbac's shocking pass inches from the grass and somehow withstood the force of his inevitable landing.

His 25-yard touchdown, Howard's second of the game and sixth of the season, secured Michigan's 24-14 victory, its first over the Irish in five years.

"As it hung up there, the one thing I thought was I had to get to the ball," said Howard. "It happened so quickly, all I was thinking is you've got to get it and pull it in."

"I thought I threw it too far," Grbac said. "I threw the ball and it was like, oh, great, he's never going to get there.

"After the touchdown pass, I was almost crying."

Lou Holtz, the Notre Dame coach, said: "That absolutely broke our backs. They don't get that and anything can happen."

Howard's acrobatic catch had become necessary because of Notre Dame's unlikely comeback. Tony Smith's 35-yard touchdown reception with 6:47 to go in the third quarter had erased all but 3 points of what had been Michigan's early 17-0 lead.

Michigan is ranked No. 3 in The Associated Press poll and No. 2 by The New York Times while Notre Dame is ranked seventh by The Associated Press and sixth by The Times.

For nearly all of the first half, it had appeared that the fourth quarter would serve as the beginning of a long-awaited celebration for the crowd of 106,138, the fifth largest in the history of Michigan Stadium.

Holtz, the coach of the Fighting Irish, has been criticized for making hopeless-sounding statements on Tuesdays, only to see miracles take place four days later.

"I'm not being negative or pessimistic," Holtz said on gloomy Tuesday. "That's the facts."

But today, problems that had usually been solved some time between Tuesday morning and Saturday afternoon created a crisis. The facts were not good for the Irish, as Holtz watched a nightmare begin to take shape.

A Quick Interception

Rick Mirer's first pass, on Notre Dame's second offensive play, was intercepted by Lance Dottin, leading to J.D. Carlson's 23-yard field goal. After a Notre Dame punt, the Wolverines drove to the Irish 29 and created the type of play that Raghib Ismail once allowed the Irish to exploit. Howard, who scored four touchdowns last week against Boston College, has inspired comparisons to Ismail, and from the 29 the Wolverines turned him loose.

Grbac pitched the ball to sophomore tailback Ricky Powers, who ran to his left but handed it to Howard on a reverse. Howard turned the right corner, faked his way past defensive back Rod Smith, used a block upfield from tackle Rob Doherty and scored for a 10-0 lead.

The Irish Try to Answer Back

This time, the Irish responded quickly, making their deepest move into Wolverine territory when Mirer found tight end Derek Brown for a 46-yard gain to the Michigan 24. But two plays later, the possession ended abruptly when Tony Brooks fumbled a handoff from Mirer. Mike Evans, a defensive tackle, recovered for the Wolverines at the 20.

The second Irish turnover put Michigan in position to establish a powerful advantage, and the Wolverines drove 80 yards in 14 plays for another touchdown.

The final play of the drive came on the Notre Dame 16. Powers picked

212

his way into the secondary and then into the end zone and the Irish were suddenly facing a situation they had not encountered all last year.

When Notre Dame took the ball with 1:45 to go in the half, they had held it for a total of just 1:18 in the quarter. But a 20-yard run by Willie Clark, a 14-yard pass to Tony Smith and a 20-yard throw to Lake Dawson helped advance the Irish to the Michigan 3.

Mirer's first-and-goal pass was just beyond the leap of Brown. But on second down, Mirer's quick throw found Jerome Bettis to bring the Irish within 10 points.

SCORE BY PERIODS

Notre Dame.........3	14	0	7	—	24
Michigan 0	7	7	0	—	14

64

ONE MAGICAL DAY

By SALLY JENKINS
Sports Illustrated

NEW YORK, Sept. 23, 1991 — This is how a guy who has a name like a British aristocrat's, who's small enough to hang from your rearview mirror and who says his greatest catch was of Michael Jackson's hat in a concert crowd lunged into stardom in a single afternoon: Desmond Howard brought a hundred thousand spectators to the swooning point, reduced his Michigan teammates to wiggling their fingers and chanting "hocus-pocus" and made Notre Dame's fleetest defenders look as if they couldn't catch an elevator.

Howard had come to be known — at least around Ann Arbor — as the Magic Man, but after the Wolverines' 24-14 victory over the Irish last Saturday at Michigan Stadium, you can throw that nickname away. It isn't enough. What do you call a guy whose catches resemble death spirals, who fractures defenses with a turn of his hip and who has scored six of his team's eight touchdowns in their first two games? Certainly, you can call him the leading Heisman Trophy candidate. Or what about just How, as in Michigan offensive lineman Matt Elliott's wonder-filled observation, "Lord only knows how he does it."

How *did* Howard catch that seemingly uncatchable 25-yard touchdown pass from Elvis Grbac, against double coverage, with 9:02 left in the game and the Wolverines, their lead having shrunk to 17-14, facing fourth down and a foot? First, he made Notre Dame defensive backs Jeff Burris and Greg Davis disappear with his speed. "I eliminated them," said Howard with a smile. Then he took a couple of smooth strides to run under a ball that seemed impossibly overthrown. He stretched his wispy, 5-foot-9 body to its full length, extended his fingers and pulled in the football as he landed belly down in the back corner of the end zone with Davis clutching at his ankles. Whereupon Howard heard the silence of the crowd, then the roar. "It felt beautiful," he said.

The cheers Howard produced traumatized Notre Dame all afternoon and helped end four years of Irish dominance over Michigan. In the process, the Wolverines established themselves as a team of imposing proportions and glamour, as well as one to be reckoned with in the national championship race. Michigan turned two Irish turnovers into 10 points to take a 17-7 lead at halftime, held the vaunted Notre Dame rushing attack to 78 yards and controlled a bloody line of scrimmage. But most telling was this: The Wolverines possessed the ball for 40:40 and devoured the last 6:30 to deny Notre Dame any chance of mounting another of its remarkable comebacks. "All that stuff about Irish luck?" said Grbac after the game. "That's bull."

Along with Howard, who's a junior wide receiver, two others were most responsible for keeping the Irish offense on the sidelines: Grbac, who's a junior, and sophomore tailback Ricky Powers. Grbac ran Michigan's no-huddle attack rhythmically, completing 20 of 22 passes for 190 yards and making flawless checks at the line. Frequently, the audibles came when he saw openings for Powers, who darted for 164 yards on 38 carries.

Grbac made the last of his astute calls from the sideline. As Notre Dame took over at its own 12-yard line with 8:57 remaining and Michigan in front 24-14, he turned to assistant coach Mike Gittleson and said, "If we get the ball back with 5 minutes to go, we win." He was correct. The Irish floundered at their 49, and with that failure, they lost control of the national championship race.

Notre Dame's four consecutive defeats of Michigan had come in various ways. In 1987, the Irish capitalized on seven Wolverine turnovers to win 26-7. In '88, Notre Dame's Reggie Ho kicked four field goals, and Mike Gillette's attempt at the game-winning field goal for the Wolverines with no time left just tailed off to the right, so the score remained 19-17 in favor of Notre Dame. In '89, Rocket Ismail set his career ablaze with kickoff returns of 88 and 92 yards for touchdowns in a 24-19 victory. Then, last year, Michigan led 24-14 in the third quarter when a pass from Irish quarterback Rick Mirer bounced off Ismail, over the head of a Michigan defensive back and into the hands of Notre Dame's Lake Dawson for a 45-yard gain that set up a crucial touchdown. Final score: 28-24.

Those experiences left Michigan with "a little hatred, I think," Grbac said. Also with a little fear. Notre Dame has a viper quality that makes the Irish most dangerous when they're most threatened. For instance, the Wolverines never entirely contained Mirer or flanker Tony Smith, whose five catches for 121 yards would have been the game's most outstanding performance were it not for Howard, who, among his other accomplishments, had six receptions for 74 yards. Mirer's 35-yard pass to Smith with

6:47 to play in the third quarter brought the Irish to 17-14. And it brought the following thought to Grbac's mind: Oh, God, this is not happening again?

Going into the game the No. 3 Wolverine players were galled by the notion, which had been engendered by those four straight losses, that the No. 7 Irish might actually be better. They are from the same neighborhoods in Detroit and Chicago and Cleveland, or from the same rural communities, out in those stretches of rolling orchards and pasture, where Michigan, Indiana and Illinois sort of melt into each other. So what made Notre Dame so perfect? "I mean I never experienced anything like this," Grbac said before the game. "It's time. It's time to get rid of this Notre Dame thing, to put the Irish where they belong."

In short, if Michigan hoped to confront top-ranked Florida State in Ann Arbor on Sept. 28 with any sort of credibility, it had to stomp on luck and on Notre Dame. Which is just what the Wolverines did with a combination of seniority, conviction and timeliness. The Irish were inexperienced, judging by their standards of the last four years; their defensive line had only one 1990 starter, and their secondary had six sophomores and two seniors filling the first- and second-string slots on the depth chart. These defenders were no match for Michigan's mammoth offensive linemen, led by 6-foot-8, 322-pound tackle Greg Skrepenak. "It's fun watching them play," said Howard of the Wolverines' blockers. "They don't just push. They lay pancakes on guys, knock them down."

Also working in the Wolverines' favor were the facts that Gary Moeller is a more confident coach in his second year in Ann Arbor and that, for a change, Michigan had opened a season with a victory, having defeated Boston College, 35-13, on Sept. 7. It felt a lot better to be 1-0 than 0-1, which had been the case since 1987 thanks to the Irish. As Howard pointed out after Saturday's game, for the first time in his career he was undefeated.

Grbac and Howard have known each other since 10th grade, when they were high school teammates in Cleveland. They are mutual admirers, although not close friends. "Elvis is the smartest guy on the football field," Howard said. "He's heady."

It takes a certain headiness to know how far to throw it to Howard, whose philosophy is, I want them to hold their breaths every time I touch the ball. He has a remarkable ability to reserve his best work for the most important moments. Howard scored four of Michigan's five touchdowns against Boston College, including a game-breaking 93-yard kickoff return. When one of his spectacular plays appears on the game films in meetings, his teammates erupt in shouts of "hocus-pocus." They call such performances the Magic Show.

Future opponents would be well advised to kick away from his reputation. Otherwise they will be able to do little to prevent him from handling the ball; the Wolverines will make sure of that. Against Notre Dame, they gave it to him on a second-quarter reverse, Howard shooting up his own sideline on a 29-yard gasp of a scoring run. He took a handoff from Powers, turned upfield and put a dazzling move on cornerback Rod Smith. No one else came close to touching him. "It was a pitch to Ricky, and Ricky handed off to me," said Howard. "What more do you want?" Where did Smith go when he disappeared, so abruptly faked out of his shoes? "I had to dimiss him," Howard said, once again with a smile.

Moeller had told Howard before the season that double coverage would not be an excuse for failing to make a reception. Triple coverage, yes. According to Moeller, Howard should have the advantage against two defenders, because he has three directions he can go — left, right or downfield. "There are only a few ways they can cover me," Howard said. "In front and behind, or on either side."

Howard's explosiveness is what provoked Moeller to make what is surely one of the bolder calls ever by a Michigan coach on that fourth and inches at the Notre Dame 25. After Moeller signalled the play in, Grbac hunched over the line, surveyed the defense, began calling the signals and then pulled up and called time out, afraid he couldn't get the play off in time. In a sideline huddle with the entire offense, Moeller reaffirmed the pass play. The Wolverines had been stopped a series earlier on the Notre Dame 35 when Powers couldn't convert on a fourth-and-1 situation, and Moeller feared another failure would be too costly. "This is our chance." Moeller told his players.

Whether it was a good call is arguable. "When it works," Moeller said later, rolling his eyes. "It takes a guy like Elvis to throw it, and a guy like Desmond to make it work and make me look smart."

Grbac told Howard as they returned to the field, "We've got to make it work, we've got to make this play." Howard had barely missed making a catch on a similar play in the second quarter, the ground jarring the ball loose at the goal line. He reminded himself to tuck the ball away this time. As Grbac got set to take the snap, he saw Burris in single coverage on Howard, who was split right and was to run a basic out pattern.

Grbac took a three-step drop and pumped once. Burris hesitated when he saw Grbac pump. "I stopped moving my feet," Burris said.

Davis, the Irish strong safety, had come over from the middle of the field to help. Grbac let the ball go. "When it left my hand it was kind of wobbly," he said. "It was really high. I thought I'd overthrown it. Des was running as hard as he could, and the ball was just floating."

Burris thought the pass had no chance. "When I saw it go up, I just kept running back," he said. "I thought there was no way he would catch that one."

But Howard had forgotten about everything — including the defenders — except making the catch. He launched himself, grasped the ball and pulled it it. "I couldn't let it go," he said. "It was too big a catch."

65

MICHIGAN, HOWARD BURY O.S.U.

By ED SHERMAN
Special to The Chicago Tribune

ANN ARBOR, Mich., Nov. 23, 1991 — The day could have been better for Michigan. The Rose Bowl could have announced Washington will have to play the Wolverines on roller skates.

Otherwise, everything went Michigan's way Saturday.

The No. 4 Wolverines thumped Ohio State 31-3 to wrap up their 14th outright Big Ten title. And a 93-yard punt return for a touchdown, plus some spectacular pass-catching, gave Desmond Howard reason to practice his Heisman pose. The only way Howard doesn't get the trophy now is if he decides not to accept it.

And, finally, Ohio State (8-3, 5-3 in the Big Ten) gave coach John Cooper a three-year extension on his contract. Wolverine fans love Cooper. Michigan's 28-point win was the largest margin in this series since 1946.

"Hey, Cooper," yelled a fan as the coach walked off the field, "lifetime contract."

Cooper now has lost four straight to the Wolverines, giving him a shot next year to become the first Ohio State coach to drop five in a row to the Buckeyes' most hated enemy.

Saturday's game was supposed to be crucial to Cooper's future, but Athletic Director Jim Jones removed any suspense when he announced the extension minutes before kickoff.

"This sends a message that the decision is not based on winning or losing against Michigan," Jones said.

Cooper has a year remaining on his current contract, which means the new pact runs through the 1995 season. Jones cited improvement in the Ohio State program under Cooper as the reason for keeping him.

"I feel like we have made some improvement," Cooper said. "Maybe it didn't show today."

Hardly.

As for "improvement," Ohio State ranks fifth in the Big Ten during

Cooper's four years, trailing Michigan, Iowa, Illinois and Michigan State. His Buckeyes are 2-11-1 against ranked teams, including 0-8 against Michigan and Illinois. And no Big Ten titles or Rose Bowls.

These Buckeyes are a long way from the days of Woody Hayes, or even Earle Bruce.

Ironically, Bruce's ouster might have helped save Cooper's job. As much as anything else, it appears Ohio State felt bound to honor Cooper's contract because the university was roasted nationally in 1987 for firing Bruce during the middle of his pact.

"I couldn't look you in the eye and say (the Bruce situation) had no effect," Jones said. "For continuity of the program, and the integrity of the institution, it was important to recognize Coach Cooper already had a contract."

Cooper was relieved.

"I've been on pins and needles all year," he said. "I don't know that I'd want to go through another season like this one."

Then there's Howard's status. The sensational junior might have played his last game at Michigan Stadium. He's scheduled to graduate in May, and with his hands on the Heisman Trophy, there doesn't appear to be much reason for him to return. Not with a multimillion-dollar pro contract waiting for him.

After the game, Howard said he planned to return to Michigan for 1992, but that's been a standard answer for players like him in that situation. Previous junior Heisman winners Barry Sanders and Andre Ware later changed their minds. Even Howard hedged.

"I'm looking forward to getting my degree and winning the Rose Bowl," he said. "Otherwise, I can't think that far ahead."

Howard, whose 213 all-purpose yards included three catches for 96 yards, can look ahead to Dec. 14, when the Heisman winner will be announced in New York. He tightened his lock on the trophy with the second-quarter punt return, faking two defenders at the Michigan 10-yard line and blowing past the Buckeyes for his 23d touchdown of the season.

Howard then celebrated by striking the Heisman pose (knee up with a stiff-arm) in the end zone. "I told my friends I'd do something special," he said.

Michigan coach Gary Moeller couldn't believe Howard would pull such a stunt. "One of my players wouldn't do something like that," he said.

But nothing was going to bother Moeller after Michigan completed an 8-0 run in the Big Ten and wound up 10-1 over all.

It was his first title as head coach, and he made no secret of his emotions.

"When you're 10-1 and you beat Ohio State, you've got to be happy," Moeller said. "I feel honored to be coaching at Michigan."

SCORE BY PERIODS

Michigan	7	17	7	0	—	31
Ohio State	0	3	0	0	—	3

66

IN HIS GRASP

By SALLY JENKINS
Sports Illustrated

NEW YORK, Dec. 9, 1991 — There is magic in any ordinary act, and its essence is practice. Turn a carrot into a goldfish, pull a bird from a handkerchief, roll a coin over your fingers a thousand times until you can make it disappear. Practice — that is the innocent art of Michigan receiver Desmond (Magic) Howard.

Howard is a young man of 21 who is experiencing his first metaphysical stirrings, and you know what metaphysical stirrings can do to a young man. First he has a stirring, and the next thing you know, he is considering the true nature of magic. Then he is meditating and wearing an Egyptian ankh — the symbol of life — around his neck, and beads, and wondering whether he is more a black man than a maize and blue one, and soon there are posters of African kings on the wall of his apartment, where he lives alone (to the consternation of the Michigan coaching staff), and then he is refusing to eat beef because of its impurities and reading Malcolm X and listening to the speeches of African-American psychologist Na'im Akbar and asking, well, Why?

Frequently, the answer is, well, Because. Howard has learned this not from books or mediatations or speeches, but from his father, J.D. Howard, a tool and die maker. J.D. played basketball as a youth with the Jolly Jokers, a dime-store version of the Harlem Globetrotters, in the days when good black athletes didn't always get scholarships. More often they got a trade like tool and die. Desmond was all J.D. got for company after he and his wife, Hattie, split up when Desmond was 13, and J.D. devoted the next several years to raising a son with otherworldly speed, a smile softer than your daughter's and a sure sense that there is more to life than all this.

Howard, now a joyous college junior, is a virtual shoo-in for the Heisman Trophy, which will be bestowed on Dec. 14. With 138 points, he shattered Michigan's single-season scoring record of 117, set by Tom Harmon in 1940, and if he decides to stay at Michigan for a fifth year, he will easily break the school record for career touchdowns (40), set by Anthony Carter from 1979 to 1982. But the numbers do not express the style of his performances or how absolutely no one has been able to stop him. Nor do they speak to what an unusual man-child he is, a gentle tofu eater who talks to troubled youngsters, an activist who aims to get a Ph.D. in social work, a meditative loner with a vibrant laugh. There is an eloquence to Howard's play, a sense that it pleases his entire body, from his eyes to the bottoms of his cleats, to simply catch the football before 100,000 people on a Saturday afternoon.

It was J.D. who explained the true nature of magic to his son. Actually, he didn't explain it so much as live it, working overtime at the Osborn tool and die plant in inner-city Cleveland in order to send Desmond to a predominantly white, private Catholic school, where he might have a chance to earn decent college board scores and an athletic scholarship and learn to speak in the fiercely educated tones that he now employs. "It wasn't cheap," Desmond says. "There was sacrifice. You learn what you owe."

J.D worked, and wonderful things would magically appear, like the latest and most expensive sneakers, fashionable athletic wear, even a car. So when you telephone Desmond's rather ascetically decorated apartment near the Ann Arbor campus and he answers with the bright greeting, "Magic!" he doesn't mean anything frivolous by it. He means work.

"To work at something until it looks easy defines my relationship to the word *magic*," he says. "It's the one aspect where I deserve the nickname." He adopted it in seventh grade and does not intend to relinquish it, even though it has taken on added significance of late.

Desmond's mother, Hattie Howard-Dawkins, who is now remarried, helped define the relationship as well. Desmond went to live with his father in part so his mother could earn her college degree. She then got a job on the Ohio Hunger Task Force, teaching day-care administrators how to plan meals for children. Before that she ran a day-care center in her home for 17 years. The size of young Desmond's allowance depended on how much he did to help Hattie, reading to the children at story hour, taking them outside to exercise, putting them down for naps. If he seems older than his years, "I think he gets it from me," she says, "because he had responsibilities."

In the midst of Hattie's struggle to go to school, raise Desmond and his three brothers and run a day-care center all at the same time, J.D., who remains on good terms with his ex-wife, suggested that he take Desmond. "Let him come with me," he said. "You go on and finish school.

223

You know my heart is with him." Hattie agreed. J.D. says now, "Without him I'd have been lost. I wouldn't have had a thing." Desmond's childhood friend Warren Morgan says, "It's like they're brothers. Desmond is J.D.'s life."

When Desmond was ready to enter high school, J.D. told him to look around at the various private schools in town and choose which he liked best. One day Desmond saw a basketball team from St. Joseph's enter a gym wearing neatly pressed uniform blazers. "When I saw those blazers, I knew that's where I wanted to go," he says.

So J.D. sent him. One afternoon when Desmond was in the 10th grade, as father and son drove home from football practice along Lakeshore Boulevard, J.D. said, "Desmond, I'd appreciate it if you'd show me how much you love your daddy." Desmond asked if J.D. wanted him to drive. "No," J.D. said, "I want you to give me the next year. Don't go out. No girls. Just do your homework, play football and run track, and I give you my word, I'll give you anything you like for your senior year."

They struck that deal and then another while watching the 1988 Summer Olympics. J.D. told Desmond to pay attention to some of the athletes from smaller countries. He pointed out the ones he thought would win medals someday. "They aren't in the gold yet, but they will be," he said, "because you can tell that when they go home, they will keep practicing. Most athletes go home from practice and sit down to dinner while their mamas pat them on the head. You do a little bit more." A couple of afternoons later, Desmond came home from practice and went for a run. "Now, Desmond, you are working on that edge," J.D. said.

Desmond didn't go to his senior prom, because he had a track meet the next day. He rarely went to the local clubs where most of the neighborhood kids hung out. His social circle was restricted to two best friends, Marcus Greene and Morgan, studious and athletic kids from families not unlike his. Both are now seniors at the University of Cincinnati, Morgan majoring in criminal justice, Greene in psychology. "The only dance he ever went to I conned him into," Greene says. "He wanted to separate himself, just keep out of trouble. He knew there were shootings sometimes. He told me, 'Accidents will happen.' "

By his senior year Desmond, who played tailback and safety at St. Joe's, had 20 major schools recruiting him and a used Plymouth to drive. J.D. gave him the car and whatever else he wanted and didn't mind driving a beat-up Oldsmobile himself. Michigan came after Desmond the hardest. Gary Moeller, now the Wolverine coach, recruited Desmond, whose 4.3 speed overrode any concerns about his 5-foot-9, 167-pound size (he is now

176). Moeller fell hard for him in his final high school game when he returned the opening kickoff 95 yards for a touchdown. "The one thing I liked about him early was he wanted the ball," Moeller says. "He got mad when he didn't have the ball. He loved his hands on the ball."

J.D. sent Desmond off to Michigan with one last cautionary lecture. He told Desmond that no matter how hard things got under then head coach Bo Schembechler, he didn't want to hear about it. "Don't bring Bo home," he said.

Ann Arbor turned out to be colder than expected that first year. Howard was so taken aback by the array of talent at Michigan that during orientation, when the coaches grouped the recruits by position, he went with the defensive backs, thinking he might have a better chance of playing at that position. Moeller found Howard sitting with the safeties and tried him at receiver to see if he could catch at all. "We stood there and said, 'Yeah, he can catch the ball,' " Moeller recalls. "It was just a quick pass, and then, first thing, he made a [tackler] miss." Schembechler didn't know the full extent of what he had, but he had an idea. Asked what he intended to do the next year, after his leading receiver, John Kolesar, graduated, Schembechler said, "I've got this crafty little devil, Desmond Howard."

Howard's success has come partly by the hand of another Wolverine from St. Joe's, junior quarterback Elvis Grbac, the strapping son of Croatian immigrants. Grbac and Howard had no idea that they would become the most decorated and prolific passing tandem in Michigan history, since all Grbac did at St. Joe's was hand off to Howard 30 times a game. Grbac completed exactly one pass to Howard during their high school days. But at Michigan they began developing a relationship that Howard now says is "almost telepathic — I can practically read his mind." The more laconic Grbac says, "It's a mutual friendship that's been growing for several years. There's something about him that just makes you play better. He understands your attitudes and quirks at crunch time. He's got a habit of being there at the right time."

The telepathy between them is, on the surface, unlikely. Grbac's family is from the village of Istra in the northwest part of Yugoslavia, where everything is farmed by hand. Grbac is the type who studies film alone late at night in the players' auditorium. He is reserved and old world. Howard is a bright flame of a personality. Yet their fathers are like-minded men who sit next to each other at Michigan games. When Grbac and Howard combined for what may have been the most memorable college football play in many seasons, both men sensed it coming and dropped their heads in fear. It was a 25-yard desperation pass to the corner of the

225

end zone with 9:02 left and Michigan holding on to a 3-point lead against Notre Dame on Sept. 14. With the crowd on its feet, Grbac called an audible, and when he pumped his arm and signaled Howard deep, both fathers sat down at the same time and hid their eyes. "We knew it was going to be a problem," J.D. says. Desmond caught the ball on his fingertips with his body parallel to the ground. The catch secured a 24-14 Michigan win and elevated Howard to the top of the list of Heisman candidates.

Howard finished the regular season with 23 touchdowns, including a Big Ten-record 19 TD receptions. He has made catches of all descriptions, and punt and kickoff returns so picturesque they should hang in art galleries. Even if Howard did not have staggering numbers, he ought to be awarded the Heisman simply for making plays look so pretty.

Howard's style is one part studied nonchalance, one part meticulous technique and one part haughty arrogance. He runs fastidious routes, but sometimes he runs them at less than full speed, reserving a step for the instant he sees the ball leaving Grbac's hand, when he "hits another gear." That was how he managed to outstrip Notre Dame's double coverage to make his scoring catch. "That would be graded out as poor technique but great ability," he says bluntly.

Moeller has told Howard that he is so talented that double coverage is not an acceptable excuse for failing to make a catch. "If you really want the ball, then you can't let two guys take it away from you," Moeller said. Howard hasn't. And when he isn't making circus catches, he is a lethal presence on special teams. Against Ohio State on Nov. 23, Howard ran back a punt 93 yards for a touchdown. It was the longest punt return in Michigan history, and upon completing it, Howard momentarily struck a pose in the end zone, his left leg held high, his arm outstretched, like the figure on the Heisman. He had planned the gesture as a way of "capping off the team's special season," he says. "I love entertaining crowds. I love hearing that silence, then the burst of noise when you make the catch."

Yet during the week, Howard is reluctant even to discuss football. So reluctant, in fact, that he moved off campus last year. First he tried an apartment with roommates, but unwashed dishes and unmade beds made him irritable. So this year he took an apartment alone in Ypsilanti, several miles from campus.

Howard rarely socializes with football players, preferring to surround himself with a small circle of intimates who are not athletes. He will not say who he is dating. "I like my privacy," he says. "I like my time to myself, not to be bothered by people. They don't mean any harm, but if they are always knocking on your door and stopping by, you can't get anything done." He is only 13 hours short of his degree in communications, which he will receive in May. After that he intends to go to graduate school, whether he enters the N.F.L. draft or returns for a final year of elibility. (He has another year of football left because he did not play a down as a freshman.) "When Desmond said he wanted to live alone, I knew we had a grown man on our hands," says Hattie.

Living alone also allows him to meditate, a habit he picked up from his mother. For 10 or 15 minutes each day, he shuts off the lights and turns on water sounds, and thinks. "It can be about anything," he says. "A big game, or a test."

Howard rarely socializes. He might go to the L.A. Club Cafe sandwich shop near the center of campus, where the proprietor fixes Howard's favorite meal, a grilled chicken sandwich with cheese fries and a strawberry shake. Or he will go to hear the more provocative public speakers who are regularly booked on campus, such as the psychologist Akbar or 1960's radical activist Angela Davis. He has more important things to do than socialize. "I want to destroy stereotypes about the black male athlete," Howard says. "It's a mission of mine to break down stereotypes about our behavior, our social life, our literacy, our academic situations. . . ."

To that end, he has developed a strong interest in the 1960's and social activism. Perhaps his closest friend on campus is Greg Harden, a 42-year-old counselor who is a consultant to the athletic department and who has led Howard on an interesting quest for his identity. At Harden's urging, Howard has explored African-American history and culture, and the result is that Howard's sense of self-worth does not depend entirely on his being an athlete. They met two years ago when Howard called Harden to tell him how much he admired a speech on substance abuse that Harden had given to the football team.

Harden suggested some extracurricular reading, and ever since he told his protege that "you dress for what you aspire to," Howard has regularly worn a coat and tie and carried a briefcase to class.

Howard and his friends at Cincinnati, Morgan and Greene, share a sense of curiosity about their race and an accompanying sense of responsibility to get their degrees. They exchange books and pamphlets in the mail, exploring the position and plight of the educated young black in America.

Howard has tried his hand at speaking and apparently has a gift for it. He has made a dozen visits to the nearby Maxey Boys Training School, a youth home, where his reception is mixed. "You play football?" some of the offenders have asked incredulously of the slight figure before them. "I play football," he affirms. His performance thrills Harden. "Some athletes have been a disappointment in not figuring out that they have access to power and getting chewed up by it instead," he says. "Desmond could be worth his weight in gold to the black community in showing blacks new ways to see themselves. He's trying very hard to do it right."

Perhaps too hard at times. Howard can display personal standards that border on priggishness. He is intolerant of others' mistakes and of people who do not live to his high expectations. "I like reliable people," he says adamantly. He admits to fussing with his former roommates over housekeeping. "I think you have a responsibility," he says. "There's no sense in trying to go out and straighten up the neighborhood if your own home isn't straight." With Howard, says Harden, "mediocrity is not an option."

But just when Howard seems a touch overbearing, a beauteous smile comes forth, and he's suddenly describing, with a sense of high hilarity, something he did on the football field. For all of his exalted aspirations, Howard has a touch of pure lowbrow vaudeville. "I've enjoyed entertaining crowds since I was young," he says. "It's a pleasure making everybody happy. My family comes to the games, and I feel like they are there in harmony, cheering for their son."

His parents meet every weekend in seats on the 50-yard line to regard with a mixture of awe and admiration what they have accomplished.

"I tell Desmond," J.D. Howard says, " 'You make this whole family feel good. Just the idea of you.' "

67

HOWARD WRAPS UP HEISMAN TROPHY

By **MALCOLM MORAN**
Special to The New York Times

NEW YORK, Dec. 15, 1991 — Back in mid-September, when the leaves were still green and Desmond Howard's football season at the University of Michigan was just one game and four touchdowns old, he sat in a restaurant in Ann Arbor, Mich., and listened to a question that seemed as much a courtesy as anything else.

What do you think of your chances of winning the Heisman Trophy?

Howard's response seemed more genuine than political. He felt his chances were slim and none. Anthony Carter, Michigan's record-setting receiver from 1979-82, had never come close. How could Howard expect anything more?

This is how: Howard made it his, a week at a time, hanging on to footballs by his fingertips, often while parallel to the ground. By early yesterday evening, Howard's grip was firm and everlasting. He was named the 57th Heisman Award winner by a margin of 1,574 points — the second largest in the history of the award — over Casey Weldon of Florida State.

But there were fewer electors than voted for O.J. Simpson of Southern California over Purdue's Leroy Keyes in 1968. Howard won 85 percent of the first-place votes, 3 percent more than Simpson.

Howard, a 5-foot-9, 174-pound junior who is scheduled to graduate in May, has one remaining year of eligibility because he did not play as a freshman. When asked about a reported offer to play in the Canadian Football League, Howard said he intended to return to Michigan as a graduate student for a final season.

"As of now, my thought process is to get a degree at Michigan, beat Washington in the Rose Bowl, and at least start on my Ph.D. in social work."

Howard became Michigan's first Heisman winner since Tom Harmon, Old 98, won the award 51 years ago. He was the 11th winner from the Big Ten Conference, and the first since Archie Griffin of Ohio State won his second consecutive trophy in 1975. Howard and Notre Dame's Tim Brown, the 1987 winner, are the only wide receivers to win.

He is the 11th junior to win and the fourth in as many years, following Barry Sanders of Oklahoma State, Andre Ware of Houston and Ty Detmer of Brigham Young. Detmer, who was brought to The Downtown Athletic Club, finished third, with 445 points. Weldon and defensive tackle Steve Emtman of Washington were also at the ceremony.

And the nationally televised presentation became the culmination of a process that began when Howard entered St. Joseph High School on the outer edges of Cleveland. "He looked like a sixth grader," said Bill Gutbrod, Howard's coach there.

Howard was a high school sophomore when he began at St. Joseph, making a three-bus trip that would last at least an hour each way. He was a running back and a defensive back, used within the offense much the way Raghib Ismail would later be used at Notre Dame.

"We didn't throw to him that much," Gutbrod said, "because every time we put him out in a slot as a wide receiver, half the team would go with him."

So Howard spent most of his time lining up as a tailback, behind Elvis Grbac, who would become his quarterback at Michigan. At St. Joseph, the two combined for one touchdown pass; Howard had more interceptions (10) than receptions (7) in his senior season.

But at Michigan, with Howard a wide receiver, the two combined for 19 touchdown passes this season and 31 over the past three seasons, National Collegiate Athletic Association records for the same passer and receiver. Howard caught 61 passes for 950 yards. His 23 touchdowns included two rushes, one punt return and a kickoff return.

The Heisman questions grew more serious after Howard's fourth-quarter, fourth-down, 25-yard catch against Notre Dame. His team's lead down to 3 points, with 9 minutes 2 seconds to play and the Irish threatening to come from behind for a fifth consecutive victory over Michigan. Howard and Grbac produced their best-remembered touchdown catch.

Less than two hours before his time would come in the Heisman Room, as invited guests were sipping cocktails elsewhere in the club, Howard found a television that was tuned to the Duke-Michigan basketball game.

At halftime of the basketball game, when the Heisman Award was being discussed, the young face on the screen was talking about how he came up with the The Pose, his memorable imitation of the Trophy after he scored a touchdown against Ohio State.

Howard's statement began a celebration. Just as Tom Harmon's performance against the Buckeyes had helped secure a Heisman — and earned a rare standing ovation for a Michigan man in Columbus — Howard eliminated any doubt.

After he weaved through the Buckeyes for a 93-yard punt return touchdown, the longest in school history, Howard made his smiling statement in the end zone, imitating a 13½-inch-high bronze trophy.

68

NOTRE DAME AND MICHIGAN SPUTTER TO A 17-17 TIE

By **MALCOLM MORAN**
Special to The New York Times

SOUTH BEND, Ind., Sept. 12, 1992 — They don't cheer ties at Notre Dame.

With boos filling Notre Dame Stadium at the end of a long, imperfect afternoon, the Fighting Irish ran two running plays to begin their final possession in the last 65 seconds and did not call their last timeout until seven seconds remained in a bizarre 17-17 tie with Michigan.

After overcoming a 10-point, fourth-quarter deficit on a 2-yard touchdown run by Jerome Bettis and Craig Hentrich's 32-yard field goal, the Irish had a chance for a last-second victory after Michigan quarterback Elvis Grbac threw the last of his three interceptions at the Irish 11-yard line with 1 minute 5 seconds to play.

But nearly 26 years after Ara Parseghian, then the Irish coach, was criticized for a conservative approach at the end of a 10-10 tie with Michigan State, the sellout crowd of 59,075 fans was shocked to see the Irish run the ball on first and second down as the final minute ticked away.

After the second of those runs, a 12-yard gain by Reggie Brooks, was negated because the Irish failed to line up with seven players on the line of scrimmage, Notre Dame lost more than 10 seconds when the Irish forgot that the clock restarts immediately following a penalty.

A pass to Lake Dawson was caught out of bounds for an incompletion with 7 seconds to go, and a final throw intended for Michael Miller was broken up at the Michigan 32 on the final play.

"I made a mistake," said Lou Holtz, the Notre Dame coach, who admitted that he forgot that the clock is restarted after a penalty. "That was the only thing I regret. That was dumb on my part. But I am convinced if we do not have the penalty, and Lake catches it in bounds, we win the football game. No doubt about it."

Michigan and Notre Dame had never tied in their 23 previous meetings, dating to 1887. The Irish had not tied at all since 1982, and had not had one at home since a 14-14 tie with Southern California in 1969. Holtz's teams had tied just five times in his previous 22 seasons here and at William and Mary, North Carolina State, Arkansas and Minnesota.

Fumbles by Dawson, Miller and Bettis had seemed to undo the work of an improved Irish defense and the memorable 20-yard touchdown run on which Brooks broke or evaded five tackles.

But interceptions on Michigan's final two possessions caused the Wolverines to lose a chance for their first victory at Notre Dame Stadium since the first game of the Lou Holtz era in 1986.

"You want to go win at the end," said Rick Mirer, the Notre Dame quarterback, "but you've got to make sure you don't lose, too. I think at the end of the game you have to be cautious not to give up what you already have."

Holtz said the decision to run was made because the Irish were not sure what pass coverage Michigan was using.

"Maybe they have a blitz on," he said. "Maybe they're playing man-to-man and bringing everyone, as we've seen them do. Then you may get sacked in the end zone or the 1-yard line because the route isn't going to come open in time.

"What you need to do is say, 'O.K., how are they going to play,' " Holtz said. "Are they going to play for the tie and back off?"

Before the Irish started out, Mirer said, Holtz asked him his opinion. Mirer said he told the coach the Irish should play to win. "I think we did that," Mirer said.

But the quarterback acknowledged having trouble as the result of conditions that are impossible to prepare for in the sterile environment of the practice field. Notre Dame's task was made more complex by the added formations the Irish hoped would cause problems for Michigan.

"It's awful hard to communicate when first of all you're doing new things," Mirer said, "and second of all you're pressed for time. You have one timeout. You can't practice things like that. You can hope you get the ball down — boom, boom, boom — make some plays, break tackles. You can't plan on it falling in place.

"We get a penalty because we didn't have enough guys on the line because we can't hear. It's hard to hear. We've got different formations. We've got split ends that are playing flanker, flankers that are playing split end. Flankers are not on the line, the split end is. You can't hear. We don't have a tight end."

The quarterback snapped his fingers quickly to emphasize the pace.

"It's almost chaotic when you're trying to make it happen at the end," he said. "We were pretty poised for the most part, and didn't give away what we already had."

Soon the boos were filling the place that had responded with stunned buzzing to late-season losses to Tennessee and Penn State in the previous two years. Soon Holtz was reminding his players that the 1966 season ended with an unofficial national championship despite the controversial tie with Michigan State.

SCORE BY PERIODS

Michigan 0	7	3	7	—	17
Notre Dame 7	0	0	10	—	17

69

MICHIGAN, OHIO STATE SETTLE FOR DEADLOCK

By THE ASSOCIATED PRESS
The Chicago Tribune

COLUMBUS, Ohio, Nov, 21, 1992 — Michigan coach Gary Moeller blamed the elements, and Ohio State's John Cooper blamed the percentages.

Sixth-ranked Michigan and No. 17 Ohio State fought to a 13-13 tie Saturday, and near the end, both were playing to avoid a loss rather than for the victory.

"You can't stand up on that field," Moeller said. "It's a joke! It was like an ice rink."

Citing fan noise, he added, "You can't hear, and we got no help from the officials. The whole world was against us. It's never been like this here."

Ohio State chose to kick a tying extra point with 4:24 left, then elected to punt rather than go for it on fourth and 4 at the Michigan 49 with 1:12 left.

"You want to gamble, guys, but you want to gamble with my chips," Cooper said. "We gave ourselves a chance to win the football game."

Kirk Herbstreit's 5-yard pass to Greg Beatty and Tim Williams' extra-point kick had tied it with 4:24 left.

Michigan (8-0-3, 6-0-2 Big Ten) took over at its 9 with 1:03 left after Ohio State (8-2-1, 5-2-1) chose to punt, and the Wolverines allowed the clock to run on two running plays.

"On our 9-yard line, we were playing not to lose. The slippery conditions made me run the ball," Moeller said.

Herbstreit attempted 47 passes and completed 28, both the second-highest one-game totals ever at Ohio State. He passed for 271 yards and had no interceptions.

Michigan led, 13-3, early in the fourth quarter, scoring on a 3-yard run by starting quarterback Elvis Grbac in the second quarter and a 1-yard run by backup quarterback Todd Collins late in the third quarter. Peter Elezovic missed the first point-after kick. He converted the second just as a steady rain started, with 1:33 left in the third quarter.

Williams had had a 38-yard field-goal attempt blocked by Jean-Agnus Charles on Ohio State's first possession, and he missed a 56-yard attempt to end the half. Williams, who kicked a 39-yarder in the first half, pulled the Buckeyes to 13-6 on a 30-yard field goal with 12:16 left.

After Michigan was forced to punt, Herbstreit completed a tense fourth-and-goal pass from the 5 to Beatty with 4:24 remaining. Williams' kick deadlocked things.

"Did I ever think of going for 2? The answer is no," Cooper said. "There was a little over 4 minutes left to go in the game, and I thought, we tie the ballgame up, we'd kick off, hold them — which we did — get the ball back and have a chance to go down and kick the winning field goal. As it turned out, we didn't make that play."

Grbac was held out of the second half after injuring his ribs on his touchdown keeper.

SCORE BY PERIODS

Michigan 0	6	7	0	—	13
Ohio State 3	0	0	10	—	13

70

MICHIGAN ON TOP
WHEN SEE-SAW STOPS

By TOM FRIEND
Special to The New York Times

PASADENA, Calif., Jan. 1, 1993 — Coming in, the 79th Rose Bowl had been difficult to market. Michigan may have been undefeated this season, but it also had a decade worth of ties — three. Washington may have been the defending national champion, but in the fall it had undergone a decade worth of internal investigation. So, there was only enough intrigue today to attract a crowd of 94,236, the smallest Rose Bowl gathering in 38 years.

Who knew? Michigan (9-0-3) and Washington (9-3) ended up playing an exhilarating, Ping-Ponging game, with Michigan winning, 38-31, on Elvis Grbac's 15-yard touchdown job to his virtuoso tight end, Tony McGee, with 5 minutes 30 seconds left in the game.

'A Wild Coach Now'

"They'll say I'm a wild coach now," Michigan's Gary Moeller said.

Not that the Wolverines easily ran out the clock. With 1:03 remaining, they let Washington's David Killpatrick steam through to block a punt, and the Huskies had possession on the Wolverines' 44-yard line. Michigan acted as if it wanted another tie for old time's sake.

"Don't worry, wouldn't have been any tie," Washington coach Don James said afterward. "I would've gone for 2."

He had no such opportunity. The Huskies could not gain a single inch when its quarterback, Mark Brunell, threw four straight errant passes. Michigan then emptied its ice bucket on Moeller.

"For all you people who laugh at the guy getting Gatorade thrown on him, it's not the greatest thing in the world," Moeller said.

"We heard some boos in the Illinois tie, and that's why I hope some of those people watched today."

Savoring the Moment

Michigan practically refused to leave the field afterward. The players climbed atop the sideline benches and sang, a cappella, the Michigan fight song.

"But I couldn't dance," said Wolverine sophomore tailback Tyrone Wheatley.

Wheatley, at that point, could hardly walk. Back spasms in the first quarter had numbed his left leg, yet — on one leg — he somehow recorded the greatest rushing game in Michigan bowl history: 235 yards on 15 attempts. His most valuable player day included an 88-yard touchdown on the first play of the second half, a Rose Bowl mark.

"Was afraid I was going to start falling down or tripping," he said, "because it felt like my leg wasn't there. It was tingling and cramping. But I kept going. Did I know I had 200 yards? Oh yeah, they told me I had two bills."

The peculiarity of it all was that former Michigan coach Bo Schembechler had questioned Wheatley's perseverance in the off-season. Wheatley — 6-feet-1-inch, 225 pounds — was also on a track scholarship and seemed to be shirking spring football drills. Schembechler pulled him aside and in his usual gruff manner asked Wheatley, "Are you a track man playing football or a football player running track?"

"Football," Wheatley had replied.

"Act like it then," Schembechler said.

Motivational Tactic

Then, on New Year's Eve, the running backs coach, Fred Jackson, tried another motivational tactic. He trotted Wheatley around the Rose Bowl Stadium, which seats 101,366, to see a plaque of past m.v.p.'s. "Last Michigan man to do this was Leroy Hoard," Jackson told Wheatley. "And he was a running back. Get it?"

Jackson left Wheatley alone at the plaque, and Wheatley said, "That stayed on my mind."

It was almost not a happy ending for Michigan, because of Brunell. Brunell — the replacement for Billy Joe Hobert, who had been put off the team for accepting a loan in violation of National Collegiate Athletic Association rules — had his career day, throwing for 308 yards and two touchdowns. As a matter of fact, Brunell had been the Rose Bowl m.v.p. in January 1991, and today he broke the career Rose Bowl total yardage record (618 yards in three games).

His elusiveness is what made him dangerous today. Michigan had jumped ahead, 17-7, in the first half, but twice in the second quarter Brunell scrambled to his left — for he is left-handed — and completed long bombs. One was a 64-yard touchdown to Jason Shelley, although Shelley seemed to fumble before crossing the goal line, and the Huskies led at intermission, 21-17.

The second half was unruly. Wheatley's 88-yard run gave Michigan a 24-21 lead, but Brunell's 15-yard slant pass to Husky tight end Mark Bruener — a combination that clicked all day — set up Napoleon Kaufman's 1-yard scoring dive, to put the Huskies ahead by 28-24. A 44-yard field goal by Travis Hanson padded the lead to 31-24.

SCORE BY PERIODS

Michigan	10	7	14	7 —	38
Washington	7	14	10	0 —	31

71

MICHIGAN SPOILS PENN STATE FESTIVITIES

By WILLIAM N. WALLACE
Special to The New York Times

UNIVERSITY PARK, Pa., Oct. 16, 1993 — The scene was ripe: it was the 1,000th game in Penn State football history, played before the largest crowd in Beaver Stadium history (96,719), against the titan of a new conference, Michigan of the Big Ten, on a beautiful autumn afternoon.

But there was no pleasure in Happy Valley. The result: Wolverines 21, Nittany Lions 13.

Penn State spoiled too many opportunities of its own and never could stop Tyrone Wheatley, the Michigan tailback. Wheatley, who rushed for only 33 yards in the loss to Michigan State last week, had that many before the first quarter ended today, and 192 yards on 32 carries in the game.

The Michigan defense contributed a four-down, goal-line stand in the second half that denied Penn State the 6 inches it needed.

So the Nittany Lions lost for the first time this season and have a 5-1 record with Ohio State as their next opponent, at Columbus in two weeks. Michigan is 4-2 and, like Penn State, is 2-1 in the Big Ten.

Michigan won the game in the second half after trailing, 10-7. The Wolverines scored two touchdowns and, in between, held Penn State at bay with their remarkable stand at the lip of the end zone.

The Nittany Lions, who had moved the football most of the game, had a first down 6 inches from the goal, but went no farther. The play selection, which had been so clever in the first half, was simple: four straight-ahead plunges. The first two were by quarterback Kerry Collins, and the last two by Ki-Jana Carter, Penn State's best running back, who otherwise gained 127 yards on 17 carries.

Joe Paterno, the Penn State coach, had an explanation.

"They are awfully good on the goal line," he said of Michigan. "They have a clever little scheme where they pinch and then loop out. If you run the sweep — we were debating that — and they loop out, you're in trouble. So you have to guess against them. I guessed they would loop out, expecting something like a bootleg pass, and I thought we could run right at them. So we went with the two sneaks and we just didn't make it go."

Among several damaging Penn State errors was an offside penalty by the usually reliable cornerback Shelly Hammonds on a Michigan field-goal attempt that turned out to be no good. Hammonds lined up outside with no chance to block the kick.

The Wolverines, who had driven down the field using basic running plays on this first possession of the second half, gained a first down from that 5-yard penalty to the 19. On third down, Todd Collins completed a 16-yard pass to Mercury Hayes in the end zone, and after the conversion kick, Penn State trailed for the first time this season, 14-10.

Oops!

After the goal-line stand, Penn State got the ball back at the Wolverine 39 and moved to the 9, settling there for a short field-goal attempt for the third time rather than a touchdown. Craig Fayak, the kicker who was successful two of three times, made this one from 25 yards.

So Penn State trailed, 14-13, with 6 minutes left to play. Next came another of those little mistakes, an out-of-bounds kickoff by Brett Conway that gave Michigan the ball on its 35-yard line.

It was then that Wheatley, a 226-pound junior with great speed who must be a prime Heisman Trophy candidate, broke the Penn State defense. Against a blitz on second down, Wheatley ran left for 47 yards down to the Nittany Lions' 6-yard line.

On third down, Todd Collins threw a pass out in the flat to his uncovered fullback, Che Foster, who scored on a 5-yard touchdown play.

The Nittany Lions, 8 points behind, had the ball twice more but never got past midfield.

Kerry Collins, the Penn State quarterback, echoed so many of his teammates' sentiments when he said: "We just made too many mistakes. And they didn't make any."

He was right. Michigan had no turnovers and was never ruffled when behind early, 10-0.

Derrick Alexander helped with a 48-yard punt return for a touchdown in the second quarter.

"At that point," said Wheatley, "I was thinking we needed something special, and Derrick came up and made a play that turned the game around."

Carter's jabbing inside runs with cuts to the outside pulled up the

Wolverines' secondary, setting up the only Penn State touchdown, a pass into the end zone from Collins to Bobby Engram, who had run past the covering Alfie Burch. It was scored as a 37-yard play and looked so easy. But Michigan was not about to give up.

SCORE BY PERIODS

Michigan	 0	7	7	7	—	21
Penn State	 3	7	0	3	—	13

72

WOLVERINES INTERCEPT BUCKEYES' BOWL PLANS

By CHRISTINE BRENNAN
Special to The Washington Post

ANN ARBOR, Mich., Nov. 20, 1993 — Woody Hayes always despised the forward pass, even more, perhaps, than he ever hated Michigan, although that's debatable. Today, 15 years after Hayes last coached an Ohio State-Michigan game, everyone found out why he felt the way he did.

The fifth-ranked Ohio State Buckeyes, undefeated entering their final regular season game, were intercepted on four consecutive first-half possessions and ended up falling meekly, 28-0, to archrival Michigan before an N.C.A.A.-record crowd of 106,867 on a frigid afternoon at Michigan Stadium.

Had the Buckeyes (9-1-1) won or tied, they would have gone to the Rose Bowl. Now, if Wisconsin, a 35-10 winner over Illinois today, beats Michigan State on Dec. 5 in Tokyo, the Badgers will be the Big Ten Conference's representative in Pasadena on New Year's Day.

Which, by the way, pleases Michigan no end. The unranked Wolverines, losers of three Big Ten games during their 7-4 season, wiped out a year of frustration with their overpowering victory. That's the nature of this 96-year-old rivalry. Ohio State may yet end up in the Rose Bowl, and Michigan appears to have settled on the Hall of Fame, but it doesn't matter to the Wolverines tonight.

All that counts to them is this: For the sixth consecutive year, an Ohio State team coached by John Cooper could not beat them.

"This is one of the most embarrassing games I've ever been involved with," said Cooper, 0-5-1 against Michigan as the Buckeyes' coach. "They outplayed us on offense, on defense and in the kicking game. Running the ball, passing the ball. . . . I'm shocked. If you had told me we'd come up here and get beat, 28-0, I'd have probably stayed home."

Gary Moeller, the beleaguered Michigan coach whose job almost certainly was saved today, was glad Cooper came.

"It was probably our lack of success during the season that helped in our victory this time," he said. "We set sail today."

And they did it, oddly enough, with their passing game. Quarterback Todd Collins threw two touchdown passes and set up a third score with a 50-yard bomb to the Ohio State 1 near halftime, while the Michigan defense smothered any semblance of an Ohio State offense. The Buckeyes, who came in averaging 32 points per game, never got closer to the end zone that the Michigan 23.

No one would have believed it early on, but that first Collins' touchdown pass — a 25-yarder to Mercury Hayes with 6:34 remaining in the first quarter — was cushion enough for Michigan's victory.

Hayes made a superb play, reminiscent of those made on this field by a man thought of more fondly around these parts than he is in Washington, former Michigan Heisman Trophy winner Desmond Howard. As the ball floated through a swirling wind toward Hayes in the end zone, the sophomore flanker changed direction and, twisting, with his feet slipping out from underneath him, caught the ball with his fingertips as Buckeye safety Walter Taylor fell over the top of him.

Two possessions later, Ohio State changed quarterbacks, benching the ineffective Bobby Hoying for late-season star Bret Powers. That decision backfired when Powers was intercepted three straight times, twice when he was trying to throw into double coverage to big-play wideout Joey Galloway.

Michigan turned the second and third interceptions into touchdowns, riding mostly on the cutback, slashing running of tailback Tyrone Wheatley, as well as Collins' home-run arm.

It was a measure of Michigan's dominance today that Wheatley, who gained 105 yards for a second consecutive 1,000-yard season, left the game near the end of the first half with a possible concussion. He never returned, but the Wolverines didn't miss him. Backup Ed Davis ran for 96 yards.

Michigan led at halftime, 21-0, but Ohio State still thought it had a chance. The Buckeyes stopped Michigan on its first possession, then nearly blocked the punt. But, when forced to punt themselves near midfield a few minutes later, disaster struck. Ohio State punter Tim Williams, trying to field a bad snap, inadvertently downed the ball when his knee hit the grass at the Ohio State 32.

Four plays later, after an uncharacteristic reverse, Michigan scored for the final time when Davis dashed 5 yards with 10:39 remaining in the third quarter.

Score By Periods

Michigan 7	14	7	0	—	28
Ohio State 0	0	0	0	—	0

73

WHEATLEY SHOWCASES TALENT AS WOLVERINES DOMINATE

By The Associated Press
The Washington Post

TAMPA, Jan. 1, 1994 — Michigan running back Tyrone Wheatley scored two touchdowns and rushed for 124 yards today in a 42-7 rout of North Carolina State in the Hall of Fame Bowl.

Wheatley, a junior, scored on runs of 26 and 18 yards, helping the 23d-ranked Woverines (8-4) win their fourth straight. It may have been the last collegiate performance for Wheatley, who has until Jan. 10 to decide if he'll skip his final year of eligibility to enter the National Football League draft.

Earlier in the week, the 226-pound tailback said he hadn't made up his mind. Today, he didn't answer questions about his future, preferring to focus on Michigan's strong finish after a 4-4 start.

"The seniors and the captains gathered everybody up and said, 'Hey, we have to play.' . . . Coach [Gary] Moeller stressed that you just can't lie down and expect everyone else to lie down with us," Wheatley said.

Wheatley, named the game's most valuable player, was far from a one-man show against N.C. State. The Wolverines' defense forced the Wolfpack (7-5) into six turnovers before a crowd of 52,649 at Tampa Stadium.

Clarence Thompson ran back one of Michigan's four interceptions 43 yards for a third-quarter touchdown. Derrick Alexander returned a punt 79 yards for a second-quarter score and Todd Collins hit Amani Toomer with a 31-yard touchdown pass.

Michigan outscored its past four opponents 153-24, including a 28-0 win over Ohio State. North Carolina State was looking to rebound from a 62-3 loss to Florida State in the final regular-season game.

"We'll try to remember all the good things that happened this season," said Wolfpack coach Mike O'Cain, "but the back-to-back losses will stay with me for a long time."

North Carolina State moved the ball well at times, but turnovers stopped two drives inside the Michigan 30. The Wolfpack finally scored on Geoff

Bender's 12-yard pass to Brian Fitzgerald with 4:53 remaining in the third quarter.

"Since the middle of the season, we've been a little embarrassed with ourselves," said Collins, who was 11 of 22 for 189 yards. "After winning the last four games, we wanted to show the country we're the Michigan of old and we can dominate people like we used to and win anytime we want."

SCORE BY PERIODS

Michigan 0	21	21	0	—	42
N. Carolina St. 0	0	7	0	—	7

74

THE LONG VIEW

By S.L. PRICE
Sports Illustrated

NEW YORK, Aug. 29, 1994 — The big money called Tyrone Wheatley. The big money stretched itself like something lovely, begging to be taken, and who resists that anymore? Even when the agents sliced it so coolly — $1.2 million for one year, $3.6 million for two, $8 million for four, then the signing bonus, incentive clauses and, yes, the endorsement deals — the package laid out for a sure-thing N.F.L. rookie would still end up feeling the same: green and crisp and nothing like life. No more driving that Escort his grandparents got him from the Ford plant, bringing it home weekends so his sister could use it. No more worrying over his 12-year-old brother, Leslie, smack at the age when so many drift into Detroit's welter of drugs and guns and punks in Mercedes. And the memory of rationing meals and of days when the rations weren't much, well, that would just . . . fade, wouldn't it? All he need do was reach out. "I would've left," says Wheatley's roommate, Michigan fullback Che Foster. "I would've taken it."

Fifteen years old and tempted to spit in God's face. Two friends dead already. Running football for Michigan, that's some other kid's vision this icy night. Just trying to get home from a basketball game at Robichaud High, race-walking alone through the streets of Inkster, Mich., breath rising in a cloud. Car pulls up and a voice drifts out: "Hey. What you got in the bag?"

Keep walking. Don't say a word.

"You're not a seller, are you?"

Don't give them anything.

"Come work for us."

Don't stop . . . But now they see the school colors, now they're out of the car and on him, and all he can hear in his head are the words: Damn . . . why? WHY? It happens quickly. He's on his butt and staring dead-on

*into the barrel of a gun; time stops, curses and threats rain down. But
no. They send him off running. He gets home, takes his aunt's 9-mm pistol
and trips back into the dark, bent on retaliation. Two hours later, feet
cold and temper cooled, he comes to this: I shoot, my life is over. And
this: You cannot depend on anyone. My brother, my aunt — they didn't
know I had the gun. If I'd shot one of those guys, who else could I blame?*

No one would have blamed Wheatley. Five years ago, maybe, there was
an onus on underclassmen who left college early to play pro football. Not
anymore. Tennessee quarterback Heath Shuler, Fresno State QB Trent
Dilfer, San Diego State running back Marshall Faulk, Alabama receiver
David Palmer, Auburn running back James Bostic, Nebraska running back
Calvin Jones and 23 others shirked their senior seasons and bolted for
the N.F.L. before the Jan. 10 declaration day. All had good reasons. But
none more so than Wheatley, who finished eighth in last year's Heisman
balloting, whose 40 touchdowns already make him the most prolific running back in Michigan history, whose freight-train combination of a
230-pound body with a sprinter's speed has elicited hosannas for three
years and now makes him the odds-on favorite to win this year's Heisman
Trophy. N.F.L. scouts pegged him as a top-five pick. "I don't know what
I would've done," says Michigan coach Gary Moeller. "It's sad. But I think
everybody has a price."

*What his mother once said: "Stay clean. Don't do drugs or drink."
But then came her back injury, disability checks, money slipping away
like a toilet flushing down. He comes home, and there's booze in a bottle,
and Pat Wheatley has become just like everyone else around Tyrone,
wishing one thing and doing another. That alcohol on her breath . . . smell-
ing like a child's first whiff of betrayal. Now she says, "It's something
you can't understand until you're out." Out? Other kids wearing new Air
Jordans and flashing money, calling him a fool for playing ball. He is
14, no dad and a mother crumbling. "Why is this happening to me?" he
says. "I'm going from house to house; I shouldn't have to depend on other
relatives to live the way I live. People say, 'Have faith in God. He'll lead
the way.' And I think, Lead me where? Where the hell am I going?"*

Question was, who *wasn't* going anymore? Look at his Michigan pals.
Wide receiver and 1991 Heisman Trophy winner Desmond Howard left
Ann Arbor as a junior in 1991. Chris Webber deserted the Fab Five after
his sophomore season, leaving Michigan basketball to Jalen Rose and

Juwan Howard; those two bailed out as juniors a year later. Flip on the TV: There's Webber and underclassmen Shaquille O'Neal and Anfernee Hardaway with contracts hovering between $5 million and $6 million a year; there's former Notre Dame junior Jerome Bettis, for god's sake, battling for the N.F.L. rushing title with the Los Angeles Rams. Yes, Tyrone tried to set an example for Leslie, be the father Tyrone could remember only from photos. He told Leslie education was the most important thing. But stay in school? Why?

His grandmother, Louise Wheatley, she kept most of it to herself. She wanted Tyrone to know that she loved him for who he was, not because the way he walked and spoke and lit up around kids reminded her so much of her own son, Tyrone Sr., dead these last 20 years. She didn't talk much about the nights she would put little Tyrone, 8 years old, to bed and then wait for the sound that always came, the boy crying hard in his sleep. "He had a great hurt," Louise says. "I didn't know what type of hurt it was. I'd ask him what he was dreaming about, but he would never say. To me, it was that his father was there, with him. . . ."

This, too, she kept to herself until it mattered, until the time came for Tyrone Wheatley to declare who he was. Twenty-two years old last January, everyone urging him to go to the N.F.L., and Tyrone thinking he would. Louise took him aside and told him how it had been the day he was born. How her son had pointed to his new baby boy, an hour old. "You see him?" Tyrone Wheatley Sr. said then. "You see my baby, Mama? He's going to be one great man."

On Jan. 10 the son walked into a room at Schembechler Hall. "A man has to do what he thinks is best for him," he began.

Tyrone Wheatley let the money be. That, of course, only made him bigger. Suddenly Wheatley wasn't just a great football player; he was an *example*, a symbol: the man who chose education over cash. "Thank you, Tyrone," wrote one columnist. "Just when I had lost faith in my generation, you stood up and let me know there's still hope." But Wheatley says he was making no statement at all. Wheatley says he factored in football — the Michigan rushing record he can break with a good final season, the Heisman, the chance for a national title — as heavily as his wish to complete his degree in four years. But maybe even that's too simple. Moeller, who has watched Wheatley for three years, says, "Tyrone's different. I don't know if even he knows exactly why he decided to stay. Maybe because he didn't want to be like everybody else."

250

Not to worry. Wheatley has little of what coaches and sports writers call *attitude*: He is never out of shape; he always credits his offensive line. After recovering from spring football practice in April, he trained a week, then won the Big Ten outdoor track championship in the 110-meter hurdles. "He's very modest about his athletic ability," says Wolverine track coach Jack Harvey. Even now, accepted as the country's best college running back and inviting comparison with Gale Sayers and Eric Dickerson, Wheatley wants to be better. "He's an example of the right way to do things," Moeller says. "There are kids who can really be jerks, and you say, 'I've got to put up with *this* guy?' But this kid you can keep around forever."

The problem with this sketch is that it reduces Wheatley to a choirboy in shoulder pads. It makes him sound charitable, giving, obedient, when Wheatley's motivations have nothing to do with being a coach's dream. In fact, his most striking characteristic may be his independence. On the morning of Wheatley's announcement Moeller drew up a draft of things the player might say. Wheatley rejected it. He refused to tell his aunt, whose house was his home through high school, about his decision to stay at Michigan until the night before the press conference; his girlfriend, Kim McClinton, heard the news on television. They have dated for five years, and he plans to marry her. But if she ever leaves him, Wheatley has told her, "that'll just give me an excuse to do even better." He has a line for people who displease him. "There's nothing you can do to upset me; there's nothing you can do to embarrass me," he says. "I can live without you."

This jarring combination of selflessness and selfishness, humility and cruel honesty, leaves even those closest to Wheatley off balance. "He's not letting anyone deviate him from his program," says Michigan offensive tackle Trezelle Jenkins. "And only he knows what it is." Says Wolverine backfield coach Fred Jackson, "You talk to him. The unexpected? He's the person you're going to get it from. He's not the natural."

Except on the field. As a freshman in the 1992 Rose Bowl, Wheatley announced himself with a frenzied 53-yard touchdown run. "It was a draw play, and he just cut outside," says Michigan quarterback Todd Collins. "Everybody saw the look on his face; it was just crazed. He was flying." He hasn't stopped yet. Wheatley tore through Notre Dame last fall, even though his team lost, rushing for 146 yards, returning four kicks for another 133 and picking up 39 more in the air.

Injuries kept him out of two games and limited him in two others, but he gained 1,129 yards last season; Minnesota coach Jim Wacker called him the best back in America. Joe Paterno, who watched Wheatley race 192 yards in State College last October — the highest rushing total surrendered by Penn State in six years — uttered the usual paeans to his gifts, plus, "He has the best stiff-arm I've seen in college football in a long, long time."

"His ability is beyond that of any person who ever put a foot down around here," Jackson says. "You don't find anybody that big, that fast, that strong, that tough in one body. He's a fast Emmitt Smith. He'll run around Emmitt."

It's not just Wheatley's size and 4.4 40-yard dash that make him so coveted. In a return engagement against Washington in the '93 Rose Bowl, Wheatley produced a 235-yard, three-touchdown performance on just 15 carries despite back spasms so troublesome that he could barely stand afterward. Three weeks later he won the 55-meter dash at the Michigan relays with a time of 6.3 seconds — in his first race with the team. Against Ohio State last season Wheatley piled up 105 yards in less than a half, then suffered a concussion. He tried sneaking out onto the field; Jackson stopped him by taking his helmet. "Where I came up, a lot of guys wanted to do easy things," Wheatley says. "I feel better if I work. I feel a lot better if I go through pain."

Better? Maybe he means normal. Wheatley does not do right because society or coaches say so. Wheatley does what he does because the pain taught him to, and if that puts him on the side of angels, so be it. He doesn't care what people think because he has learned he can't depend on most people. "I forgive a person real easy," Wheatley says. "But I won't forget. I'll know next time to never, ever let you have the opportunity to get close."

Here is Wheatley's postfootball plan. He is majoring in administrative education. He's aiming to be a principal, but before that he wants to teach, he want to work with physically and mentally disabled kids. Growing up in Inkster, near the Detroit airport, he was approached by three kids whom others shunned: too slow, too dumb, retarded. Over time he forgot those labels. "Those three people touched me, asked me for my time," Wheatley says. "Why did they ask *me*? Things happen for a reason. And I really enjoyed it.

Superman? That's what they were calling him coming out of Robichaud High, what they called him after that breakout in the Rose Bowl. But what would they call him now, after 14 days in the hospital? He took a helmet in the back during the spring game, and they tell him his spleen his bruised; but this isn't like any bruise he has known. Tubes in his arms, up his nose,

*catheter jammed in his crotch . . . 30 pounds lost, his sophomore season
in jeopardy . . . can his eyes sink any farther into his head? "It was so
gross, my teammates didn't want to come see me," he says now. That hurt.
That taught him something valuable. "I could've died," he says. "No
one knew if I could come back from it. I'm Tyrone Wheatley, I had
everything, and all of a sudden I'm reduced to where people don't come
see me because of the way I look?" He gets home, and for 10 days he
can't ride in cars, walk, nothing. He's on the couch. "And the people who
were there before I was hurt weren't there for me anymore," he says. Except for the three. The kids everyone always laughed at — in they come
to show they care. Too slow, too dumb, retarded: his friends. They make
him laugh. They joke. They ask him, "Do you feel pitiful?" And Superman smiles and says, "Yes, actually, I do."
"Now you see how we feel," they say. "People see you, and they know.
And then they treat you different."*

It might have been different, if his dad and mom hadn't gone to that
party on Dexter Street. But it was April 15, 1973, a cousin's birthday. Were
the men looking for the cousin? Who knows? Tyrone Sr., 20 years old,
never had any trouble with the law, worked the line at Ford. Three men
came into the house on Dexter. They thieved some, grabbed a TV, and
on the way out one of them said, "This is your last party." He shot Tyrone
Sr. in the head, then rifled through his pockets. Pat was unharmed, but,
says Louise Wheatley, "to see her husband, oh . . . she passed out once
she knew he was dead."

For a while Pat held the family together, raised Tyrone Jr. and his sister,
Ava, worked construction until the back injury ended that. She began
drinking, and Tyrone, at 14, didn't know what to do. "I couldn't take it,"
he says. "Here's the woman who raised me, who would go to any extreme
in the world for me. Yet she turned into something she always told me
to fight against. It grabbed her. It hurt me . . . It destroyed me a little."

He made himself tougher. He demanded his mother get help. He told
her he was moving out, began a circuit of stays with grandparents, an uncle,
Pat's sister, Jeanette Boyd. He want to Robichaud High, became a star.
Jeanette would hear him repeating, "I can't wait. I can't wait till I get an
opportunity."

"For what?" she would ask.

"Anything," Tyrone would say. He forgave his mother, says she has been
sober for two years, says, "She helps keep me going now." But he never
forgot. "It's not that I'm angry," he says. ."I don't *trust* too much. Don't

promise me anything, because I'm not going to look for you to keep your promise. Just say you're going to try."

For himself he leaves less room. His decision to stay in school was an unspoken pledge to Leslie made good. "I want him to know there's more than just money," Wheatley says. "A person with morals cannot be bought. I told him this is the choice I made. Not to win the Heisman, not to break records — this is something I felt I should do. If you want a path to follow, I'm going to set the best path."

This is a world of pressure, far heavier than a stadium full of 100,000, and it is chilling to see Wheatley negotiate his way, allowing no weakness. Jackson says he has never seen anyone so rigid. "He doesn't smoke, doesn't drink, doesn't do anything anybody else does," Jackson says. "And that makes him strong. He gathers strength from not being what the odds say he should be."

Midnight. Tyrone and Kim are on the track, both practicing starts, over and over. She is tired. He doesn't care. "One more," he says.

She is beginning to hurt. She wants to stop now.

"Not till you get it right," he says.

Her hands are bleeding. She is crying. "Why do you train so hard?" she says.

"One more," he says. "One more . . ."

This is not meanness. This is survival.

Tyrone Wheatley is a senior at the University of Michigan.

75

MICHIGAN BEATS IRISH AT GUN

By MALCOLM MORAN
Special to The New York Times

SOUTH BEND, Ind., Sept. 10, 1994 — Another comeback. Another giddy go-ahead touchdown. But just when the legend of Ron Powlus seemed ready to take on enormous proportions after his first game at Notre Dame Stadium, it was Todd Collins, the Michigan quarterback, who engineered the decisive drive that left the Fighting Irish lying in pain on the grass.

A 42-yard field goal by Michigan kicker Remy Hamilton, with 2 seconds to play, gave the Wolverines a remarkable 26-24 victory that brought back painful memories of Notre Dame's loss to Boston College last November. This time, at the end of a warm, late-summer afternoon with much of the stadium still in sunlight, Hamilton's kick between the south goalposts, his fourth field goal in as many attempts, jeopardized Notre Dame's championship hopes.

Powlus's 7-yard pass to a leaping Derrick Mayes, just inside the back line in the center of the end zone with 52 seconds to play, had given the Irish a 24-23 lead. But Collins, starting at his 16-yard line with 46 seconds to play, scrambled for 15 yards and then completed three consecutive passes — 26 yards to tight end Jay Riemersma, 9 to flanker Seth Smith, and 9 yards to Smith to place the Wolverines at the Irish 25. The last pass by Collins, which he made while lunging forward and in the grasp of Irish linebacker Bert Berry, gave Hamilton his chance.

Three Notre Dame turnovers led to Hamilton's first three field goals, including the 35-yard kick that gave the Wolverines a 20-17 lead with 39 seconds to play in the third quarter and the 32-yard kick for a 6-point lead with 2:15 to play. Irish senior tailback Lee Becton, who committed the first two fumbles, had lost a fumble just once in his previous three seasons and had gone 233 carries without losing the ball.

Notre Dame had taken a 17-10 lead midway through the third period, on an 8-yard run by sophomore fullback Marc Edwards that was set up by a pass interference penalty against Michigan defender Tyrone Noble in a third-and-16 situation.

But the Wolverines, forced to cope with the absence of four injured senior starters, including tailback and Heisman Trophy candidate Tyrone Wheatley, found themselves in a position to control the final 22 minutes. They tied the score on a 3-yard pass from quarterback Todd Collins to Riemersma with 4:08 to play in the third quarter, and benefitted from Becton's second fumble to take the lead.

And just when a fumble by Collins, Michigan's first turnover of the day, gave the Irish the ball at their 23 with 5:02 to play and led the crowd to believe it was about to witness the first miracle of the Ron Powlus era, the sophomore committed a basic and costly mistake.

On the second play of the possession, after Becton's 14-yard run increased the noise and anticipation of a dramatic finish, Powlus stumbled backwards as he took the snap from new center Mark Zataveski. The loose ball was recovered by Michigan linebacker Steve Morrison, and the Irish drive was ended before it had a chance to really begin.

The focus of the week, and the loudest cheers from the capacity, shirt-sleeved crowd of 59,075 during the pregame introductions, centered on the Notre Dame Stadium debut of sophomore quarterback Ron Powlus. But the most dramatic shift at the beginning of the game — and one of the most significant for the championship hopes of the Irish — was the return of a reliable running game.

Notre Dame's total of 161 rushing yards last week against Northwestern, a game in which they were outgained on the ground by the Wildcats, created concerns about a restructured offensive line. The Irish hoped that the problem would soon prove to be a temporary struggle of an emerging unit, and from the first series, their judgment seemed to be correct.

With Michigan forced to respect the passing of Powlus, who threw for 291 yards in his first game last week, the Irish were able to achieve a balanced attack from the beginning. On their third play from scrimmage, after Powlus' quick pass to junior wide receiver Derrick Mayes created a 13-yard gain, senior fullback Ray Zellars gained 16 yards up the middle for Notre Dame's longest run of the season.

SCORE BY PERIODS

Michigan 7	3	10	6	— 26
Notre Dame 10	0	7	7	— 24

APPENDIX

THE STATS: 1969-1993

16 BIG TEN CHAMPIONSHIPS

11 ROSE BOWL GAMES

20 BOWL GAME APPEARANCES

56 ALL-AMERICA SELECTIONS

170 ALL-BIG TEN SELECTIONS

THE RECORD

Year	Won	Lost	Tied	Big Ten Ranking	A.P. National Ranking
1969	8	3	0	1st	9th
1970	9	1	0	2nd	9th
1971	11	1	0	1st	6th
1972	10	1	0	1st	6th
1973	10	0	1	1st	6th
1974	10	1	0	1st	3rd
1975	8	2	2	2nd	8th
1976	10	2	0	1st	3rd
1977	10	2	0	1st	9th
1978	10	2	0	1st	5th
1979	8	4	0	3rd	18th
1980	10	2	0	1st	4th
1981	9	3	0	3rd	12th
1982	8	4	0	1st	—
1983	9	3	0	2nd	2nd
1984	6	6	0	6th	—
1985	10	1	1	2nd	2nd
1986	11	2	0	1st	8th
1987	8	4	0	4th	19th
1988	9	2	1	1st	4th
1989	10	2	0	1st	7th
1990	9	3	0	1st	7th
1991	10	2	0	1st	6th
1992	9	0	3	1st	5th
1993	8	4	0	4th	21st
	230	57	11		

ALL- AMERICA

Year	Player	Position
1969	Jim Mandich	End
1969	Tom Curtis	Safety
1970	Dan Dierdorf	Offensive Tackle
1970	Marty Huff	Linebacker
1970	Henry Hill	Middle Guard
1971	Mike Taylor	Linebacker
1971	Reggie McKenzie	Offensive Guard
1971	William Taylor	Running Back
1971	Thom Darden	Defensive Back
1972	Randy Logan	Defensive Back
1972	Paul Seymour	Offensive Tackle
1973	David Gallagher	Defensive Tackle
1973	Dave Brown	Defensive Back
1974	Dave Brown	Defensive Back
1975	Don Dufek	Defensive Back
1976	Rob Lytle	Running Back
1976	Calvin O'Neal	Linebacker
1976	Jim Smith	Wide Receiver
1976	Mark Donahue	Offensive Guard
1977	John Anderson	Linebacker
1977	Mark Donahue	Offensive Guard
1977	Walt Downing	Center
1978	Rick Leach	Quarterback
1979	Curtis Greer	Defensive Tackle
1980	Ron Simpkins	Linebacker
1980	Anthony Carter	Wide Receiver
1980	George Lilja	Center
1981	Kurt Becker	Guard
1981	Anthony Carter	Wide Receiver
1981	Ed Muransky	Offensive Tackle
1981	William (Bubba) Paris	Offensive Tackle
1981	Butch Woolfolk	Tailback
1982	Anthony Carter	Wide Receiver
1983	Stefan Humphries	Offensive Guard
1983	Tom Dixon	Center
1985	Mike Hammerstein	Defensive Tackle
1985	Brad Cochran	Defensive Back
1986	Garland Rivers	Defensive Back
1986	John Elliott	Offensive Tackle

1986	Jim Harbaugh	Quarterback
1987	John Elliott	Offensive Tackle
1987	Mark Messner	Defensive Tackle
1988	Mark Messner	Defensive Tackle
1988	John Vitale	Center
1989	Tripp Wellborn	Safety
1990	Dean Dingman	Offensive Tackle
1990	Greg Skrepenak	Offensive Tackle
1990	Tripp Wellborn	Safety
1991	Erick Anderson	Linebacker
1991	Desmond Howard	Wide Receiver
1991	Matt Elliott	Offensive Guard
1991	Greg Skrepenak	Offensive Tackle
1992	Joe Cocozzo	Offensive Guard
1992	Chris Hutchinson	Defensive Tackle
1992	Derrick Alexander	Defensive Tackle

About the Editor

Francis J. Fitzgerald is a contributing editor to Athlon Sports. A noted researcher and editor, he lives in Washington, D.C.